Gadamer, History
and the Classics

Studies in Literary Criticism and Theory

Hans H. Rudnick
General Editor

Vol. 15

PETER LANG
New York • Washington, D.C./Baltimore • Bern
Frankfurt am Main • Berlin • Brussels • Vienna • Oxford

Alison Forsyth

Gadamer, History and the Classics

Fugard, Marowitz, Berkoff and Harrison Rewrite the Theatre

PETER LANG
New York • Washington, D.C./Baltimore • Bern
Frankfurt am Main • Berlin • Brussels • Vienna • Oxford

Library of Congress Cataloging-in-Publication Data

Forsyth, Alison.
Gadamer, history and the classics: Fugard, Marowitz, Berkoff and Harrison rewrite
the theatre/ Alison Forsyth.
p. cm. — (Studies in literary criticism and theory; vol. 15)
Includes bibliographical references.
1. Gadamer, Hans Georg, 1900– Contributions in hermeneutics.
[1. Drama—20th century—History and criticism.] I. Title.
II. Studies in literary criticism and theory; v. 15.
PN1861 .F64   809.2'045—dc21   00-050653
ISBN 0-8204-5265-3
ISSN 1073-2004

Die Deutsche Bibliothek-CIP-Einheitsaufnahme

Forsyth, Alison:
Gadamer, history and the classics: Fugard, Marowitz, Berkoff
and Harrison rewrite the theatre / Alison Forsyth.
–New York; Washington, D.C./Baltimore; Bern;
Frankfurt am Main; Berlin; Brussels; Vienna; Oxford: Lang.
(Studies in literary criticism and theory; Vol. 15)
ISBN 0-8204-5265-3

© 2002 Peter Lang Publishing, Inc., New York

Printed in the United States of America

To my Mother and Father

Table of Contents

Acknowledgments

I owe a special debt of gratitude for many different forms of encouragement and support from the following individuals who participated directly in the evolution of this book: Grahame Smith, who supervised my doctoral studies and from which this book has grown; Michael Anderson, Denis Walder and Nicholas Royle for their constructive, encouraging and positive input with respect to the thesis from which a large part of this study has developed; Bill Rubinstein for his advice and support during the publication of the book; Phyllis Korper, my editor, for showing enthusiastic interest in the book content and being so patient and helpful during the various stages of production; Daniel Meyer-Dinkgrafe for his quietly understated but nonetheless much appreciated intellectual backing; past colleagues at the Universities of Stirling and Aberystwyth and present colleagues at Staffordshire University. Most of all I would like to add a fond thank you to my parents for their unconditional and ever present support throughout my research and the book production process.

I gratefully acknowledge permission to reprint material from the following sources: *Truth and Method* Second Edition, translation revised by Joel Weinsheimer and Donald G Marshall (London: Sheed and Ward, 1993) and (New York: Continuum, 1993); Edward Bond and Casarotto Ramsay and Associates Ltd for permission to reprint from *Rough Notes on Olly's Prison* copyrighted Edward Bond, 2001.

Introduction

The aim of this study is to elaborate and extend our present knowledge of rewriting as a critical paradigm by explaining the creative and political potential of performative rereading and rewriting. The Dramatic Rewrite, it is argued, produces new and altered states of understanding from a dialogue *with* as opposed to making a reiterative statement *of* tradition, as represented by 'the classic'.

With close reference to the hermeneutic project of Hans Georg Gadamer, particularly that put forward in *Truth and Method* (*Wareheit und Methode*, Tubingen Mohr, 1960) it is intended to show, by detailed critical consideration of selected plays by Marowitz, Fugard, Berkoff and Harrison, that the Dramatic Rewrite is distinct from other artistic negotiations with earlier works of art, such as parody, appropriation, allegory, montage and pastiche. As opposed to foregrounding the concerns of the past through reconstruction and recontextualisation or highlighting present issues through allegorical appropriation it is argued that the Dramatic Rewrite creatively *mediates* with the past and present, with knowledge gathered through the force of tradition (*Erfahrung*) and the immediacy of the moment (*Erlebnis*), to performatively, and thus transiently, produce a different and new understanding or what Gadamer refers to as 'transformation into structure'.

In Chapter One it is argued that, as the classics are representative of the community of cultural consciousness, regardless of whether one opposes, venerates or remains indifferent to their status, they are the most productive resource for a creative mediation with the past for the present, and that the Dramatic Rewrite elicits performative *Erlebnis* by negotiating with the classics' cultural cachet, their subsequent appropriation and 'intratextuality' and the focus they provide as literary vortices of cultural consciousness and, by extension, socio-historical issues.

Chapter Two extends the earlier consideration of the classic to discuss the specific relevance of Gadamer's phenomenological hermeneutics for 'rewriting' the classics as well as explaining the Rewrite's potential to engage in dialogue with the past from the present.

Chapters Three, Four, Five and Six focus on the Dramatic Rewrite in practice, with specific and detailed discussions about Marowitz's post-Holocaust treatment of *The Merchant of Venice*, Fugard's rewritten *Antigone* for what was an Apartheid-riven South Africa, Berkoff's approach to *Oedipus Rex* through its psychoanalytical intratext, and Harrison's revivification of Satyr drama for the twentieth century in the form of *The Trackers of Oxyrynchus*.

In conclusion, it is argued that the Dramatic Rewrite performatively transforms the classic from being a symbol of textual 'endurance' or cultural 'survival' into the vibrant and thus finite experience or *Erlebnis* that is hermeneutic 'life'.

Chapter One

What is a Classic?

Absorption and Synthesis

The most common response to the question of how one reaches a decision as to what is and what is not a classic invariably comprises a vague, essentialist notion about quality, merit and superiority, but such responses do not explain the criteria which evaluatively set certain literary texts against others. Is it just a matter of personal choice or *aesthesis* as espoused by Bloom[1] and others, or are we merely acquiescing with the institutional value judgements, often economically motivated, made by critics, publishers, curricula designers and academics as discussed by Arthur C. Danto[2], George Dickie[3] and, more recently, Barbara Herrnstein Smith?[4] Conversely, Pierre Bourdieu and other cultural sociologists see the evaluative criteria for deciding what is a classic as being class-based and class-perpetuated, whereby the ruling class covet the self-distinguishing and self-aggrandisement offered by the construct that is the classic, which they accordingly bestow with notions of rarity, expensiveness, provenance and cultivation accessible only to those who have enjoyed an elitist education.[5] According to Bourdieau, the self-distinguishing evaluation on the part of the ruling classes is bolstered by the insidious cultivation of self-subordinating inhibition amongst the excluded or lower classes when confronted with this ideologically constructed classic.

Besides such theoretical analyses of what constitutes our evaluation of a classic, all of which contribute toward grasping the complexity of the construct, is the hermeneutically grounded notion of the "eminent text" as formulated by Hans Georg Gadamer. Gadamer incorporates and addresses all of the aforementioned approaches toward defining a classic and synthesises them into his definition of tradition and the eminent text:

> The classical is something that resists historical criticism because its historical
> dominion, the binding power of the validity that is preserved and handed down,
> precedes all historical reflection and continues in it.[6]

In this respect, Gadamer views the various analyses of the evaluation of
the classic as belonging to the discourse of aesthetics, which should and
must be acknowledged, but which are nonetheless absorbed by hermeneutics, because there is no absolute progress and no final exhaustion of
what lies in a work of art. As Gadamer explains:

> Every work of art, not only literature, must be understood like any other text that
> requires understanding, and this kind of understanding has to be acquired. This
> gives hermeneutical consciousness a comprehensiveness that surpasses even that
> of aesthetic consciousness. *Aesthetics has to be absorbed into hermeneutics.*[7]

Thus, although Gadamer does not discount the sociological, institutional and personal *aesthesis* theories, he puts forward a far more strident claim for the classic as being a potential source of hermeneutic truth,
which is founded on, but ultimately subsumes and absorbs the aesthetic
discursivity that has created its status. Because Gadamer sees history as a
potential source of truth, the classic, as part of history, is also a source of
truth. In this respect, the classic or classical is far more than just a description of style or period. Thus, although the classic is often represented as
the stylistic apogee of art in a given epoch or period and as such is a
development to which an immanent telos gives unity, Gadamer elabo-
rates how the classic of a defined period is subject to the "uprooting"[8]
movement of history and absorbed by and into the general nature of
tradition in which only the part of the past that is not past offers the
possibility of historical knowledge. However, as Joel Weinsheimer has
pointed out, this does not mean preservation as mere cultural storage,
but rather processual and continual preservation by a constant interpretative putting to the test ". . . of what, in thus proving itself, brings into
being something true."[9] Weinsheimer continues:

> A history of the classic is not merely research because it is also a testing, proving,
> and thus a participation in the truth of the classic. So also the classic does not
> exist in itself; its truth does not persist of itself but only through historical partici-
> pation, the constant mediation with the present of the historian. For this reason,
> what the classic says to us is not merely a statement about the past but a truth
> addressed to the present.[10]

Thus, intrinsic to the classic's status is its continual interpretative mediation between the past and the present, and not the ritualistic endorsement

of past, ideologically motivated evaluations which confine the classic to the status of a literary museum piece.

Gadamer's notion of interpretation is more complex than that put forward by Barthes who emphasises the part of the reader as being the activating force behind the disclosure of meaning in a text, because he stresses the dialogic or conversational aspect of meaning. For Gadamer, the interpreter is not attempting to decode or decipher a fixed meaning hidden in the text whereby interpretation is no more than ". . . the continuing determination of an object-world waiting to be recognised."[11] Rather, Gadamer sees interpretation as a conversation between two interlocutors about a given subject that has become illuminated, through historically effected consciousness, during and as a result of the vicissitudes of passage of time. Thus, for Gadamer, interpretation does not arise as a result of the interpreting "subject" (reader) interpreting the interpretative "object" (text), rather it is the content-subject of the text thrown up by history that reanimates the written word into speech with an interlocutor in the present. As Risser points out:

> For Gadamer, instructed by Heidegger, thinking has its context in language, and consequently the overcoming of every fixation of meaning occurs through the future development of conversation . . . the text remains plural by virtue of the structure of the interpretation itself.[12]

The text therefore is the alive and present half of a conversation and not a dead and past historical source for critical historical research. In this respect, what animates the text into such a conversation is not the reader alone but the dialogic 'good will' to come to an understanding about the present subject-content of the text with the text, as thrown up by a specific and contingent historical moment and a consciousness of that moment.

Tradition as the Community of Cultural Consciousness

Gadamer points out that after the First World War the concept of the classic became increasingly difficult to interpret, for it appeared somewhat incongruous and unbefitting in a fragmented, shattered and disrupted world to attempt to express the unity of a stylistic ideal.

Indeed, much of the hotly contested canon debate, in which the classic is necessarily embroiled, has been motivated by a vehement reaction against what is perceived as the artificial homogeneity and monolithism of "our" literary tradition. However, such critiques fail to emphasise the role of the interpreter in the interpretation of our tradition, namely that the classics

are only truly reinforced, or indeed discarded, by our hermeneutic negotiation with them. It is only our concerted hermeneutic negotiation with
the classics that alters, transforms and prevents the canon, or indeed the
much vaunted more popular or "representative" canon, from being the
very homogenous, unrepresentative and cultural monolith so vilified by
the critical canon-busters, a view echoed by Bourdieu:

> To deny evaluative dichotomies is to pass a morality off for a politics. The domi-
> nated in the artistic and intellectual fields have always practised that form of
> radical chic which consists in rehabilitating socially inferior cultures or the minor
> genres of legitimate culture . . . To denounce hierarchy does not get us any-
> where. What must be changed are the conditions that make the hierarchy exist,
> both in reality and in minds. We must—I have never stopped repeating it—work to
> *universalize in reality the conditions of access* to what the present offers us
> that is most universal.[13]

In this respect, the value of art, not just literature, is produced through
interpretation and as such is inescapably a temporarily constituted and
continual activity. However, Gadamer posits that such interpretative "value"
is more likely to be produced by our engagement with the eminent text
because, by its very status, it invites continual rereading. The rereading
suggested by the classic is not by virtue of its intrinsic transcendental
superiority, but because of its enhanced hermeneutic significance as a
text that has become embedded and situated in the tradition that is the
community of cultural consciousness. The past evaluative decisions which
are constituted by and reflected in the classic, are as much a part of
tradition as the text itself, and thus, any engagement we have with the
classic assumes wider socio-historical dimensions. In this respect, Peter
Osborne's critique of Gadamer's "suprahistorical"[14] concept of the classic
is misplaced, for it is the classic's very involvement in history, not only by
virtue of antiquity or age, but by its significance in subsequent intratextuality
that leads Gadamer to assign a quality of timelessness as a mode of historical being[15] to the eminent text—a status which depends for its valida-
tion, not through reification but by continual interpretative 'understanding':

> From such functions of artistic media, what we call a work of art remains quite
> distinct. Even if, for example, statues of gods, choral songs, and attic tragedy and
> comedy are found within cultural systems, and even if every "work" belongs origi-
> nally to a context of life that has passed away, nevertheless the doctrine of aes-
> thetic non-differentiation implies that this relation to the past is, as it were, re-
> tained in the work itself. Even in its origin it had gathered its "world" in itself and
> was therefore "intended" as itself, as this statue of Phidias, this tragedy of Aeschylus,
> this motet of Bach. The hermeneutic constitution of the unity of the work of art
> is invariant among all the social alterations of the art industry.[16]

It is futile, according to Gadamer, to demolish an "unpopular" canon in favour of a more "popular" one because, if we are seriously interested in the evaluation of literature, such an interest must be premised upon a proactive and interpretative involvement which in turn reflects, alters and transforms the significance of a given text in the community of cultural consciousness.

To fully comprehend Gadamer's definition of a classic it is necessary to distinguish between tradition as ritualistic reiteration and tradition as that which exists because it is continually reinforced by hermeneutic application. Although a text may well be normatively referred to as a classic, and indeed may even belong within a corpus of works attributed to a culturally feted literary icon like, for example, Shakespeare, according to Gadamer such a text is more vulnerable to the hermeneutic challenge by very dint of the heightened status which has made the text undoubtedly more complicitous in not only our cultural tradition but also our socio-historical heritage and its effects. It is the classic's embedded significance as tradition that in part arouses and engages our historically effected consciousness into subsequent dialogue about a specific subject-content. Thus, because the classic has invariably enjoyed cultural status throughout the centuries, far from securing a suprahistorical and transcendental textual position that is above and beyond worldly concerns, the classic is more deeply enmeshed and complicit with the everyday world which we inhabit. It is the very socio-historicality which inheres in the classic, be it by way of its past appropriation and misappropriation, its intratextuality or its implication in past political ideologies, which Gadamer exploits for his hermeneutic project based on historically effected consciousness. As John Guillory explains:

> Literary works must be seen rather as the vector of ideological notions which do not inhere in the works themselves but in the context of their institutional presentation.[17]

Thus, for Gadamer what constitutes a classic is the interpretation of the text, and because of the text's previous evaluative stature and implication in our cultural heritage our hermeneutic engagement is given an even greater intratextual breadth and depth than it would with, for example, a contemporary or lesser known work, an evaluation endorsed by Italo Calvino, ". . . every re-reading of a classic is as much a voyage of discovery as the first reading."[18] As Weinsheimer states:

> A text has no consequences except in it being continually understood . . . The text is an unfinished process, one that is continually completed in the history of its being understood.[19]

For Gadamer, the classic represents tradition as the community of cultural consciousness. Central to his appreciation of the eminent text is its ability to engage our sense of cultural memory, which Gadamer does not summon up for the purposes of reification or that which Andreas Huyssen has cited as ". . . the hermeneutically-oriented culture-as-compensation model."[20], but rather as a route to the self formation of *Bildung* through "understanding". Indeed, Huyssen has observed the noticeable resurgence of interest in the "temporal anchoring"[21] proffered by cultural memory in the face of the late twentieth century's seemingly headlong projection into an accelerated pace of life that obliterates memory, a cultural trend which attempts to salvage the time for what Gadamer designates as the reflection of *phronesis* amidst the accelerated pace of *techne* and *poiesis*. Indeed, despite his disparaging critique of phenomenological hermeneutics, Huyssen's appeal for cultural memory is strikingly similar to Gadamer's exposition of the historical nature of "understanding":

> It [cultural memory] represents the attempt to slow down information processing, to resist the dissolution of time in the synchronicity of the archive, to recover a mode of contemplation outside the universe of simulation and fast-speed information and cable networks, to claim some anchoring space in a world of puzzling and often threatening heterogeneity, non-synchronicity, and information overload.[22]

Such an approach necessarily requires that we do not abdicate from our hermeneutic responsibility to the text, a prerequisite that far from being authoritarian or elitist is founded upon a particularly democratic reader-reception theory, that does not necessarily perpetuate the evaluation of predecessors, although such past value judgements will invariably inform one's historically contingent and situated dialogic interpretation with the source text in the present. As Gadamer explains:

> It was not defining some canon of content specific to the classic that encouraged me to designate the classical as the basic category for effective history. Rather I was trying to indicate what distinguishes the work of art, and particularly the eminent text, from other traditionary materials open to understanding and interpretation. The dialectic of question and answer that I elaborated is not invalidated here but modified: the original question to which a text must be understood as an answer has, as suggested above, an originary superiority to and freedom from its origins. This hardly means that the "classical work" is accessible only in a hopelessly conventional way or that it encourages a reassuringly harmonious conception of the "universally human." Rather, something "speaks" only when it speaks "originarily", that is, "as if it were saying something to me in particular." This hardly means that what speaks in this way is measured by a suprahistorical norm. Just the reverse is true: what speaks in this way sets the standard.[23]

Polarised opinions which ascribe to tradition either reactionary or liberational, negative or positive properties, are prejudices formed according to political agendas external to the text. Frequently such extratextual political agendas are foisted onto texts, or are invoked to decry the classics, as a result of the texts being erroneously confused with being representative of the ruling hegemonies of the past which lauded the self-same texts. However, a will to mastery which extratextually objectifies the text before interpretation takes place is always doomed, unlike the conscious foregrounding and testing of one's prejudice and presuppositions in a dialogue with the source text on the basis of the good will to reach an understanding, for as Risser observes, ". . . In the coalescing of text and interpretation, the text only emerges in its effect . . ."[24].

Undoubtedly, texts may well have been feted by the ruling class in the past, and perhaps for dubious ideological ends, or maybe the author of such texts received state patronage and thus was motivated by the ruling powers, but to deduce, as a result of such historical antecedents, that the text is intrinsically corrupt or the textual promulgator of social division is both dogmatic and unproductive. It is only by assuming one's hermeneutic responsibility[25] in recognition of one's own situated and contingent historical interpretative position that the classic is freed from, although still associated with (and thus bringing a dimension of commonality to the interpretation), past historical associations and evaluations for a different understanding in the present. As Jonathan Miller points out:

> With texts that come from the more or less distant past, it is often claimed that their meaning inevitably changes with the passage of time, and that it is only profitable to read them for contemporary meanings or for meanings which are interestingly relevant to the modern imagination. Hirsch points out that if this attitude is taken to its logical conclusion the reader encounters no one but himself each time he engages with a text, or an utterance, from the distant past. In any case, it is not the meaning of the text that changes with the passage of time but its significance. The mere fact that a modern reader can recognise implications which would have been unrecognisable to the original author does not imply that the meaning has altered.[26]

The Ideal Text

The term "classic" or "the classic" is used with abandon when discussing art and literature but any attempt to define what constitutes a classic is fraught with conflictual opinions and contradictions. Of course "classic" is essentially an evaluative term, but in order to come close to a definition of the word it is helpful to consider not only what shapes and directs such an evaluation but also, and in the first instance, to discuss the socio-historical roots of such an aesthetic differentiation based on a process of exclusion and inclusion.

The first documented reference to a "classic" in aesthetic terms is attributed to Aulus Gellius in the second century in his statement ". . . a classic writer is distinguished from the rabble."[27] The class-based distinctions associated with the *classicus scriptor* and the *proletarius* and by extension, their relationship to aesthetic judgement, were alluded to even earlier by Aristotle when he discerned a distinct division between the make-up of theatre audiences according to their appreciation of either epic and tragedy:

> It may be asked which of the two forms of representation is the better, the epic or the tragic. If the better form is the less vulgar, and the less vulgar is always that which is designed to appeal to the better type of audience, then it is obvious that the form that appeals to everybody is extremely vulgar . . . Thus epic is said to appeal to cultivated readers who do not need the help of visible forms, while tragedy appeals to meaner minds. If then it is a vulgar art, it is obviously inferior to epic.[28]

Guillory has drawn attention to the fact that although ". . . selections of texts historically have the appearance of having selected themselves,"[29] in the antique period the concept of an ideal author centred on a grammatical criterion whereby, to quote Quintilian, the *grammatici* were concerned to teach both "the art of speaking correctly"[30] and the skilful interpretation of the poets. Indeed it was these early expositions of the rules governing interpretation that not only set a precedent for the art of interpretation, but which also set a model for what could now be designated as "literary" writing. *Grammaticus sensus*, that is, interpretation based upon the verification of what words originally mean, was the result of such institutionalised prescription and this interpretative practice was the norm as early as the classical age of Athens, when Homer's language was no longer immediately intelligible to the Athenians or to the Alexandrians. In this respect, the phenomenon of linguistic change and the ageing of linguistically fixed utterances lie at the source of the impulse to determine *sensus litteralis*. Gadamer refers to the earliest antecedents of what we refer to, today, as literature:

> The concept of literature is not unrelated to the reader. Literature does not exist as the dead remnant of an alienated being, left over for a later time as simultaneous with its experiential reality. Literature is a function of being intellectually preserved and handed down, and therefore brings its hidden history into every age.[31]

It was from such institutionalisation of literary skills, based on rhetorical aptitude and linguistic fluency, and the subsequent desire to realise the original meaning of earlier texts that the impetus for canon formation came about. A result of such interpretative strategies as *grammaticus sensus* was that all notions of historical distance were erased by an impulse to preserve and recover an originary sense. Thus as early as the classical age of Athens we can identify the desire to draw the canonical text, which Homer represented for the Athenians and Alexandrians, out of its historical remoteness into the present to make it not only comprehensible but also "present" as proof of its undiminished validity and its right to canonical status.

Another interpretative strategy, which was partly to supersede the concept of *sensus grammaticus*, was *allegoresis*, which had been practised by the Sophists, the Cynics and was further elaborated by the Stoics. Such a strategy arose especially out of the dissatisfaction with Homer's representation of and pronouncements about the Gods, an unease expressed by the pre-Socratic philosopher Xenophanes[32], and later Plato who wanted to drive all poets as heretics out of his "ideal" Republic.[33] *Allegoresis* allowed the Stoics to make the reactionary claim that the ideas of their own time had been anticipated and prefigured in allegorical disguise by canonical authors like Homer, and this led them to conflate the historical distanciation between their own reception and the production of Homeric classics so that they might invoke the classics as an endorsement and justification of their present social practices. In this respect, the foundations of canon formation can be seen to reflect a concern to diminish historical distanciation either by eradicating the interpretative historical standpoint, in the manner of *sensus grammaticus*, or by shifting a text from another era into their own historical horizon, like *allegoresis*[34].

Thus, the concept of the classic came about as a result of the ancients' notion of a literary ideal, a model for other writers to follow. However, as the corpus of literary models proliferated a more complex process of retroactive evaluation of literature evolved. Although the evaluation of certain texts as classics has been to a large extent dictated and perpetuated by institutions representative of the dominant ideology or to refer to Althusser, the ISAs, it is erroneous to consider the texts upon which classic status is bestowed as being in any way a product or necessarily reflective of the dominant ideology the institutions embody and promulgate. Moreover, most classics are not considered to be classics during their own period of production, and are only given the cultural kudos of canonical status retrospectively according to an evaluative process of retroaction of signification. Unlike the *grammatici's* "model" of a classic which was self-consciously prescribed by the ancients at the time of its inception, later literature which might be considered classic today such as, for example, the works of Shakespeare, were popular rather than being self-consciously classic at their point of production. It is only through a process of institutional evaluation and the retroactive conferral of classic status that the works of Shakespeare have evolved into what we know today as canonical, although this process is often elided with the prescriptive notion of the classic which the Greeks instituted at the point of or at least soon after the text's production. In this way, the complex intratextuality which is intrinsic to the source text's secondary production as a classic becomes obscured, giving the mystifying impression that the classic status is a pregiven or intrinsic quality rather than a retroactive and appropriative expression of value. Andre Lefevere's explanation of the canon as a literary system is worth quoting in full in order to make clear the distinction, which is frequently blurred, between the texts which are subsequently deemed to be classics and the canonical structure:

> Significantly, though, works of literature canonised more than five centuries ago tend to remain secure in their positions, no matter how often the dominant poetics is subject to change. This is a clear indication of the conservative bias of the system itself, and also of the power of rewriting, since what happens in this case is that the work of literature itself remains canonised while the "received interpretation" or even the "right interpretation" in systems with undifferentiated patronage, quite simply changes.[35]

The notion of the classic as a literary ideal, an aesthetic model to which other authors should aspire, was a view that was to be reinvoked and consolidated during the Augustan period. Raymond Williams has pointed out that "literature" as an aesthetic category and academic discipline did not emerge until the eighteenth century and it was with the institutional concretization of "literature" that the stultifying "stable" standards of good and bad, high and low literature arose.[36] The eighteenth century may be considered as the historical period in which the classics were to become most closely linked to a notion of literary standard, canonicity and dominant ideology.

However, the classic texts which are the object of historically situated criticism should not be constrained by such critical evaluation for all time, and although many texts hailed as classics during the eighteenth century were unarguably synonymous, or at least presented in such a manner as to be synonymous with the dominant ideology, the associations which were forged at that time were often artificially appropriative and frequently had the effect of devaluing art to the level of the status symbol. Indeed, Gadamer addresses the problem whereby a classic can degenerate to the level of historical object for the purposes of progressive research, and he further warns against the danger of 'appropriating' the other persons in one's understanding and thereby failing to recognise his or her otherness. The critical approaches of different periods must be recognised as being deeply permeated with and formulated by ideological, cultural and even theological concepts, emphasising the imperative for any competent criticism to address and interrogate past critical appraisals in the full awareness that literature, to a large extent, has been constituted by the criticism that has read and passed judgement on it. Matthew Arnold (1880, Introduction to T. H. Ward's *The English Poets*) drew attention to the need for such critical circumspection although, somewhat ironically, he often failed to exhibit and apply a consciousness of his particular historically contingent interpretative standpoint when making his own critical pronouncements:

> In the present work, [Arnold is referring to his article "The Study of Poetry"] therefore, we are sure of frequent temptation to adopt the historic estimate, or the personal estimate, and to forget the real estimate; which latter, nevertheless, we must employ if we are to make poetry yield us its full benefit . . . The exaggerations due to the historic estimate are not in themselves, perhaps, of very much gravity. Their report hardly enters the general ear; probably they do not always impose even on the literary men who adopt them. But they lead to a dangerous abuse of language. So we hear Caedmon, amongst our own poets, compared to Milton. I have already noticed the enthusiasm of one accomplished French critic for 'historic origins.'[37]

Too often the prevailing literary criticism and judgements of a given period, like that of, for example, the neo-classical period, become absorbed into the mainstream of the literary criticism of subsequent ages and are not always carefully distinguished as being the result of a specific ideological, and thus biased, agenda. Indeed, as Weinsheimer observes, it was during the neo-classical period that the damaging notion of "surviving" the passage of time became one of the key criteria for canonical status, as illustrated by Johnson's remarks about Shakespeare (1765, *The Plays of William Shakespeare*)

> The Poet of whose works I have undertaken the revision may now begin to assume the dignity of an ancient, and claim the privilege of established fame and prescriptive veneration. He has long outlived his century, the term commonly fixed as the test of literary merit.[38]

At this time the classic became synonymous with being a textual survivor within a historical continuity, which, as opposed to being evidence of cultural continuity, had the essentialist effect of creating the perception that the classics were the cultural vestiges of eternal truths and transcendent values. When the age of a text becomes the chief criterion for assessing its value, and we assume a sense of culture on the basis of "knowing" the ancient texts, we have reached a stage whereby we have distanced ourselves from ever reaching a true "understanding" of the classics, for as Marowitz states " . . . [i]t is the malleability of a classic that we should celebrate, not simply its age."[39] John Lahr, commenting on Peter Sellars' 1993 Gulf War adaptation of Aeschylus' *The Persians* also emphasises the vibrant immediacy of cultural continuity over misplaced admiration and distant veneration for texts which merely survive a chronological test of time:

> A classic is a house we're still living in . . . you're going to fix it up and add a new wing. It's not an exhibit, it's meant to be lived in and not admired.[40]

For Johnson it was the very historical distanciation that revealed those works which were classic from those which were not, and as opposed to hermeneutically celebrating the classic for intrinsic merit, he evaluated such works on the basis of their having passed the test of time, as illustrated by the following remarks:

> There is a kind of intellectual remoteness necessary for the comprehension of any great work in its full design and true proportions[41]

According to this deterministic critical trajectory, the classic does not merely 'survive' with and through culture, but it actually begins to shape and create our sense of culture, a point elaborated on by Herrnstein Smith:

> . . . it will begin to perform certain characteristic cultural functions by virtue of the very fact that it has endured—that is, the functions of a canonical work as such—and be valued and preserved accordingly: as a witness to lost innocence, former glory, and/or apparently persistent communal interests and "values" and thus a banner of communal identity; as a reservoir of images, archetypes and topoi—characters and episodes, passages and verbal tags—repeatedly invoked and recurrently applied to new situations and circumstances; and as a stylistic and generic exemplar that will energise the production of subsequent works and texts (upon which the latter will be modelled and by which, as a normative "touchstone" they will be measured.).[42]

Undoubtedly, this naively temporal bound attribution of classic status played a part in consolidating the negative and reactionary connotations and opinions about the classic which persist today, but as Gadamer has perceptively emphasised, such a phenomenon tells us more about the eras which gave rise to such prescriptions, than enlightening us about the 'value' of the classics. Augustan literary criticism highlights how the evaluation of art, by way of the refusal to develop a consciousness of its own historically contingent interpretative position, can actually become divorced from any hermeneutic interaction with the work of art, a rift which, as Herrnstein Smith observes, invariably leads to the familiar but futile " . . . searches for 'true' or objective value and for uniquely 'correct' interpretations or determinate meanings."[43] Indeed, an insight into Augustan criticism highlights how easily the ideological coherence of the canon can become confused with the potential hermeneutic singularity of the classic, a distinction emphasised by Weinsheimer:

> While the canon is plural but determinate, grammatical usage suggests that "the classic" by contrast, is essentially singular and indeterminate . . . Classicality is a property of the work and even its being. Both adjective and noun, classic is what a classic is. Canonicity, in contrast, is not a quality or characteristic of the work (still less its being) but rather the result of what has happened to it—namely, canonisation, a process which the work undergoes and which alters nothing in it. The claim of the classic is essential; the claim of the canonical is either institutional, conventional, or historical, but in any case accidental.[44]

Bergonzi has pointed out that by the early nineteenth century "English" evolved into a multi-faceted concept which encompassed nation, language, literature and the academic discipline. The retrospective conferral of literary value on texts during the nineteenth century came to assume a distinctly nationalistic drive, as well as including texts which were written in other countries and in other languages suggesting that canon formation acquired an almost imperialistic impetus.[45] Also in a similar vein to Samuel Johnson in the eighteenth century, Matthew Arnold's criticism which reflected the dominant ideology of the nineteenth century society he inhabited, was to have a noticeable impact upon the formation of the canon and subsequent aesthetic evaluations. Both critics emphasised that any real artistic and literary merit depended on how far the texts reflected and represented the moral dictums and norms of the societies in which they were received, namely their own, as illustrated by Arnold's own explanation:

> We find attraction at times . . . in a poetry of revolt against them [morals]; in a poetry which might take for its motto Omar Kheyam's words: 'Let us make up in the tavern for the time which we have wasted in the mosque.' Or we find attractions in a poetry indifferent to them; in a poetry where the contents may be what

they will, but the form is studied and exquisite. We delude ourselves in either
case; and the best cure for our delusion is to let our minds rest upon that great
and inexhaustible word, life, until we learn to enter into its meaning. A poetry of
revolt against moral ideas is a poetry of indifference towards life.[46]

Such prescription towards literary evaluation reflects an ideological agenda
that suggests that a particular moral outlook can be a critical criterion,
and thus an essential feature of and yardstick for "good" or "high" art,
and indeed Arnold identified the critical failure to observe such prescriptive methods as "charlatanism":

Charlatanism is for confusing and obliterating the distinction between excellent
and inferior, sound or unsound or only half sound, true and untrue or only half
untrue.[47]

Although the benevolent paternalism of Arnold's cultural project is well
known, his criticism further propounded the artificial division between
"high" and "low" art and it undoubtedly contributed to the later criticism
levelled against the classics as being reflections of established and ideologically driven power structures. It is not unreasonable to view the
Arnoldian project, that propounded the duty of educated and enlightened
guardians of society to cultivate 'the masses' in compensation for and as
protection against a perceived loss of spirituality in Victorian Britain, as
an example of cultural control. Arnold drew clear distinctions between
high and low art, believing that "society" (which in reality meant the
ruling societal guardians and watchdogs) should assume a prescriptive
role when making decisions about aesthetic distinctions and he praised
the Academie Francaise " . . . for creating a form of intellectual culture
which shall impose itself on all around," going on to make an impassioned plea for a similar cultural paternalism in England (1861, "On Translating Homer"):

I think that in England, partly from the want of an Academy, partly from a national habit of intellect, but which that want of an Academy is itself due, there
exists too little of what I may call a public force of correct literary opinion possessing within certain limits a clear sense of what is right and wrong, sound and
unsound . . . Anyone who can introduce a little order into this chaos by establishing in any quarter a single sound rule of criticism, a single rule which clearly
marks what is right as right, and what is wrong as wrong, does a good deed.[48]

Thus throughout the nineteenth century culture was seen to be synonymous with the ruling classes and the maintenance of the status quo, a
cultural hegemony which was perceived to be threatened by the rapid

dissemination of independent printed material and uncensored publications. Indeed the "deterioration" of cultural standards was observed by and commented upon by Arnold in his essay "The Function of Criticism" (1867):

> I am bound by my own definition of criticism: *a disinterested endeavour to learn and propagate the best that is known and thought in the world.* How much of English Literature comes into this 'best that is known and thought in the world"? Not very much, I fear, certainly less at this moment, than of the current literature of France and Germany.[49]

Indeed, Edmund Gosse, expressed his fear at the rise of the democratising spirit in the form of the flourishing printed matter in the nineteenth century:

> One danger which I have long foreseen from the spread of democratic sentiment is that the tradition of literary taste, the canons of literature, are being reversed by a popular vote. Up to the present time the mass of educated and semi-educated persons, who form the vast majority of readers, though they cannot and do not appreciate the classics of their race, have been content to acknowledge their traditional supremacy.[50]

De Quincey also passed comment on the democratisation of the access to literature (1863, "The Art of Conversation"):

> But a class of readers, prodigiously more extensive has formed itself within the commercial orders of our great cities and manufacturing districts . . . But the interest of literature has now swept downwards through a vast compass of descents . . . It still remains true that the busier classes are the main reading classes whilst from their immense numbers, they are becoming effectually the body that will more and more impress upon the moving literature its main impulse and direction.[51]

Examples like these clearly illustrate how the canon may deviate from being a gauge of cultural value into a prescriptive agenda founded on socio-political control and determinism, and even when culture is in benevolent and paternalistic hands such attitudes reveal how the aesthetic evaluations of the traditional liberal humanist are often set within carefully guarded and prescribed parameters:

> However much [the classics] . . . may be seen to question secular vanities such as wealth, social position and political power, and remind their readers of more elevated values and virtues and oblige them to confront such hard truths and harsh realities as their own morality and the hidden griefs of obscure people . . . [they] would not be found to please long and well if they were seen radically to undercut the establishment interests or effectively to subvert the ideologies that support them.[52]

Many Victorian cultural critics were undoubtedly perturbed by the rising accessibility of the printed word, for such availability threatened the rarefied cultural superiority they had cultivated and which had enabled them to bolster their own sense of self-importance within the class system. In this respect the "distinction" attributed to texts on the grounds of aesthetic value appeared to degenerate into a "distinction" rooted in social divisiveness and elitism. The repercussions of the criticism motivated by such an agenda was not only to carry over into the twentieth century but also the criticism of, say, Matthew Arnold and Samuel Johnson was even to attain canonical status itself and thus elude closer critical scrutiny. Moreover, a further consequence of the cultural enshrinement of the criticism penned by Arnold and Johnson was that the misconception of the classics as intrinsically elitist was further consolidated and affirmed.

The Evaluating Institutions

The concept of the classic, besides having clearly prescriptive roots and being based on a decidedly ahistorical interpretative strategy, has from its inception been closely linked to socio-economic factors, a relationship that was to become even more formalised and entrenched with the institutionalisation of education. Institutions and establishments that form part of the dominant ideology at any one time, such as the academy, publishers and critics, are integral to the conferral of approval and status upon designated works of art, and they form an essential part in the process of canon formation. Indeed, with respect to the role played by the academy in canon formation and its decision as to what constitutes a classic text, it is noteworthy that as early as the sixth century Magnus Felix Ennodius described his student as a "classicus" who attends classes, and much later Littre, the nineteenth century lexicographer, defined the "classique" as that which is taught in classes. Gadamer also endorses the connection between the inception of "the classic" and the academy when he states "they [the authors and their works] were preserved in the history of Western culture precisely because they became canonical as writers of the 'school'."[53]

However, although the notion of the classic was originally conceived as an ideologically prescribed and sanctioned model to which all other authors should aspire this developed into a far more complicated concept as differing communities within a more heterogeneous social structure reacted against these primary literary models. Today literature deemed canonical at any given time is the result of an interactive dynamic between the past and the contemporary, besides being the consequence of a variety of institutional "evaluative" practices. Even though the concept of evaluation behind the classic is founded on the ancients' idea of a literary ideal, it is foolishly short-sighted to view the classics as elitist, for as previously discussed, the rise of printed matter in the nineteenth century followed by the technological developments of mass communication during this century has transformed the conferral of literary value into a far more heterogeneous and sophisticated affair. Herrnstein Smith has identified the multifarious evaluative influences and procedures which help to shape our perception of literary value:

> The recommendation of value represented by the repeated inclusion of a particular work in anthologies of "great poetry" not only promotes but goes some distance toward *creating* the value of that work, as does its repeated appearance on reading lists or its frequent citation or quotation by professors, scholars, critics, poets and other elders of the tribe; for all these acts have the effect of drawing the work into the orbit of attention of potential readers and, by making the work more likely to be experienced at all, they make it more likely to be experienced as "valuable." In a sense value creates value.[54]

The major institutional evaluations about literature are taken by the academy, critics and publishers, and this is further shaped by the ongoing effect of the poet-critic tradition which reinforces certain texts' status by way of derivative references and allusions to their literary predecessors in their own work.

The poet-critic tradition is another section of the larger evaluative community that is instrumental in the production of new and different forms of art as well as creating the climate for the appreciation of novel art forms which flourishes in response to the given literary selections and evaluations of its own age. The poet-critic tradition is an essential component in the transformation, mutation and shaping of the evaluative procedure, and because it is one stage removed from the artwork it is often a less highlighted but nonetheless deceptively powerful aspect of the way any given culture reaches notions about literary value, for as Gerard Genette has pointed out, ". . . a period is manifested as much by what it reads as by what it writes, and these two aspects of 'literature' act upon one another."[55] Of course the poet-critic tradition is totally bound up with the previously considered evaluative powers of the academy, in that present and future poets and critics have been educated and thus intellectually formed by exposure to the very texts which the academy has evaluated or continued to evaluate as classic. T. S. Eliot alluded to the dialectic dynamic which produces literary language when he considered the mechanics of the poet-critic tradition (1920, "Tradition and the Individual Talent")

> We dwell with satisfaction upon the poet's difference from his predecessors, especially his immediate predecessors; we endeavour to find something that can be isolated in order to be enjoyed, whereas if we approach a poet without this prejudice we shall often find that not only the best, but the most individual parts of his work may be those in which the dead poets, his ancestors, assert their immortality most vigorously.[56]

Edward Shils' comprehensive study of the tradition and its formation also refers to the poet-critic tradition, as well as drawing attention to the popular misconception, as illustrated by Artaud's infamous call to ". . . let the dead poets make way for the others"[57], of treating originality and tradition, the new and classic, as mutually exclusive:

> . . . works of literature in the present assimilate one work or an epoch of works by succeeding generations. However great any novelist of the twentieth century might be, his works do not render superfluous the reading of any other great works from the past. [58]

Thus, besides the overt institutional evaluation of literary texts, the more covert intertextual activity of the poet-critic tradition contributes to canon formation, for by alluding to, criticising, and even parodying earlier works they tacitly imply a certain criterion of the continuity of value through change. Just as Gadamer has likened the literary critic to a weaver who adds and thus extends the tapestry of tradition that supports us, Shil has made the following observation about the often disruptive effect new art has upon that self-same tradition

> Each time a new work is added to the gallery of surviving works by which the tradition of literature is constituted, the tradition changes. It changes not by addition alone, but by the changes which occur in the understanding of the works which are already in the tradition. The generation subsequent to the tradition has before it a tradition which is different from that faced by its predecessors.[59]

Barbara Herrnstein Smith has astutely observed that evaluation, including literary evaluation, is always compromised, because value is always in motion, and unless we continue to treat the classic as a prescriptive literary model in the manner of the *grammatici*, it is erroneous and an abdication of hermeneutic responsibility to equate a literary text with the dominant ideology which has conferred the cultural cachet of classic status upon that text, or, for that matter, the dominant ideology which continues to adhere to a text's cultural kudos for ideological or extratextual purposes. As Herrnstein Smith explains:

> For like all value, literary value is not the property of an object *or* of a subject but, rather, *the product of the dynamics of a system*. As readers and critics of literature, we are within that system; and because we are neither omniscient nor immortal and do have particular interests, we will, at any given moment, be viewing it from *some* perspective. It is from such a perspective that we experience the value of the work, and also from such a perspective that we estimate its probable value for others. There is nothing illusory in the experience, however, or necessarily inaccurate in the estimate. From that real (if limited) perspective, at the real (if transient) moment, our experience of the value of the work *is* its value. Or, in the terms I should prefer: our experience of "the value of the work" is equivalent to *our experience of the work in relation to the total economy of our existence.*[60]

The necessary distinction between the classic status bestowed on texts which fall beneath the canonical panoply erected during any particular age, and the material text, provides the interpretative space occupied by the Rewrite, which neither affirms or refutes the classic's status, but rather harnesses its cultural cachet to provide the intratextual foundation between its production, "classic" status and current reception for its own dramaturgy. In this respect, the Rewrite can be seen, amongst other things, as a performative exploration of the dynamics of the valuing and evaluating system which constitutes and perpetuates the present day category of "literature"[61] including the evaluative variables of good/bad, classic/non-canonical and major/minor which sustain it. Thus, despite the correct identification of the inception of "the classic" with prescriptive and establishment ideology this does not preclude the suitability of such texts for a radical aesthetic interaction with daily *praxis* in the present. Indeed, it is the Rewrite's exploitation of the classics' imbrication with dominant ideology that contributes toward and facilitates a new and potentially radical aesthetic experience in the present.

Although the canon and its formation are and have been closely allied to the interests and perspectives of the ideologically motivated powers that be at any given time, the decisions about literary value are not totally formulated by such institutions, but rather these institutions base their decisions as a result of a complex response to the overall social and political climate of opinion of the larger community they represent. The unseen but complex social dynamic which operates behind cultural evaluation is cited by Herrnstein Smith:

> . . . in accord with the changing interests and other values of a community, various potential meanings of a work will become more or less visible (or

"realisable") and the visibility—and hence value—of the work for that community
will change accordingly. The problem here can be seen as the interlooping of two
circles, the hermeneutic and the evaluative.[62]

Herrnstein Smith cites the overlap of the hermeneutic and evaluative dimensions of our approach to texts as problematic, but Gadamer's theory
of the eminent text regards such an interpretative collision as a prerequisite to gaining access to the path which affirms a work of art's hermeneutic "value". As opposed to negating the inevitable prejudice engendered
by the pre-evaluated authority of the classic, Gadamer views the eminent
text's evaluative stature as providing the most fertile ground to develop
and arouse either negative or positive prejudices—a prerequisite for hermeneutic dialogue. In this respect the perception of the eminent text's established value and authority is the best source for the prejudice which instigates hermeneutic experience, because unlike contemporary art the classic
exhibits the genuine productivity of the course of events. Thus, unlike
contemporary art which does not represent the evaluative kudos, bolstered by the productive intratextuality created by temporal distance, the
classic is an ideological vortex of evaluative and historical ideas which
arouses the prerequisite prejudice for the attainment of hermeneutic understanding. As Gadamer explains:

> Everyone is familiar with the curious impotence of our judgement where temporal
> distance has not given us sure criteria. Thus the judgement of contemporary
> works of art is desperately uncertain for the scholarly consciousness. Obviously
> we approach such creations with unverifiable prejudices, presuppositions that
> have too great an influence over us for us to know about them; these can give
> contemporary creations an extra resonance that does not correspond to their
> true content and significance. Only when all their relations to the present time
> have faded away can their real nature appear, so that the understanding of what
> is said in them can claim to be authoritative and universal.[63]

Status and Literariness

John Guillory has emphasised the degree to which linguistic and knowledge "capital" is still very much implicated in any literary evaluation, and
similarly, Gadamerian hermeneutics presupposes a level of intellectual
competency. Guillory explains:

> I regard these two kinds of capital [linguistic and knowledge] as ultimately more
> socially significant in their effects than the "ideological" content of literary works,
> a content which the critics of the canon see as reinforcing the exclusion of minor-
> ity authors from the canon by expressing the same values which determine exclu-

sionary judgements. Literary works must be seen rather as the vector of ideological notions which do not inhere in the works themselves but in the context of their institutional presentation, or more simply, in the way in which they are taught.[64]

Undoubtedly, our appreciation of certain classics has sometimes become more dependent on and shaped by the academy which, in the past, has been instrumental in the conferral of the very canonical status such texts enjoy. However, "linguistic capital" does not and should not apply to most classic texts, and if it does, it is not the texts that should be lambasted as elitist relics, but rather it is the competence or indeed the tacit elitism of the educational experts that should be scrutinised. In addition, certain critics believe that the classics are defunct today because they do not represent societal and cultural heterogeneity, but as Guillory astutely points out such an argument is founded upon a conception of "the literary canon as a hypothetical image of social diversity, a kind of mirror in which social groups see themselves,"[65] reducing literary evaluation to the "imaginary politics" of image and representation. Critiques like that postulated by Henry Louis Gates Jr. are not only predicated on the erroneous assumption that representation can redress social exclusion, but also they fail to perceive how a fruitful engagement with the classics can reveal far more about how social exclusion can arise, as well as revealing how productive hermeneutic play through the reinscription of the excluded can be utilised to great pedagogical effect:

> . . . the teaching of literature has meant teaching an aesthetic and political order in which no women and people of colour were ever able to discover the reflection or representation of their images, or the resonances of their cultural voices.[66]

Too often, as illustrated above, critics confusingly combine socio-historical critique with the merits and failings of the texts which comprise the canon. Indeed, the performative re-evaluation of the Rewrite addresses such problems, by negotiating with the classic as opposed to making the relatively empty gesture of replacing it with a more representative image. Thus, if certain social groups consider themselves to be alienated by the classics, either because of knowledge or linguistic capital, or indeed by restricted access, it is surely, as Guillory suggests, not because the texts are elitist but because the channels through which those texts are taught or produced are failing to make the classics accessible. Bourdieau and other cultural sociologists have argued that the classics are tools of the ideologically driven powers to cement social division through what he describes as the administered reception of art, but this critique, I would suggest, ultimately persists in confusing the evaluative appropriation of the text with the text itself, as opposed to being instrumental in highlighting an intrinsic textual elitism.

Thus, the literary language of canonical texts cannot be cited as elitist per se, although invariably the longer such works endure, the more difficult the reading of them may become and thus all the more dependent on the resources of educational expertise. With respect to the "linguistic capital" of the classics one can clearly see how, yet again, the relationship between canonical texts and institutions becomes so consolidated in the popular imagination that an erroneous equation is made that confuses the restricted accessibility to the classics, often perpetuated by educational inequality and social injustice, with the unjustifiable charge that the classic texts' are intrinsically elitist. As Guillory explains:

> . . . the argument that such social bias is the determinant of canon formation has been so generally accepted in critical discourse that it is now capable of being elaborated into a general critique of aesthetic judgement. In its most extreme form this critique seeks to discredit the concept of the aesthetic altogether, as intrinsically repressive . . . [t]he extrapolation of a critique of aesthetics from the critique of the canon is mistaken in its fundamental premise. This premise takes the form of "aesthetic value" on the grounds that aesthetic values cannot be distinguished from any other values in the social realm, not even economic value.[67]

The blinkered response to aesthetic value which trenchantly couples art with, for example, economic "use value", also fails to consider the dynamics of cultural formation as postulated by, for example, Bakhtin, who in his analysis of Rabelais' *Gargantua and Pantagruel* illustrates culture as being processual and evolutionary, rather than being founded on a perpetual reaction against a perceived static and atrophying reiteration. Indeed, if the classics do become increasingly rarefied and exclusive, which is the natural trajectory of the "use value" argument, they will disappear not only by pricing themselves out of the market but by failing to fulfil their cultural responsibility to the community at large, with the result that a more popular art form would replace them. Indeed, in an age of mass media and communication which facilitates easy access to a wide range of art forms the use value argument appears to be somewhat outmoded, although Bourdieau's and Herrnstein Smith's theses about the double discourse of value pertaining to art is still useful when considering the commodification of art.[68] However, there is and has been since the middle of the eighteenth century the notion of the aesthetic which as Murray Krieger has comprehensively explained undoubtedly plays a role in the conspiracy of the acquisitive society. Indeed, Lord Kames' opinions illustrate the popular endorsement of the aesthetic as precious commodity during the eighteenth century:

> A flourishing commerce begets opulence; and opulence, inflaming our appetite for pleasure, is commonly vented on luxury, and on every sensual gratification: selfishness rears its head; becomes fashionable; and infecting all ranks, extinguishes the *amor patriae*, and every spark of public spirit. To prevent or retard such fatal corruption, the genius of an Alfred cannot devise any means more efficacious, than the venting of opulence upon the Fine Arts; riches employ'd, instead of encouraging vice will excite virtue.[69]

Caygill considers Kames' work as representative of an eighteenth century settlement between ". . . the traditional fear of the luxurious corruption of virtue and the aspiration to justify the virtues of commercial society through moral sense."[70] Such aestheticisation transforms art objects into precious objects, but literature must be distinguished as a special category whereby although a propensity for literature to succumb to such aestheticisation certainly exists, it is less likely to occur because of the literary hermeneutic potential of words, which already have meaning or the potential for meaning prior to the artist's use of them. In this respect literature is a distinct aesthetic medium from the plastic arts which are ". . . usually regarded as a neutral element open to being manipulated by the artist into his medium."[71] Besides the preciousness with which the eighteenth century critics and institutions invested Fine Art, the commodification of the aesthetic can take the form of a throwaway, self gratificatory and ephemeral consumerism, although both forms exemplify the aestheticisation of hermeneutics whereby fashion or modishness suppresses and supersedes the meaning and understanding which is so central to Gadamer's hermenuetic of aesthetics. As Barthes perspicaciously observes with respect to the hermeneutic ideal of re-reading a text:

> Rereading, an operation contrary to the commercial and ideological habits of our society which would have us "throw away" the story once it has been consumed ('devoured') so that we can then move onto another story, buy another book.[72]

To equate the classics solely with economic "use value" does not truly account for their undoubted popularity today, (although, as stated, this can lapse into faddishness and consumerism). In addition, such an approach overlooks the fluctuating fortunes which undoubtedly beset the reception of what are deemed to be classic texts, and as such does not confront cultural formation in its whole and complex totality, a point raised by Terry Eagleton:

When Shakespeare's texts cease to make us think, when we get nothing out of them, they will cease to have value. But why they 'make us think', why we 'get something out of them' (if only for the present) is a question which must be referred at once to the ideological matrix of our reading and the ideological matrix of their production. It is in the articulation of these distinct moments that the question of value resides.[73]

Indeed, the convincing counter-argument to those who would abandon all notions of literary value on the grounds of an encroaching and unavoidable elitist commodification of art, is that the result of such an approach will be a "free for all" culture, whereby having dispensed with any criteria for evaluating art, literally anything, that is, non-art, would be art and art would be non-art. Such an unhierachicized textuality, and the potential cultural demise it presents for all, is explained by Weinsheimer:

For when nothing is excluded, literature (now called "text") becomes an all-inclusive category. The universe becomes a universe of discourse, the world is textualized, literaturized and the literature professors reclaim their lost empire . . . In certain respects, pantextualism has merely universalised the puristic aestheticism from which we were fleeing insofar as it acknowledges no Other of the text, no non-text to puncture its pretensions to universality and resist its imperialist ambitions. When Froula recommends a pedagogy of interrogation that "calls into question" the best that has been thought and said . . . we begin to wonder whether despite all this questioning some questions are nevertheless precluded— indeed precisely the ones that would call the authority to the questioner into question . . . What text does the pantextualist reverence? . . . if there are not, how does critical thought that venerates no text escape venerating itself and thus becoming uncritical?[74]

Bakhtin's work on cultural formation is helpful with respect to understanding how the evolution of different and new art forms is not predicated on replacing what came before, or indeed based on the premise that all new art must necessarily stand in stark contrast to its cultural predecessors. Instead, Bakhtin asserts that all new art is actually founded on a relationship, a cultural symbiosis between itself and received culture, of which the classic forms a part, as explained by Guillory:

"Literary language" [and by extension other literary works] . . . forms at the interface between the language of preserved literary texts and the context-bound speech that continually escapes total regulation and hence *changes*. It is different from both.[75]

Bakhtin's study of Rabelais' *Gargantua and Pantagruel* reveals socio-linguistics as an area of struggle, the outcome of which is new, although often transient, literary genres and language, which are dependent on the effect of a dynamic dialogue with the canonical models which precede them. For example, during the Renaissance, Rabelais' work brought folk humour into artistic dialogue with official ideological discourse, not in order to effect a parodic inversion but to expose an effect of distance through a reinscription upon the official literary discourse. In this way Rabelais revealed the crumbling foundations upon which official ideology was built, so that:

> The culture of folk humour that had been shaped during many centuries and that had defended the people's creativity in non-official terms in verbal expression or spectacle could now rise to the high level of literature and ideology and fertilise it . . . The thousand year old laughter not only fertilised literature but was itself fertilised by humanist knowledge and advanced literary technique.[76]

Thus, although many of the ancient classics were evaluated during the antique and early modern period according to socio-linguistic criteria and thus set a linguistic precedent for subsequent literature, the copying of models was to be superseded by the dynamics which help to formulate our ever-changing idea as to what constitutes "literariness". As Bahktin has shown literary language is one of the most dynamic sites of change and is an aesthetic gauge for the continuous struggle between the "standard" dominant linguistic norms and the vernacular discourse of heteroglossia.

Because the increasing literariness of the classics can restrict our access to them, the misconception arises that these texts are intrinsically elitist, but in reality it is often the very perception or indeed experience of the classics' literariness, or to put it another way difficulty, that gives rise to the evolution of literary language itself in new and different forms. As such, a concept of traditional value and received standards is a necessary and integral part of cultural formation, an opinion intrinsic to Gadamerian hermeneutics which Joel Weinsheimer lucidly explains:

> Since art in Gadamer's view is just as interpretative as the interpretation of it, his hermeneutics necessarily forgoes the possibility of any specifically aesthetic hermeneutics. But then its whole point is to affirm that all creation as well as all understanding is mimetic, interpretive, traditionary: always dependent on precedent while always transforming it as well.[77]

In addition, it is the very literariness of the classics that presents the greatest hermeneutic challenge to our sense of hermeneutic responsibility, which to refer to Blanchot's metaphor, is an irresistible force akin to the combination of familiarity and strangeness presented by the Sirens' song which challenges us to listen for the unheard in the heard:

> What makes them seductive is . . . the future of what they say. Their fascination is due not to their current song but to what it promises to be.[78]

Blanchot discusses the distinction between a classic which demands literariness, and non-literary reading, and he concludes that the latter is a submission to a text that is no more than a " . . . stoutly woven web of determined signification."[79] Going on to analyse language and its every-day usage, Blanchot likens understanding to the rolling of the boulder which blocks the entrance to Lazarus' tomb:

> To roll the stone, to move it away, is certainly something marvellous but we accomplish it each instant in our everyday language and we converse each instant with this Lazarus.[80]

However, when confronted with literary language, our communication is not merely at the level of repeating the well told story of raising the dead, however fantastic and imaginative it may be, but rather it is actually being present at the event of resurrection when " . . . a vast deluge of stone . . . strikes the earth and the sky."[81] Indeed, Chladinius observed that once a story becomes " unexpected, improbable or fanciful" like so many biblical legends then it is "in need of interpretation"[82], and Blanchot's metaphorical allusion to *understanding* being akin to physically witnessing Lazarus's resurrection, as opposed to hearing a repeated story or received *knowledge* is both illuminating and insightful when explaining the experience of *Erlebnis* in our reception of art. A sense of hermeneutic responsibility in the reader or spectator arises not only because of an ineluctable and indefinable aesthetic quality created by the classics' literariness, but as a consequence of the classic being a text embedded in our cultural tradition, and furthermore actually constituting that tradition which has shaped and formed us in the present. As Weinsheimer states:

> The classic makes history and thus is not merely the object of historical research but also its condition.[83]

In this respect, the classic is more than a text, it is the textual manifestation of tradition which, whether we read the text or not, has shaped and formed our cultural situation and thus represents an inescapably strong link which exerts an irresistible pull on our cultural consciousness in the present. In other words the classic is a timeless present that is contemporaneous with every other present. As Gadamer explains, the Enlightenment philosophers tended to dismiss our sense of responsibility to the authority of tradition, such as the classics, with an "extremism"[84] which unfairly equated *all* authority with being diametrically opposed to reason and freedom: to be in fact, blind obedience. However, Gadamer asserts that as opposed to the imposition of power, tradition, and the authority it exerts cannot actually be bestowed but must be earned if someone is to lay claim on it. In this respect, Gadamer sees the authority of tradition as being founded on knowledge, similar to the authority which a teacher represents and exerts over a student. For Gadamer, the authority of tradition, like the authority of the teacher over the student, is not the inflexible enforcement of dogma but rather the facilitation of a potentially liberating and adventurous hermeneutic experience in understanding:

> That which has been sanctioned by tradition and custom has an authority that is nameless, and our finite historical being is marked by the fact that the authority of what has been handed down to us—and not just what is clearly grounded—always has power over our attitudes and behaviour. All education depends on this, and even though in the case of education, the educator loses his function when his charge comes of age and sets his own insight and decisions in the place of the authority of the educator, becoming mature does not mean that a person becomes his own master in the sense that he is freed from all tradition.[85]

The Crystalline Classic:
Mediation between *Poiesis* and *Praxis*

Ultimately, Gadamer's conception of the value of the classic is not one which rests upon and reinforces the notion of a fixed, determinate or intrinsic textual superiority which we, as readers, are hermeneutically challenged to find and reveal. Instead, Gadamer asserts that the value of the classic must be hermeneutically produced in response to our consciousness of the vicissitudes of the *praxis* of our existence. Similarly, the Rewrite performatively produces the value of the classic, or even *a* value in *a* classic, as a result of the dramatists' consciousness of the 'hap' of their historical existence, which in turn has emphasised a specific subject-content that is pertinent to both text and interpreter.

Thus, at the root of Gadamerian hermeneutics is the attempt to negotiate the conjunction between *phronesis* and *praxis* with *techne* and *poiesis*[86] historically, whereby classic texts as being both a cause and product of our tradition are approached with an historically effected consciousness as bearing testimony not only to our past but also to our present realities which have been and are shaped by our cultural past. As Danto observes, historical meaning can only be produced by the present ". . . retroactive re-alignment of the past."[87]

Gadamer emphasises the distinction between the deliberatively and teleological projection of the knowledge which informs *techne* and *poiesis* and the retrospective insight of understanding based on the unfamiliarity of experience which is *phronesis* and *praxis*, in order to show how truth might be disclosed from a dialogue with tradition, although as Robert Bernasconi points out:

> There is a fundamental difficulty in providing pure examples of *praxis*, for it is not the object of a representation or of will, but is determined by the situation which calls for it. And yet, it is also true that the situation does not have its meaning in advance of the action, but is only shown to be the situation that it was retrospectively, in the light of the action. This retrospective determination of the situation and thus of the action itself arises, as Arendt has argued, in the construction of a story about it. But such storytelling is itself a form of *poiesis*. It would seem that *praxis* shows itself only by submitting to the manner of revealing characteristic of *poiesis* so that it does not show itself, except as a trace.[88]

As Bernasconi observes, in order that we might comprehend our Being we retrospectively objectify and narrativise it, and as such we subsequently foreclose the openness and uncertainty which has been presented to us by the day to day *praxis* of life. Our propensity to structure the events of life through narrative and tropes has led Riffaterre to conclude that in essence all narrative truth is based on such a grammatical organisation:

> Narrative truth is thus a linguistic phenomenon, since it is experienced through enactment by reading, it is a performative event . . ."[89]

However, Gadamer develops and further investigates our narrativising propensity as being in continual, although often imperceptible, flux, whereby our historical consciousness of hap[90] continually alters, transforms and even overrides what he considers to be transient, but finitely stabilising narrative structures.

Gadamer views static and historicist narrativisation as ultimately repetitive and unproductive, and instead puts forward his claim of historical understanding, based on a continual highlighting and subverting which is the result of historical hap, as a route to truth as in the self-formation that is *Bildung*.[91] A part of such historical understanding is our hermeneutic engagement with the classics, which cannot be infinitely contained by the closed and discrete narrativisation from the present, because our present is always changing and altering in accordance with our historical condition.

In this respect, Gadamer categorically refutes a hermeneutic which is based on decoding or deciphering an objective but hidden meaning in a text, because any real or true meaning in a text comes into being through a dialogue with the text in the present as a result of unforeseen praxis or hap, and with respect to the eminent text or classic such a dialogue is more likely to be required and facilitated. As James Risser explains:

> Such a text is not simply open to interpretation, but in need of interpretation in a special sense. The interpreter steps in when the text is not able to do what it is supposed to do, namely, to be heard and understood on its own. But such a text does not disappear in our understanding of it, for it continually stands before us continually speaking anew.[92]

The Rewrite according to this Gadamerian interpretation revisits the received *poiesis* of the classic as a result of the hap of the *phronesis* which informs and continually disrupts our daily *praxis*. The plays which fall into the category of the Rewrite are performative interpretations infused with historically effected consciousness, that alter and enlarge received knowledge and narrativised *poiesis* by engaging with the unforeseen events and hap of daily *praxis*. Gadamer emphasises that the meaning of the text does not alter, but rather its significance changes, and it is this altered significance which informs the subject-content which in turn provides the focus for dialogue between the source text and the reader as re-reader. To elucidate this point it is useful to equate the Rewrite with the interpreting judge who adapts the law to particular circumstances or hap placed before him in court. Similarly, the Rewrite is the performative interpretation of the classic in the light of historical hap whereby "application [is not] . . . subsequent to understanding, nor for that reason, is application reductive or distortive."[93] In other words Gadamer introduces that which Charles Larmore refers to as "creative insight"[94] born of historical contingency, but which is commonly referred to as *phronesis*, as essential to the interpretative quest for understanding and truth.

Gadamer advocates an observance of the original Aristotelian distinction between *poiesis* and *praxis* in order to emphasise the productive development of a hermeneutic sensibility that effects the conjunction of *poiesis* and *praxis* based on separateness, to attain unity from their difference. It is important to note that such an approach is distinct from Hayden White's theory of the "poetising" nature of reality, that posits that *poiesis* is not an activity that hovers or transcends, or otherwise remains alienated from life, because it is life. Thus, although Gadamer states that *poiesis* and *praxis* should not be considered antithetical he stresses that neither should they be considered indistinguishable to the point that fiction and reality become interchangeable, for as Vidal-Naquet states:

> Interpretation falls into the category of a lie when it denies the reality of the events of which it treats and into the category of an untruth when it draws false consciousness from reflection on events whose reality remains attestable on the level of "positive" historical inquiry.[95]

Just as *poiesis* and *praxis* must be apprehended separately but not considered to be an antithetical construct, so too Gadamer asserts that the abstract antithesis between history and the knowledge of it must be discarded. In this respect, Gadamer emphasises the fundamental distinction between the natural scientist's goal-oriented research and the disclosive, less predetermined nature of understanding for the human scientist, and although he concedes that the following formulation is too undifferentiated, and requires further investigation, it is useful for the purposes of explaining the distinct properties of *poiesis* and *praxis*, *techne* and *phronesis* and their subsequent usefulness when considering our historical approach to textual hermeneutics:

> Hence historical research is carried along by the historical movement of life itself and cannot be understood teleologically in terms of the object into which it is inquiring.[96]

Similarly, the Rewrite attempts to negotiate the fact that *all* culture is implicated in a web of inescapable guilt or *Schuldzusammenhang* and as such it exemplifies an approach which does not merely treat the classic as a fitting object of historical research, but, because of its heightened intratextuality, as the very condition of history.

Harold Bloom's work on the Western canon (1994) emphasises "the anxiety of influence"[97] which is created by the classic and the way in which misreadings ensue under the weight of such an influence:

> The anxiety of influence is not an anxiety about the father, real or literary, but an anxiety by and in the poem, novel or play. Any strong literary work creatively misreads and therefore misinterprets a precursor text or texts. An authentic canonical writer may or may not internalise her or his work's anxiety, but that scarcely matters: the strongly achieved work is the anxiety.[98]

Bloom's emphasis upon the aesthetic superiority and strength of the classic as being the overriding reason for its canonical status is perhaps valid,[99] but the foundation for his argument is the further articulation of the *poiesis/praxis* antithesis which Gadamerian hermeneutics attempts to break down. Bloom's acknowledgement of the authority of the classic is close to the view espoused by Gadamer who states authority cannot actually be bestowed but it is earned and such authority rests upon the acknowledgement and hence on an act of reason itself which, aware of its own limitations, trusts to the better insight of others. Of course, "trusts to the better insight of others" does not mean blind and unproductive acquiescence but rather a good will participation in the tradition which informs the community of cultural consciousness. However, unlike Gadamer, Bloom's refusal to consider the classic's involvement in our socio-historical tradition, and the way in which texts are, as shown through the disclosive power of time, to have been misread for a variety of social, political, religious and moral reasons, is the result of reading devoid of an historically effected consciousness. Bloom's adherence to *aesthesis* in his reception of texts depends upon a process of ahistorical abstraction, which rests on disregarding everything in which a work of art is rooted, and to refer back to Gadamer "uprooted". By adopting such a blinkered response to the classic, Bloom is depriving the classic and the reader of the classic access to further potential hermeneutic dimensions which exist not in spite of, but due to the classic's canonical status. In this respect, Tony Bennett's observation that the text is not the issuing source of meaning[100] is useful, but could well be moderated to the opinion that the text is not the *only* issuing source of meaning, an opinion which is dramaturgically posited by the Rewrite. The Rewrite is neither venerational or oppositional to the classic, rather it is the performative result or *Erlebnis* of a dialogue conducted over the centuries with the classic, and as such dramaturgically represents a hermeneutic encounter with a part of our cultural tradition.

E. D. Hirsch has also drawn our attention to the necessity of an awareness that knowing the present moment can only occur in terms of previously known types, and therefore to further understand the present we can only do so by seeing its connection with what came before and which thus produced the present moment:

> One would never invent or understand a new type of meaning unless he were capable of perceiving analogies and making novel subsumptions under previously known types.[101]

Similarly, on the other side of historiographical dialogic coin, historical "meaning" is the outcome of a narrative structure, albeit finite, being imposed upon events from a position subsequent to them, emphasising that:

> The meaning of historical actions and events from which they are perceived and historical understanding is necessarily perspectival and partial.[102]

Gadamer confronts both the way in which we research the past to explain our present and also our imposition of narratives to justify our past actions from a present perspective. Gadamer hermeneutically transcends the incrementalism of received knowledge provided by objective historicism and the atrophying results of self-justificatory imposition with his thesis which not only disrupts linear and chronological teleology but which also transforms our consciousness through a relationship with tradition typified by "excursion and return."[103] The accusation that Gadamer's approach is essentialist, and, by extension, so is this interpretation of the Rewrite, should be reconsidered in the light of the acknowledgement that it is not the essentialism of the romantically nostalgic or the product of "auratisation", and as such is not the "naturalised" essentialism lambasted by Barthes. The essentialism to be found in the Gadamerian hermeneutic which informs this interpretation of the Rewrite is not a timeless, almost religious essentialism but one which is firmly rooted in history and hails from a particular historical occasion or "monad". As Gadamer elucidates such serendipitous and unfamiliar monadic moments, or what I would refer to as contingent essences, are the very foundations of our experience of experience:

> Nature no longer provides the exemplary model for art to follow. And yet, even though it follows its own path, the work of art does come to resemble nature: there is something regular and binding about the self-contained picture that grows from within. We might think of the crystal here. The pure regularity of its geometrical structure is entirely natural, and yet surrounded by a wealth of shapeless chaos, we encounter it as something rare, adamantine, brilliant.[104]

Gadamer's dissolution of the antithetical abstraction between *poiesis* and *praxis*[105] emphasises that the classics do not merely help us to an objective understanding of past times, or provide us with eminent texts which we can experiment with through the imposition of modern theoretical models, rather that they are cultural artefacts which raise questions and interrogate the interpreter in the present who is in possession of an historically effected consciousness, and who responds with it in the face of historical hap in our daily *praxis*. As Weinsheimer states:

The full process of interpreting the classic consists in a reciprocal questioning, a dialogue whereby the interpreter too becomes the interpreted.[106]

As opposed to seeing the classics as cultural statements which will be revealed to us through objective interpretative endeavour, our cultural tradition is a series of questions which resound to the interpretation born of a historical effected consciousness, and thus initiate a dialogue. For Gadamer great texts are not the ones that espouse eternal verities but are those in which subsequent generations are able to find a living significance for themselves. To merely accept our cultural tradition as past except for the purposes of objective historical research is merely to consign the classic to the monolithic ideological coherence of canonicity, as relics invested with artificial cultural kudos, useful for the purposes of political allegories or appropriations and the perpetuity of canonised reading practices. Such a sterile approach to our cultural tradition is to condemn the classics to be little more than historical facts and lifeless dates which are repeated to give us some kind of empirical grounding for our cultural status, a state of affairs which Yehuda Amichai has commented upon:

No one knows where Moses was buried but we know all about his life. Nowadays everything is the other way around. We know only where the burial places are. Where we live is unfixed and unknown. We roam about, we change, we shift. Only the burial place is known.[107]

Thus, although Bloom may well espouse a return to *aesthesis* which accommodates misreadings, he fails to consider the way in which such misreadings are very often culturally implicated in shaping social and political norms and even more so when considering a socially performative artform like drama. Indeed, as any cultural historian will concede, our reception of art and literature is to a greater or lesser extent shaped by critics and institutionalised experts, and this is one of the processes addressed by the very dramaturgical form of the Rewrite.

Bloom's notion of misreading under the anxiety of influence is pertinent to our understanding of the Rewrite, but it does not cover the wider implication of rewriting as opposed to rereading the classics. By turning rereading into rewriting, a self-conscious critical performance focused on the classic's multiplicity of modes of signification, past and present, is elicited. As Marcel Cornis-Pope has remarked in rereading the classics, however hermeneutically focused, there is a sense of "deja-lu" which does not encompass "a performative response to the latent cultural force and goals that drive literary texts."[108] The Rewrite, however, is the performative result of a hermeneutic which foregrounds the perspectives and system of values that collude in any rereading, or for that matter, misreading of a text, past and present. By revealing the misreadings of misreadings not only is the classic potentially released from the negative distortions which have resulted from canonicity, but also a new historically contingent hermeneutic dimension which encompasses a critique of past misreadings, and thus the foundations for socio-historical norms, is actively produced for the present. Rereading and by extension rewriting compels us to consider the way in which our reading practices and thus understanding may become canonised, fossilised and anachronistically untrue, an effect symptomatic of the negation of phenomenologically hermeneutic sensibility and historically effected consciousness.

The plays under consideration, according to this Gadamerian model of interpretation exemplify the recognition of the unsatisfactory project of historical objectivism which fails to question its own historicity. By rewriting the classic, a Gadamerian phenomenology is effected, for the Rewrite both elicits and includes in itself the varying interpretations through which the classic is and has been transmitted. Indeed, Gadamer's analysis of the game emphasises that the text or artwork, like play, lives in its presentations and the variety of performances or interpretations of a text are not simply subjective variations of a meaning locked in subjectivity but belong to the ontological possibility of the work.

In this respect Gadamerian hermeneutics appear to be refuting so many of the artificially and self conscious theoretical historical categorisations which abound today, for as indicated by their neologistic labels they exempt themselves from the historical processes of which they form a part. In this respect, Gadamerian hermeneutics does not merely highlight historical aporias or temporal gulfs, but rather such historical and cultural distanciation is negotiated in order to elicit mediation for integration through difference. It is such a crucial distinction between *identifying* aporias and *mediating* them, that sets Gadamerian hermeneutics and by extension the project of the Rewrite apart from, for example, postmodernist theories about art. As opposed to recycling past literature in order to emphasise and self-consciously construe, in a postmodernist fashion, art as defined by polyvalent and ahistorical "rhizomic" disorder[109], rewriting the classics is an approach which performatively frees the classic from its material textuality, to elicit the interpretation not of the text, but the interpretation of the subject of the text, as elucidated by the hap of history.

In a sense, the Rewrite is the performative form of rereading the classic with an historically effected consciousness which simultaneously embraces and endorses the cultural cachet of the classic in order to critique the possible distortions and misreadings which canonicity fosters. As opposed to indulging in Bloom's private search for the personal and present mode of signification and *poiesis* in the text, the Rewrite actively releases a plethora of modes of signification within the classic, as both an aesthetic and socio-historical resource for the present realities of daily *praxis*. The Rewrite dramaturgically encapsulates the negotiation of past narrativized *poiesis* in our tradition with our experiential *phronesis*, which, as a result of hap intrudes upon our existence, and as opposed to interpretatively objectifying the past of the text, past and present, *poiesis* and *praxis*, are mediated, to disclose a new and different understanding and truth. As Martin Heidegger perceptively observes:

> Whatever and however we may try to think, we think within the sphere of tradition. Tradition prevails when it frees us from thinking back to a thinking forward, which is no longer a planning.[110]

Notes

1 In *The Western Canon: The Books and School of the Ages* (New York: Harcourt Brace, 1994) Harold Bloom espouses a personal interaction or *aesthesis* with a text in order to evaluatively affirm or disavow their cultural status, leading him to assert that Shakespeare is *"Nature's own artist"* (p.54) and:

> Shakespeare and Dante are at the centre of the Canon because they excel all other western writers in cognitive acuity, linguistic energy and power of invention. (p.46)

and

> Shakespeare is almost as free of ideology as are his heroic wits . . . (p.56)

Although Gadamer also emphasises that the text's value is in its performative interpretation, he also endorses and includes the worldly concerns of hap and intratextuality which inform the signification and value we contingently receive from our reading of the classics.

2 Arthur C. Danto, "The Artworld" in *Journal of Philosophy* (1964) states " . . . to see something as art requires something the eye cannot descry—an artworld."

3 G. Dickie adheres to the view that art is "created" by institutional powers, stating ". . . artefactuality is conferred on the object rather than worked on it." *Art and the Aesthetic* (New York: Cornell University Press, 1974) p. 45.

4 Barbara Herrnstein Smith, *Contingencies of Value: Alternative Perspectives for Critical Theory Today* (Cambridge, Mass: Harvard University Press, 1988)

5 Pierre Bourdieau, *Distinction: A Social Critique of the Judgement of Taste* trans. by Richard Nice (London: Routledge, 1994)

6 Gadamer, *Truth and Method* trans. by Joel Weinsheimer and Donald G. Marshall (London: Sheed and Ward, 1993) p. 287. [hereafter referred to as *TM*]

7 Gadamer, *TM* p. 164.

8 Gadamer, *TM* p. 289.

9 Joel Weinsheimer, *Gadamer's Hermeneutics: A Reading of Truth and Method* (New Haven and London: Yale University Press, 1985) p.174. [hereafter this text will be indicated by (a)]

10 Weinsheimer, (a) p. 174.

11 Gadamer, *Philosophical Apprenticeships*, trans. Robert R. Sullivan (Cambridge: The MIT Press, 1985) pp.189–90.

12 James Risser, "Reading the Text" in *Gadamer and Hermeneutics* (London: Routledge, 1991) p. 99.

13   Pierre Bourdieu and Loic J. D. Wacquant, *An Invitation to Reflexive Sociology* (Chicago: University of Chicago Press, 1992) pp. 84–85.

14   Peter Osborne criticises what he deems to be Gadamer's suprahistorical concept of the classic in *The Politics of Time: Modernity and Avant-Garde* (London: Verso, 1995) p. 130. With reference to Gadamer's hermeneutics he states: "Under such circumstances, it is hard to make sense of the transhistorical, except as the manifestation of the suprahistorical . . ."

15   For a further explanation of the way the classic enables the present to be made more present through the past, see *TM* p. 288.

16   Gadamer, *TM* pp. 578–579.

17   John Guillory, *Cultural Capital: The Problem of Literary Canon Formation* (Chicago, London: University of Chicago Press, 1993) p. ix.

18   Italo Calvino, *The Uses of Literature* trans. by Patrick Creagh (San Diego: Harcourt Brace, 1986) p. 127.

19   Weinsheimer, (a) p. 14.

20   Andreas Huyssen, *Twilight Memories: Marking Time in a Culture of Amnesia* (New York and London: Routledge, 1995) p. 25.

21   Huyssen, p. 7.

22   Huyssen, p. 7

23   Gadamer, *TM* pp. 577–578.

24   Risser, p.104.

25   See Chapter II for a more detailed consideration of the concept of hermeneutic responsibility. Gadamer's contention that language lays claim to our attention, and as such the work speaks to us before we interrogate it is complex, but Joel Weinsheimer has put forward a convincing explanation here of what he terms *anspruchsvoll* – the way language speaks to us *(uns anspricht)* in such a way as to make a determinate claim *bestimmter Anspruch).* [Joel Weinsheimer's *Gadamer's Hermeneutics: A Reading of Truth and Method*, New Haven and London: Yale University Press, 1985 pp. 84–5, pp. 209–12.]

26   Jonathan Miller, *Subsequent Performances* (New York: Viking, 1986) p. 71.

27   Aulus Gellius cited E. R. Curtius, *European Literature and the Latin Middle Ages* trans: by Willard R. Trask (New York: Harper and Row, 1953) p. 250.

28   Aristotle, "On the Art of Poetry" in *Aristotle, Horace, Longinus: Classical Literary Criticism* trans. by T. S. Dorsch (London: Penguin, 1965) p.74.

29   John Guillory, *Cultural Capital: The Problem of Literary Canon Formation* (Chicago and London: University of Chicago Press, 1993) p. 62.

30   Quintilian, *Institutio Oratoria*, 4 Vols. trans: by H. E. Butler (Cambridge: Harvard University Press, 1969) 1:63

31   Gadamer, *TM* p. 161.

32   Pindar, Xenophanes and Heraclitus all represent early expressions of literary criti-
     cism, especially with respect to Homer. For further examples and a more detailed
     discussion reference should be made to J. W. H. Atkin's *Literary Criticism in
     Antiquity* (London: Methuen, 1952).

33   Peter Szondi, *Introduction to Literary Hermeneutics* trans: by Martha
     Woodmansee (Cambridge: Cambridge University Press, 1995) p. 6. Szondi ex-
     plains the institutional formation of literary interpretation, and discusses the an-
     cients' use of allegorical exegesis. Szondi also cites Wolf-Harmut Friedrich's illu-
     minating analysis of the ancients' allegorical interpretation of Homer:

     > The Homeric epics were canonical for the Greeks; they remained inalien-
     > able cultural possessions even when the world in and for which they had
     > arisen no longer existed. Thus in our culture allegoresis developed out of
     > the discussion of Homer; it arose especially out of dissatisfaction with his
     > pronouncements about the gods. The pre-Socratic poet-philosopher
     > Xenophanes protested the slandering of them by Homer and Hesiod, and
     > Plato wanted to drive the poets as heretics out of his republic. The answer
     > is allegorical interpretation which had already been practiced by the Soph-
     > ists and then by the Cynics, and had been elaborated by the Stoics. By
     > presenting the gods as personifications of cosmic or moral forces, one
     > eliminated everything offensive : the wounding of Aphrodite by Diomedes
     > now meant the victory of Greek virtue over barbarian unreason, her adul-
     > tery with Ares meant a reconciliation of opposing life forces [. . .] in the
     > second century before Christ, the stoically inclined philologist Crates of
     > Peramum believed he could find all the scientific knowledge of his time
     > already contained in Homer. [Wolf Hartmut Friedriech "Allegorische Inter-
     > pretation" in *Fischer Lexikon, Literatur,* ed. Wolf-Hartmut Friedrich and
     > Walter Killy (Franfurt am Main, 1965), vol.2. pt. 1. p. 19.]

34   *Allegoresis* works on a similar basis to *figura*, that is establishing a connection
     between two events or persons, the first of which signifies not only itself but also
     the second, while the second encompasses the first. Examples included Lazarus
     awakening from the dead as figura of the Resurrection, and Moses as the figura of
     Christ.

35   Andre Lefevevre, *Translation, Rewriting and the Manipulation of Literary Fame*
     (London: Routledge, 1992) p. 19.

.36 Raymond Williams, *Marxism and Literature* (Oxford: Oxford University Press,
     1977)

37   Matthew Arnold, "Essays in Criticism: Second Series. The Study of Poetry" in
     Selected Prose ed. P. J. Keating (London: Penguin, 1987) p. 345.

38   Samuel Johnson, *Johnson on Shakespeare: The Yale Edition of the Works of
     Samuel Johnson,* vol. 7 ed., Arthur Sherbo (New Haven: Yale University Press,
     1968) p. 61.

39   Charles Marowitz, *Prospero's Staff: Acting and Directing in the Contemporary Theatre* (Bloomington: Indiana University Press, 1986) p. 38

40   John Lahr, "The Dying Wave" in *New Society* 2nd January, 1986. pp.26–27.

41   Samuel Johnson, op.cit. p.111

42   Barbara Herrnstein Smith, *Contingencies of Value: Alternative Perspectives for Critical Theory* (Cambridge, Mass: Harvard University Press, 1988) p.50.

43   Barbara Herrnstein Smith, p. 11.

44   Joel Weinsheimer, *Philosophical Hermeneutics and Literary Theory* (New Haven: Yale University Press, 1991) pp. 131–132. [hereafter referred to as (b)]

45   Bernard Bergonzi, *Exploding English: Criticism, Theory, Culture* (Oxford: Clarendon Press, 1990) p. 26.

46   Matthew Arnold, "The Study of Poetry" in *Selected Prose* (ed) P. J. Keating (London: Penguin, 1987) p. 344.

47   Matthew Arnold, p. 341.

48   Matthew Arnold, "On Translating Homer" *On the Classical Tradition* (ed) R. H. Super (Michigan, Ann Arbor: University of Michigan Press, 1960) pp. 171–172.

49   Matthew Arnold, "The Function of Criticism" in *Lectures and Essays in Criticism* (ed) R. H. Super (Michigan, Ann Arbor: University of Michigan Press, 1962) pp. 283–4.

50   Edmund Gosse, *Some Memoirs* ed., William Bellows (London: R. Cobden Sanderson, 1929)

51   Thomas De Quincey, "The Antigone of Sophocles as Represented on the Edinburgh Stage" in *De Quincey's Works: The Art of Conversation and Other Papers* (Edinburgh: Adam and Charles Black, MDCCCLXIII) Vol. XIII, pp. 199–233, pp. 206–207.

52   Herrnstein Smith, p.51.

53   Gadamer, *TM* p. 497.

54   Herrnstein Smith, p.10

55   Genette, Gerard, See "Structuralism and Literary Criticism" in *Modern Criticism and Theory: A Reader* (ed) David Lodge (London: Longman, 1988)

56   T. S. Eliot, "Tradition and The Individual Talent" in *Selected Prose of T. S. Eliot* ed., Frank Kermode, (London, Faber and Faber, 1975) p. 38.

57   Antonin Artaud, "No More Masterpieces" in *The Theatre and Its Double* trans. V. Corti (Montreuil, London: Calder, 1993) p. 78.

58   Edward Shils, *Tradition* (London: Faber and Faber, 1981) p.148.

59   Shils, p. 156.

60   Herrnstein Smith, pp. 15–16.

61   Raymond Williams, *Marxism and Literature* (Oxford: Oxford University Press, 1977) 45 ff. Williams draws attention to the modern sense of literature, that is particular kinds of writing like poetry and drama which dates from the late eighteenth century as opposed to the earlier use of the term literature which encompassed all written material.

62   Herrnstein Smith, p.10

63   Gadamer, *TM* p. 297.

64   John Guillory, p. ix

65   Guillory, *TM* p. 7.

66   Henry Louis Gates Jr., "On Canon Formation and the African American Tradition" in *South Atlantic Quarterly* 89 (1990) p. 105.

67   Guillory p. xiii.

68   The double discourse of value refers to the interchangeable but often indistinct ideological and economic dimensions to the evaluating process. For a detailed discussion of this process see John Guillory's *Cultural Capital* and Pierre Bourdieu's *Distinction*.

69   Lord Kames as cited in Howard Caygill, *Art of Judgement* (London: Basil Blackwell, 1989) p. 65.

70   Howard Caygill, *Art of Judgement* p. 69.

71   Murray Krieger, *Words About Words About Words: Theory, Criticism and the Literary Text* (Baltimore, London: The Johns Hopkins University Press, 1988) p. 160.

72   Roland Barthes *S/Z* trans. Richard Millar (New York: Hill and Wang, 1974) pp. 15–16.

73   Terry Eagleton, *Criticism and Ideology* (London: Verso, 1986) p. 169.

74   Weinsheimer, (a) pp. 127–128.

75   Guillory, p. 67.

76   Mikhael Bakhtin, *Rabelais and His World* (Cambridge, Mass: MIT Press, 1968) p. 72.

77   Joel Weinsheimer in the Preface to Szondi, P *Introduction to Literary Hermeneutics*, trans: by Martha Woodmansee (Cambridge: Cambridge University Press, 1995) p. xix.

78   Maurice Blanchot, "Eurydice and the Sirens" in *Foucault* (New York: Zone Books, 1989) p. 41

79 Maurice Blanchot, *The Gaze of Orpheus and Other Literary Essays* (Station Hill, 1981) p. 95.

80 Maurice Blanchot, *The Space of Literature* trans. by Ann Smock (Lincoln, London: University of Nebraska, 1989) p. 195.

81 Blanchot, p. 195

82 Ernestus Martinus Chladenius, 319, p. 196. [as cited by Szondi]

83 Weinsheimer, (a) p. 129.

84 Gadamer, *TM* p. 280.

85 Gadamer, *TM* pp. 280–281.

86 Robert Bernasconi has drawn attention to the efforts of both Arendt and Gadamer to explain that the predominance of *poiesis* and *techne* in our study of the human sciences has led us to place a distorted emphasis upon the production and making which represents the source of art and meaning as opposed to the active and performative dimensions of reception at the destination of art:

> Aristotle initially understands poiesis to be an activity that aims at an end distinct from the activity, whereas praxis is an activity whose end is nothing other than the activity itself. [Bernasconi, R., *Heidegger in Question: The Art of Existing* p. 2.]

For the earliest reference to these concepts see Aristotle's *Nicomachean Ethics*, and for more recent discussions see Arendt's *The Human Condition* (Chicago and London: University of Chicago Press, 1970) Chapter V and Gadamer's *Truth and Method* pp. 278–289.

87 Arthur Coleman Danto, *Analytical Philosophy of History* (Cambridge: Cambridge University Press, 1965) p. 168.

88 Robert Bernasconi, *Heidegger in Question: The Art of Existing* (New Jersey: Humanities Press, 1996) pp. 8–9.

89 Michael Riffaterre, *Fictional Truth* (Baltimore, Maryland: The Johns Hopkins University Press, 1990) p.xiv.

90 For a more detailed explanation of the source and meaning of the term hap see the footnotes to Chapter Two. Hap, in the context of this study, is not merely alluding to event but rather to the consciousness of event. Such conscsiousness of event or hap may not even come about until the event has passed or after the event has been taking place for some considerable period of time.

91 For Gadamer, the concept of *Bildung* is distinguished from intentional and goal oriented cultivation because ". . . cultivation of a talent is the development of something given, so that its practice and maintenance is a means to a mere end." Instead, *Bildung* is the cultural tradition which one imbibes and assimilates and as Weinsheimer suggests it is ". . . not disposed of, used up like a means" because "*Bildung* does not supersede culture but preserves it."

92   James Risser, "Reading the Text" in *Gadamer and Hermeneutics*, p.100.

93   Weinsheimer, (a) p. 192.

94   Charles Larmore, "Moral Judgement" in *Review of Metaphysics* 35 (1981) pp. 275–296, p. 293.

95   Pierre Vidal-Naquet, cited by Hayden White in "The Politics of Historical Interpretation: Discipline and Desublimation" *Critical Inquiry* 9/1 (1982) pp. 113–137

96   Gadamer, *TM* p. 284–285.

97   Although Bloom refers to the intertextual "anxiety of influence" in his more recent work (*The Western Canon*, 1994) this phrase dates back to his seminal study *The Anxiety of Influence: A Theory of Poetry* (New York: Oxford University Press, 1973).

98   Bloom, p. 8.

99   Gadamer discusses the authority of the classics [*Truth and Method* pp. 279–281] and in a similar vein to the *aesthesis* expressed by Bloom he asserts that ". . . authority cannot actually be bestowed, but is earned . . ." [p279] He goes on to explain the bilateral and consensual nature of any real authority including tradition (which should be distinguished from authoritarianism):

> That which has been sanctioned by tradition and custom has an authority that is nameless, and our finite historical being is marked by the fact that the authority of what has been handed down to us—and not just what is clearly grounded—always has power over our attitudes and behaviour . . . The fact is that in tradition there is always an element of freedom and of history itself. Even the most genuine and pure tradition does not persist because of the inertia of what once existed. It needs to be affirmed, embraced, cultivated. It is essentially preservation and it is active in all historical change. [Gadamer, *Truth and Method* pp. 280–281]

100   See Tony Bennett, *Formalism and Marxism* (London: Routledge, 1979)

101   E. D. Hirsch, *The Aims of Interpretation* (Chicago and London: University of Chicago Press, 1976) p. 105.

102   G. Warnke, *Gadamer: Hermeneutics, Tradition and Reason* (Stanford: Stanford University Press, 1987) p. 19.

103   Weinsheimer's explanation of the excursion and return of consciousness is a useful elucidation of Gadamer's hermeneutic project (a) p.70:

> In Bildung one leaves the all-too-familiar and learns to allow for what is different from oneself, and that means not only to tolerate it but to live in it . . . The being of spirit, Gadamer writes, is only return: that means, it can only come back to itself—without, as it were, setting out. To be only in return means that the traveler, recalling Heraclitus, is different from and more than when he sets out. But to reverse the Heraclitan maxim, he can only go home again: the 'more' that he is upon return is that he is more fully himself.

104   Hans Georg Gadamer, *The Relevance of the Beautiful* trans. by Nicholas Walker (Cambridge: Cambridge University Press, 1995) p. 93. [hereafter referred to a *RB*]

105   The classical distinction made by Aristotle separates poesis from praxis (*Eudemian Ethics*, II, I; *Nicomachean Ethics* I,I)

106   Weinsheimer, (a) p.129.

107   Cited in James Young, *Writing and Rewriting the Holocaust: Narrative and the Consequences of Interpretation* (Bloomington, Indiana University Press, 1990) p. 172.

108   Marcel Cornis-Pope, *Hermeneutic Desire and Critical Rewriting: Narrative Interpretation in the Wake of Post-structuralism* (New York: St. Martin's Press, 1992) p.25.

109   Rhizomic meaning is referred to by Deleuze and Guattari in *Anti-Oedipus: Capitalism and Schizophrenia* trans. by Robert Hurley, Mark Seem, Helen R. Lane (London: The Athlone Press, 1983). The word "rhizome" refers to plants that do not grow vertically but rather grow in a variety of unpredictable and unforeseen ways and at somewhat unusual angles. Deleuze et al. use this term to suggest the freedom and disruption of linearity in the artistic and cultural production and reception in the schizophrenic society they espouse.

110   Martin Heidegger, *Identity and Difference* trans. by J. Stambaugh (New York: Harper and Row, 1969) p. 41.

Chapter Two

Gadamer's Hermeneutics and Rewriting the Classics

The Limits of Method

Ostensibly and on a superficial level the interpretative model used to discuss and analyse the plays under consideration is based on Gadamer's hermeneutic project as enunciated in *Truth and Method*, which he describes as being rooted in the classical discipline concerned with the art of understanding text. However, *essentially* Gadamer's hermeneutic project is *not* a model for interpretation, rather it is an attempt to understand "understanding", and it is posited here that similarly the Rewrite is based on a re-reading of not only a specific text but also a re-reading of our past reception of a classic, thus providing a dramaturgical investigation of our understanding of past understanding. In this respect, Gadamerian hermeneutics should be distinguished from the exegetical tradition that sought to perfect a hermeneutic *method* as a means of bringing forth the esoteric or secret meanings of sacred texts in order to reveal an ultimate truth.[1] Additionally, it is helpful to be aware of the distinction between Gadamerian hermeneutics and the hermeneutic project of critics, like Peter Szondi, who are motivated by a quest to define a specific literary hermeneutic system or ". . . material theory of interpretation."[2] As Weinsheimer observes:

> . . . the *Introduction to Literary Hermeneutics* can fruitfully be read as an underground polemic with *Truth and Method* that frequently erupts to the surface. For Szondi, we have seen, hermeneutics has become so preoccupied with analysis of understanding that it has come to consider itself superior to its one-time task of being a material theory concerned with the rules and criteria of interpretation.[3]

Just as Gadamerian hermeneutics is concerned to elucidate the fundamental conditions that underlie the phenomenon of understanding, and in particular understanding texts, the Rewrite performatively "encounters" the classic and expresses a hermeneutic of understanding within its own dramaturgical parameters:

> . . . understanding belongs to the encounter with the work of art itself, and so this belonging can be illuminated only on the basis of the *mode of being of the work of art itself.*[4]

The Rewrite is a performative experience borne of a particular and unforeseen situation similar to the concept of *Erlebnis*[5] which, alongside its negotiation with tradition or *Erfahrung,*[6] underpins the discussion of understanding in Gadamer's *Truth and Method*. It is therefore erroneous to simplistically designate Gadamer's hermeneutic project as providing an interpretative model for this study of the Rewrite, not least because Gadamer himself strenuously emphasises the incongruity of method and the attainment of any real level of "understanding". Rather, just as Immanuel Kant contended in the *Critique of Judgement* (1790) that beauty cannot be prescriptively decided but is apprehended through reflective judgement, so too Gadamer asserts that understanding, the condition of which is history, can only be attained by reflective judgement about the prejudgments and prejudices that after centuries of aesthetic consciousness constitute our being.[7] Thus, despite the title of his work, Gadamer should not be misconstrued as providing a methodology for the understanding of texts. Indeed, to understand our "understanding" and, by extension, truth, Gadamer challenges the universality and exhaustiveness of "method" as the exclusive means whereby knowledge worthy of being called true or understanding is disclosed, as:

> . . . one has not rightly grasped their [the human sciences] nature if one measures them by the yardstick of a progressive knowledge of regularity.[8]

The Rewrite as Performative *Erlebnis*[9]

Another reason why a hermeneutic methodology is incompatible with Gadamer's hermeneutics is due to the centrality of his conception of the hermeneutic experience as *Erlebnis* that is, being alive to experience, in the face of *Erfahrung*, a knowledge which can be gathered from others or tradition. *Erlebnis* suggests immediacy of experience, and as such is not intentional, deliberative or premeditated, but rather is the unforeseen result of our historical contingency and daily *praxis*. The presentness of our experience is continually changing and thus cannot be truly methodologised or predetermined according to an objective historicist agenda, and as a result, Gadamer convincingly argues, our relationship to the past or to our tradition cannot and should not be treated as static. Indeed, it is our very adherence to the notion of permanence in our presentness that corrupts our reception of the classic into an atavistic, stultifying and most importantly untrue interpretation. Dilthey embraced the concept of *Erlebnis* in his own hermeneutics, by scientifically incorporating such experience as epistemological "units of meaning" for further research. However, in contradistinction, Gadamer considers *Erlebnis* phenomenologically, the consequences of which lead to his consideration of such monads of experience as constituting a transformative part of the larger temporal whole of our experience. As Weinsheimer explains:

> [For Gadamer] . . . the meaning of an experience, then is not emphatically given: and thus experience cannot serve as the datum of research. Its meaning is not given but always to be given. It takes time, and this time—the lifetime necessary to understand the meaning of experience—is precisely the episodic time that the experience interrupted. The wholeness of an experience ruptures the everyday seriality of time, and yet its unity of meaning is such that it needs that continuing flow to explicate it. An experience gives wholeness to, and acquires meaning from, that seriality.[10]

Similarly the Rewrite is performative *Erlebnis* which negotiates with experience of tradition or *Erfahrung*, which just as it is precipitated by a transient experience also contributes to the larger but unending whole of experience in its own transience. In this respect, the Rewrite does not pertain to offer a better or more sophisticated reading of the classic, rather it is the dramaturgical experience of the classic born of historically effected consciousness for that moment, that time, that transient present. As Gadamer states:

> Historical thinking has its dignity and its value as truth in the acknowledgement that there is no such thing as "the present" but rather constantly changing horizons of future and past.[11]

As Weinsheimer explains, such an experience of the infinite is akin to the symbol, but Gadamer clearly distinguishes true experience from the symbol because the latter is the result of subjective production as opposed to the unforeseen and, as the later discussion of the Holocaust and Apartheid, will reveal, the unimaginable or incomprehensible nature of experience. Instead of resorting to the aesthetic discourse of the symbolic Gadamer posits that our *Erlebnis* or experience of hap[12] is beyond aesthetic or for that matter any other categorised area of consciousness until its actual event, but it has the effect of altering our perspective of certain things which we may have "known" previously. In this respect *Erlebnis* phenomenologically alters the narrativised *poiesis* which provides the foundations for our epistemologically gathered but perpetually unfinished "knowledge" of the world.

Like *Erfahrung,* the experience that is *Erlebnis* signifies the process of acquisition, but moreover, also the residual content of what is so acquired, that is, both the immediacy or the origin of experience and its lasting significance. For example, although one may argue that the written form of text does not represent the vibrant speech of conversation, Gadamer considers that a phenomenologically inspired interpretation brings fixed language once again into speech, but not in a reconstructive way, but through the return to speech as a new event or *Erlebnis*, whereby a written tradition, once deciphered and read, is to such an extent pure mind that it speaks to us as if in the present. Gadamer likens the capacity to read and to understand what is written to a secret art, whereby the constraints of time and space are almost magically shaken off and the sheer presence of the past is attained.

Prejudice and Interpretative Responsibility

Gadamer acknowledges that the quest for truth through understanding cannot be methodological because it is always over and above our wanting and doing, and is dependent on the historical situatedness of our encounter with the text that we are attempting to understand. In this respect, like the post-structuralist denouncement of authorial intention, Gadamerian hermeneutics reflects and develops Mallarmé's observation that the subsequent interpretations of a text are always far more than not only the author but also the potential interpreter could have anticipated or known. The multiplicity of meaning in a text is a result of the fact that, as Cook states, ". . . meaning can only be apprehended temporally and historically."[13] To highlight his point about the situatedness, or to use Weinsheimer's useful term, the hap of our encounter with a text, Gadamer refers to the Aristotelian distinction between the inductive method which guides the craftsman and the philosopher's acknowledgment of *phronesis* and the fact that moral knowledge can never be knowable in advance, for:

What is right for example cannot be fully determined independently of the situation that requires a right action from me, whereas the *eidos* of the craftsman wants to make it fully determined by the use for which it is intended.[14]

For Gadamer *phronesis* is attained through a *negotiation with* as opposed to a *denial of* our prejudices, and although he acknowledges that Enlightenment thinkers attempted to expand knowledge through rationalistic discourse, their rationalism precluded any sense of doubt or prejudice as essentially flawed and thus untrue. Gadamer further draws our attention to the way in which the Enlightenment not only circumscribed *phronesis* through what was in effect methodologised rationalism but also how their adherence to logic gave rise to a continuing suspicious and irrational attitude to all forms of authority, which it immediately deemed might serve as an impediment to the application of reason:

If the prestige of authority displaces one's own judgement, then authority is in fact a source of prejudices. But this does not preclude its being a source of truth, and that is what the Enlightenment failed to see when it denigrated all authority.[15]

This confusion of authority with subjection and abdication of reason prevails today and is the source of many "canon-busting" debates, but postmodern polemics of this kind fail to confront what has already been stated but which is worthy of emphasis, namely the *hermeneutic* reality that authority cannot actually be bestowed, it must be earned.[16] This statement is not an endorsement of Johnsonian "prescriptive veneration"[17] or in any way a welcome return to the Arnoldian ideal that reading the classics is acquainting ourselves with the best that has been thought and said in the world, rather it is an awareness of the reader's responsibility or to use Weinsheimer's words, *anspruchsvoll*[18] to engage his interpretative ability to destroy the shroud of atavistic reading practices which so often condemn the classics to cultural entombment. Central to such interpretative responsibility is the reader's liberating consciousness that true meaning is eventful, produced in an event of dislosure, and is not something fixed by or in the text. In effect, philosophical hermeneutics attempts to preempt our systematic desertion of hermeneutic responsibility for the vicarious but untrue "guidance" of procedural method, for as Weinsheimer states *pace* Gadamer:

It is not interpretation but instead our conception of interpretation that requires alteration.[19]

Thus, as opposed to assuming an interpretative posture which starts off from the Enlightenment premise of objectively avoiding prejudices or with the mission to evade "misunderstandings" (a hermeneutic tradition dating from Schleiermacher and which survives in the form of Paul Ricouer's 'hermeneutic of suspicion[20]) Gadamer posits that misunderstandings are not only inescapable if we are to recognise our own interpretative contingency, situatedness and finitude, but also misunderstandings provide a productive source from which to test our prejudices, and thus reach a different hermeneutic understanding:

> Misunderstanding arises naturally because of changes in word meanings, world views and so on, that have taken place in the time separating the author from the interpreter.[21]

In this respect, Gadamer considers the conscious bringing forth of one's prejudice or presuppositions when engaging with the classic as potentially productive if, as a result of the subject-content thrown up by the *Erlebnis* of hap, we have the "Platonic" good will to enter into dialogue about, and not the deliberative superimposition of, our prejudicial perspective. Gadamer asserts that true interpretation during the course of hermeneutic play dissolves the inherent inequality and untruth of the interpreting subject interpreting the interpretative object, in contradistinction to the following assertion by Pierre Maranda:

> Only when one has reduced a society or a piece of literature to congruency with one's own prejudices does one have a proper feeling of understanding.[22]

Similarly, Stanley Fish has stated that ". . . no one can achieve the distance from his own beliefs and assumptions"[23] to attain a self conscious reflexivity about one's interpretative mores, but by rewriting the classic, one's perspective born of dialogue with the source text's significance with respect to a specific subject content thrown up by historical hap is focused and incorporated within the community of cultural consciousness suggested by canonical status. The classics presuppose rereading because of their established and longstanding status, and by extension their implication in the socio-historical interaction with culture.

Gadamer's emphasis on the situatedness of the hermeneutic endeavour is not new but is the development of a discussion of hermeneutic perspective and point of view initiated by Chladenius in the eighteenth century. Indeed, Chladenius actually highlighted the perspectival aspect

of our understanding of history and may be considered to be a precursor
to Gadamer's development of the concept of effective history and hap:

> History is always one and the same thing, while the idea of it is varied and
> manifold; history contains nothing contradictory, whereas in the idea of history
> and in various ideas about it there may be something contradictory; in history
> everything has its sufficient cause, but in the idea of it things may occur which
> appear to happen without sufficient cause. [24]

However, despite Gadamer's reaffirmation of the situatedness of the interpretative standpoint, it has often been suggested that Gadamer fails to
consider his own ontological perspective with, for example, his attributed
assumption that the history of social relations between, men and women
is normative. Schott[25] criticises Gadamer's quest for truth as being detached from the contingencies of empirical identity, and for assuming a
"universal" understanding of language that is premised on the exclusion
of marginalised groups, like women. A feminist's response to Gadamer's
hermeneutic project is illustrated by Schweickart, who states:

> The question of how we read is inextricably linked with the question of what we
> read. More specifically the feminist inquiry into the activity of reading begins with
> the realisation that the literary canon is androcentric and this has a profoundly
> damaging effect on women readers.[26]

However, such alienating arguments appear to be confusing the production of the classics with their reception, that is, a hermeneutically sensitive reception in the present, for as Gadamer retorts, nobody is ever
excluded from the interpretative framework even though they may well
have been barred from literary production, for:

> In this game nobody is above and before all the others; everybody is at the centre,
> is "it" in this game. Thus it is always his [or her] turn to be interpreting.[27]

Schott et al. justifiably point out that marginalised groups or subjects do
not possess the self-affirmation that is both a condition and consequence
of naming oneself as an interpreter, and this is where the dramatists
considered in this study play a part and who, I would argue, exemplify an
approach akin to Gadamerian hermeneutics in their historically conscious
treatment of tradition. By harnessing a politically sensitive or topical "occasion" with a dramaturgical re-reading of the classic, the Rewrite not
only instigates the classic's liberation from restrictive canonised reading
practices, but also it actually facilitates the reinscription of the marginalized

"voice" on to our conscious reception of the classic in the present. In this respect, the Rewrite dramaturgically poses the rhetorical question that surely the fact that so many of the classics did not exoterically represent those identified as the "marginalised" sectors of today's society when they were produced does not preclude the classics as a suitably consensual platform on which to discuss, re-present and address issues pertinent to "marginal" groups today?[28] Thus, just as Schott may deem Gadamer's "white, European and male" interpretative position as inescapably prejudiced, so too, her own feminist interpretative posture is itself based on prejudice, further emphasising Gadamer's point that it is only by questioning and testing these very prejudices through interpretation that a hermeneutic "understanding" might be attained. Similarly, Wa Thiong'o Ngugi's diatribe against the admittedly 'western' classics, in particular Shakespeare, fails to make the distinction between literary texts and the brutal colonising forces that used these texts to supplant the indigenous culture, and as such he is forfeiting the opportunity to perceive these classics from his own hermeneutically interpretatively empowered position:

> These writers who had the sharpest and most penetrating observations on the European bourgeois culture . . . Sometimes their greatness was presented as one more English gift to the world alongside the Bible and the needle. William Shakespeare and Jesus Christ had brought light to darkest Africa.[29]

However, as How astutely observes, this does not mean that Gadamerian hermeneutics becomes an ad hoc interpretative relativism, because, in view of the conflation of received tradition (*Erfahrung*) and the immediacy of the life experience of *Erlebnis*, ". . . for Gadamer, the living of life eliminates relativism."[30]

The Rewrite has the performative potential to assume a variety of interpretative stances, including those which are unorthodox and 'marginal', and such a dramaturgical form may be considered to be a means to understand our understanding of the classic in and for the present in a similar way to that posited by Gadamerian hermeneutics. The intrinsic openness of the Rewrite's performative and dramaturgical re-reading of the classic emphasises it own transient and contingent, but no less valid, interpretative position which is not only based on an acknowledged prejudicial treatment of the past for the present, but which also exhibits a freedom from the determinism associated with teleologically projected "methods" of interpretation, in keeping with David Linge's astute observation:

There is no presuppositionless, "prejudiceless" interpretation, for while the interpreter may free himself from this or that situation, he cannot free himself from his own facticity, from the ontological condition of always already having a finite temporal situation as the horizon within which the beings he understands have their initial meaning for him . . . Every apprehension of meaning is a finite apprehension from within the pretheoretical givenness of man's historical situation.[31]

Understanding as History is History

Integral to Gadamerian hermeneutics is the acceptance that all understanding is "situated" and by extension is historical, because history is prior to the individual experience and thus shapes and influences it. Because understanding is historical, it is inextricably bound up and shaped by the prejudices which are historical reality itself, such as the tradition which encompasses what we regard to be "the classics", a point expanded on by Weinsheimer:

> . . . the elimination of prejudice, were it to succeed, would ultimately be the elimination of history—precisely the history which the historian exists to understand. But the historian cannot purify himself of prejudice because he, like those he studies, belongs to and is a creature of history . . . Knowing and being are here united. We can know history because we are historical . . . History is what prejudices us, and if there is any knowledge produced by history, it is prejudiced knowledge. But if this conjunction of knowledge and prejudice is not to be a mere contradiction, there must be legitimate, justified, appropriate prejudices produced by history. That is to say history must be productive of truth.[32]

In this respect, Gadamerian hermeneutics differs from the essentially reconstructive hermeneutic project of Schleiermacher[33] and Dilthey[34] whereby the interpretative position is negated in the name of hermeneutic objectivity, following on from the Cartesian ideal of the autonomous interpreting subject who supposedly (although idealistically) extricates himself from history and any resultant prejudices, in the name of reason and the rationalistic impetus for a sense of progress. Likewise, Gadamer contests the recuperative, and thus idealistically repetitive project of the Romantics' quest to reconstruct the past out of a sense of admiration for what he describes as the primeval age of myth, and which for differing reasons, but to the same effect, programmatically obliterates the temporal distance between the interpreter and the interpreted in an attempt to reinvoke the myth of the past, as explained by Weinsheimer:

> The primeval wisdom sought by the Romantics was merely the reverse image of the primeval stupidity shunned by the Enlightenment.[35]

Instead, Gadamer recognizes that our historicity is an ontological condition and as such the interpreter's own present contingency, situation and, by necessity, prejudice are always constitutively involved in any process of understanding, and that to ignore the facticity of the interpreter's situation can only lead to a blinkered and reproductive procedure. Thus, as opposed to adopting either a similar methodological stance to Dilthey which advocates interpretative self-transposition into the world of the source text[36], and thus the negation of the temporal distance that separates the interpreter from his object of interpretation, or embracing Betti's theory[37] which advocates that the sustained objectification of the text's alienness through distance is the very process that occasions interpretation, Gadamer embraces the temporal distance between the text and interpreter as a productive source for mediation which acknowledges the interpreter's own present as a vital extension of the past. In this respect, Gadamer sees temporal distance as a bridge to an understanding between past and present, text and reader, which conflates the artificial and misleading distinction between the interpreted object and the interpreting subject that has and continues to dominate our reception of art, for as observed by Weinsheimer:

> On one level, objectivity consists in humble self-effacement, but on another it is marked by a distinct arrogance insofar as it makes individual self-consciousness the locus and arbiter of truth.[38]

Gadamer asserts that the temporal distance between our interpreting stance and the text is instrinsic to our understanding, because it facilitates *dialogue with* rather than enforcing the *avoidance of* our past and present misunderstandings as founded on prejudice, as well as enabling us to free ourselves from the phantasm of an objective methodologism that is no more than a selectively and non-expansive cognitive reproduction based on handing on a "dead" meaning.

> *Understanding is to be thought of less as a subjective act than as participating in an event of tradition;* a process of transmission in which past and present are constantly mediated. This is what must be validated by hermeneutic theory, which is far too dominated by the idea of procedure, a method.[39]

The Rewrite, unlike parody, allegory or recontextualisation, does not attempt to foreclose the temporal distance and intratextuality between its own performative critical re-reading and the source text, but rather, and in a similar way to Gadamer's hermeneutics of understanding it encompasses the historical gulf as a source of *mediative* understanding not only *of* the past, but of the past *for* the present. The temporal distance between the text and its reception is the very testing ground for the prejudices we possess and which are formulated, with respect to our interpretation of the classics, by our anticipations about such retrospection. It is only by testing our presuppositions (which according to Gadamer are inescapably part of the historical being that we are) that we escape from the self affirming repetition of interpretative stasis, under the guise of knowledge, and enter into the hermeneutic and liberating space that is "understanding". Of course, the classic, or to use Gadamer's terminology, the 'eminent' text[40] is more likely to arouse our presuppositions and prejudices by virtue of its historicality and cultural authority, a process that is clearly illustrated by the Rewrite. For Gadamer, the eminent text has the potential to speak "originarily" or as if it were "saying something to me in particular". However, such a power does not encourage a reassuringly harmonious conception of being universally human, rather, in Gadamer's opinion, this illustrates the classic's power to speak in a way that sets a standard. The recognition of the classic or eminent text's power to set a standard for our understanding is one of the strongest justifications for returning to the past resource as offered up by the classic to exercise our hermeneutic faculties in the present.

Not Appropriation, Parody or Recontextualisation: The Hap of History

If one is to heed Gadamer's strident advocacy for the interpretative productivity of temporal distance, the Rewrite, according to this analysis, is clearly distinct from appropriation, parody or recontextualisation. As opposed to being the product of *intratextual* re-cognition as the result of historical hap, appropriation, parody and recontextualisation is predicated on intentional and *intertextual* repetition. Linda Hutcheon's comprehensive study of parodic art clearly sees it as an aesthetic form of intertextual repetition ". . . with critical distance which makes difference rather than similarity" and she goes on to say, ". . . like Genette, I see parody as a formal or structural relation between two texts."[41]

Appropriations, parody and recontextualisations are intentional and purposive, but also they have a very clear intertextual structure which implies a decoding impetus to expose the encoded intent of the original work, as explained by Hutcheon:

> Both parody and pastiche not only are formal textual imitations but clearly involve the issue of intent. Both are acknowledged borrowings.[42]

In this respect, parodic art-forms are predicated on an originary sense of the source text, as opposed to being the performative *Erlebnis* predicated on intratextual and unforeseen hap. Such hap cannot be intended and it is only after the event of hap, after we have become conscious of our failure to imagine its occurrence, that, in aesthetic terms our new and different "understanding" of the text is precipitated. Parody, appropriations and recontextualisations with their "carefully controlled responses"[43] are thus quite distinct from the Rewrite and even though, as Hutcheon explains, they are 'intramural' as opposed to "extramural" artforms[44], they are an intended structural intertextual engagement, and are thus created under a quite distinct impetus compared to the engagment with the subject of the source text as a result of unforeseen and unimagined intratextual hap.

Like Walter Benjamin's metaphorical descriptions of "straying" and exploring the labyrinth, occasionality or hap denies any absolute or objective aperspectival position, and as such encompasses a notion of serendipitous and historical contingency. In this respect the occasionality or hap which motivates the Rewrite preempts any inclusion in any particular dogma or method and must be clearly distinguished from the appropriative "will to power" alluded to by Nietzsche or the underlying notion of authorised and premeditated transgression formulated by Hutcheon. Indeed, it is the very intent motivating parodic and appropriative art that can often lapse into the 'will to power' that lies behind the propagandist's agenda, adding weight to Orwell's astute observation that ". . . propaganda in some form or other lurks in every book."[45] Parodic and appropriative art can easily represent aesthetic means for concerted ideological ends, in much the same manner that state controlled criticism, such as Stalin's socialist realism programme, can assume the role of cultural censor. Similarly, Eagleton observes how literature and criticism (and by extension, parodic and appropriative art) can become a spiral of mutual reinforcements whereby the literary text and criticism "naturalize" each other and ". . . [u]nder the form of illumination, criticism renders natural the text's necessary self-blindness."[46] Indeed one only has to survey the dangerously adept use of appropriation and parody executed by the Nazis to emphasise the form's propensity to furnish propaganda. As Foulkes explains:

> . . . the Nazis wanted to appropriate the German classics for their own purposes and thus in 1934 books appeared with such titles as *Schiller as Hitler's Comrade-in-Arms: National Socialism in Schiller's Dramas*.[47]

Tim Benton's "Rome Reclaims its Empire" also highlights how important appropriative art was to Mussolini's vision for fascist Italy, and how he attempted to resurrect a heroic and idealised version of classical Rome for the 1930's, leading Bottai to muse:

> The revival of the grandeur of Rome is the highest aspiration of Italian poets, who, from Dante, to Leopardi, and D'Annunzio, have prophesied the triumphal events of Empire, in which—thanks to Il Duce—our generation can take that leading role.[48]

Similarly, propagandists resort to either parodying or appropriating the classics in order to add ideological and cultural credence to their "message", and it is such a potential for the historicist management of the past that distinguishes parodic and appropriative art from the self-consciously historically contingent impetus behind the Rewrite.

Unlike the purposive impetus behind appropriation, parody or recontextualisation the Rewrite's central concern is with the subject of the text which comes to attain a certain dialogic pertinence through hap, for as Richard Wolin points out ". . . truth is not something to be grasped by the intentionality of the knowing subject."[49] As revealed by Benjamin's unmapped adventures in Paris and Berlin the understanding which arises out of true interpretative *Erlebnis* is the result of hap, unplanned and serendipitous and as such cannot be summoned up by an appropriative "will to power". Truth is, as Benjamin observes "an intentionless state of Being . . . Truth is the death of intention."[50] The 'transformation into structure' elicited by *Erlebnis* is a progressive stage that cannot be premeditated or planned and as opposed to being a stylistic or structural play of meaning within the same discursive parameters, clearly elucidated by reference to the etymological roots of parody (parodia— "counter song" or "besides"), the Rewrite engages in dialogue with the source text to reach a different, transformed and progressive "understanding".

Just because the Rewrite is in opposition to the purposive methodology behind appropriation and parody, so too it is antithetical to postmodernist pastiche that indulges in contextual freeplay and "playgiarism"[51] in an attempt to intentionally deny and thus supersede history. Rather the "hap" of Gadamerian occasionality is unintended experience in full recognition of our historical limits and finitude:

> . . . real experience is that whereby man becomes aware of his finiteness. In it are discovered the limits of the power and self-knowledge of his planning reason.[52]

It is the historical "hap" that both creates and gives structure to the occasion for the adventure of experience with tradition, as opposed to the imposition of an extratextual agenda or theory onto the text.

Gadamer likens our experience with art to play and he identifies the unpredictability to every game that one no more wants to dispense with than one does its boundaries and restrictions. It is this unpredictability within the structural parameters of tradition which signifies hermeneutic hap, the hap of the historically contingent interpretative stance, which forestalls what Weinsheimer refers to as the "hegemony of method".[53]

Gadamer's philosophical indebtedness to the Platonic dialogues is in evidence, for as opposed to the determinism which typifies propaganda, or to quote Benjamin the "aestheticisation of politics"[54] as exemplified by many of the political appropriations of the classics, Platonic conversations ". . . say something only to him who finds meanings beyond what is expressly stated in them and allows these meanings to take effect within him."[55] In this respect, Gadamer highlights the importance of philosophical inquiry for the attainment of truth, a point he emphasises by way of his allusion to Socrates' response to Thrasymachus' work as constituting power politics:

> A justice which is postulated and advocated using mere power as its rationalisation cannot suffice to explain why what is based on power is valid as just and not merely as what is coerced.[56]

The Re-Read Textual Subject

James Risser perceptively draws attention to the fact that although deconstructionist critics hail the text as being interpretatively central and claim that there is nothing outside of the text, the text they refer to is far from simple and is no longer ". . . defined by its markings: title, margins, beginning, end, and authorship."[57] In this respect the interpretative stance assumed by the deconstructionist is not so far removed from that of Gadamer's philosophical hermeneutics which not only advocates interpretative freedom from *mens auctoris* but breaks down normative autonomous textual boundaries through its consciousness of effective history:

> What is fixed in writing has detached itself from the contingency of its origin and its author and made itself free for new relationships. Normative concepts such as the author's meaning or the original reader's understanding in fact represent only an empty space that is filled from time to time in understanding.[58]

This is not to suggest that philosophical hermeneutics expounds a view of the work of art as an autonomous and self-sufficient unit, for once art proclaims itself to be pure art, it is, through such a process of aesthetic abstraction, in effect non-art, a criticism which Gadamer levels against aesthetic consciousness as epitomised by Friedrich Schiller's moralistic dictum to "Live aesthetically!" (1794, *Letters on the Aesthetic Education of Man* and *On Naive and Sentimental Poetry*)

> . . . the idea of aesthetic cultivation—as we derived it from Schiller—consists precisely in precluding any criterion of content and in dissociating the work of art from its world. .[59]

Thus, exponents of both deconstruction and philosophical hermeneutics view the text as interpretation, for it is only interpretation that brings the text into being, in contradistinction to aesthetic differentiation which in its assertion of the self-contained autonomy of the object that is the work of art ultimately abdicates from any real interaction with the textual subject matter and by extension "understanding" of the text. Just as Gadamer emphasises that art can never be just art, because art is always interpretation, he also makes the important addendum that true textual interpretation is not merely concerned with formalist deconstructive techniques which play with tropes, structures and etymological discrepancies, but rather with the interpretation of *the subject of the text*. According to Gadamer, because interpretation is concerned with the *subject* of the text, the prejudices which we possess and which have evolved historically are engaged, with the consequence that art, which comes into being through interpretation, is inescapably *historical interpretation*:

> Prejudices are not necessarily unjustified and erroneous, so that they inevitably distort the truth. In fact, the historicity of our existence entails that prejudices, in the literal sense of the word, constitute the initial directedness of our whole ability to experience. Prejudices are biases of our openness to the world. They are simply conditions whereby we experience something—whereby what we encounter says something to us. This formulation certainly does not mean that we are enclosed within a wall of prejudices and only let through the narrow portals those things that can produce a pass saying "Nothing new will be said here." Instead, we welcome just that guest who promises something new to our curiosity. But how do we know the guest whom we admit is one who has something *new* to say to us? Is not our expectation and our readiness to hear the new also necessarily determined by the old that has already taken possession of us?[60]

Thus, it is Gadamer's tenet that all interpretation (which is inescapably historical) is based on the testing of prejudice concerning the subject matter or *Sache* of the text that clearly distinguishes philosophical hermeneutics from Jacques Derrida's deconstructionist interpretative play that not only avoids raising the question of truth but explicitly subverts the claim of truth.[61] Szondi has interpreted Gadamer's emphasis on our understanding of the subject of the text, as opposed to the text, as more epistemological than hermeneutic, but in Gadamerian phenomenological hermeneutics it is historical 'hap', situatedness or phenomena which inform our perspective on the subject matter of the textual dialogue. As opposed to deconstructing a text to stress its irreconcilable *differance*, aporias and fragmentation, Gadamer expands on the deconstructionist approach by emphasising the hermeneutic possibility for a finite and transient "monad" of unity out of difference through the interpretative Socratic dialogue between the present and the tradition that informs our present, for as Risser observes:

> Socrates is not only the gadfly, he is also the midwife who seeks to bring wisdom to birth, and would have us distinguish sophistry from dialectic.[62]

The Temporal Conversation and Historically Effected Consciousness

Gadamer distinguishes between understanding and epistemological knowledge, the latter of which presents history (and by extension the classics) as a chronicle of known facts, knowledge as retrievable data, if searched for according to a predetermined methodology. Gadamerian hermeneutics places less emphasis on epistemological procedure and advocates the implementation of phemomenological hermeneutics which he stresses is not concerned with adhering to a procedure of understanding but rather focuses on clarifying the conditions in which understanding takes place. Gadamer is not proposing a new and better method for determining the "correct" meaning of texts, whereby his phenomenological hermeneutics proposes a method of understanding to be used to avoid misunderstanding or to make the unfamiliar familiar. Instead Gadamer's phenemonological hermeneutic primarily seeks to determine what is involved in the understanding process itself, and in so doing he posits a hermeneutic that stresses the value of contingency and transience as the defining feature of understanding as opposed to the binding incrementalism of knowledge. In this respect Gadamerian hermeneutics is similar to legal hermeneutics and the implementation of jurisprudence, whereby specific understanding of individual cases is exercised to avoid the inevitable injustice and inequity of universal judgements based on dogmatic repetition:

> The judge not only applies the law *in concreto*, but he contributes through his very judgement to developing the law ("judge-made law").[63]

Gadamer's hermeneutic approach is not therefore concerned with trying to rediscover and decipher the lost meaning of a text which historical change has obscured, for to do so is to indulge in reconstruction not understanding. Rather, Gadamer draws attention to our own historicity, to emphasize how an historically effected consciousness as a bridge to mediation between past and present, text and interpreter, fills out the temporal gulf between us and the object of our interest. Historically effected consciousness is not a means whereby temporal gulfs between interpreter and text are overcome but rather it facilitates the mediation of continuity through which the past already functions in and shapes the interpreter's present horizon.

Just as Gadamer asserts that objective historicism is flawed because it takes no account of its own eventfulness and contingency in its interpretative stance, so too he does not consider language as the linguistic vehicle through which we express ideas but rather that the *eidos* or concept coalesces with speech. This approach to language also applies to the production of literature, and which, as Krieger has stated, is the main distinction between literature and the plastic arts, which mould and construct their artefacts with inert and non-communicative materials.[64] Thus for Gadamer, *pace* Heidegger, concepts and ideas are not considered to underlie speaking but rather to evolve in it, just as the text is not seen to be the "object" underlying its interpretation, or the past is the "object" of historical analysis, for as Heidegger states in his seminal essay "The Way to Language"(1959):

> We not only *speak* language, we speak *from out of* it. We are capable of doing so only because in each case we have already listened to language. What do we hear there? We hear language speaking.[65]

In this respect, Gadamer echoes the Heideggerian distinction between articulated sound or speech and language, a distinction which we compulsively blur with a subsequent and retroactive "rift-design" whereby we "propriate" or attempt to "own" and thus methodologise language. However, according to Gadamerian hermeneutics we are not to think of the spoken word, interpretation or historical research as being part of a universalizing and reproductive process or a reactive imitation of a particular idea, text or event, but rather as the perfection or completion, however transitory, of the idea, text or event coming into being:

> A word is not a sign that one selects nor is it a sign that one makes or gives to another . . . Experience is not wordless to begin with, subsequently becoming an object of reflection by being named, by being subsumed under the universality

> of the word. Rather experience of itself seeks and finds words that express it. We
> seek the right word—i.e., the word that really belongs to the thing—so that in it
> the thing comes into language.[66]

Indeed, philosophical hermeneutics is completely distinct in this respect
from structural linguistics which, as Culler points out, is more concerned
to "determine the nature of the system underlying an event" rather than
attempting to hermeneutically "discover what a sequence means."[67] Also,
too often in our attempt to discover systems we lapse into the imposition
of potentially unproductive methodology which distorts and obstructs the
route to meaningful understanding, akin to the blanket response made by
certain critics when they equate the classics with what they perceive to be
the ideologically driven system of canonical inequality and elitism.
Gadamerian hermeneutics is not the search for a deep meaning hidden in
the text, although the descendants of the structuralist tradition often confuse Gadamer's emphasis on the temporal impetus for the production of
a *different* meaning in a text with ideas about revealing a lost and *secret*
meaning embedded within the materiality of the original text. Such unfounded attributions are revealed by Derrida's proclamation that the
"Schleiermachers and veilmakers are routed"[68] by the patricidal demise
of the author and textual "origin" perpertrated by post-structuralist critics:

> The hermeneutic project which postulates a true sense of the text is disqualified
> under this regime . . . The veil [is] no more raised than it is lowered.[69]

Gadamer's notion of historically effected consciousness posits that self-
consciousness arises out of historical life as opposed to history being the
invisible progressive trajectory toward the fulfilment of self consciousness,
and by extension he asserts that knowledge of the world cannot be detached from being in the world. Thus, even when we speak, research or
interpret we cannot be objectively detached because, as we would be well
aware if we developed our historically effected consciousness, we are inescapably a part of an historical ongoing process.

A Gadamerian hermeneutic informs the interpretation of the plays under
consideration, and they represent the negotiation of the critical juncture
between past and present, the classic and the modern, in keeping with
the "effective history" espoused by Benjamin:

> . . . it is not a question of presenting written works in the context of their time
> but of articulating the time which grasps them—namely ours—in the time in which
> they originated.[70]

In contrast to the postmodern project which historically constitutes and
situates itself by narrativizing the past as a series of disjunctures and

discontinuities by employing pastiche and montage to form a grand narrative proclaiming the end of grand narratives, the Benjaminian hypothesis is an appropriate paradigm for understanding the rewriting of the classics. Instead of "binding the not yet realised future through idealistic utopianism or through theoretical attempts to foreclose history"[71] the historically effected consciousness is the milieu which facilitates the rescue of obscured, ignored or more importantly emergent meanings and truths from the past for the present, even though such a resuscitation will be the ephemeral and transitory experience that is *Erlebnis*.

By rereading and subsequently rewriting the classics as a result of specific occasionality or hap, the lost, dormant and potentially emergent hermeneutics within the texts are, not just revealed *despite* temporal distance, but mediatively produced for and in the present *because of* historical distanciation. Such an interpretation of the project represented by these plays is closely aligned to Gadamerian hermeneutics which makes clear distinctions between a hermeneutic "dialogic" negotiation between the past and present about the subject of the text and one-sided monologic repetition of the statement of the text. Indeed the conditions and cognitive assumptions which distinguish 'monologic' and 'dialogic' discourse have been considered by Mikhael Bakhtin, and his analysis is pertinent to our discussion of the dialogue of historically effected consciousness as represented by the Rewrite:

> The contexts of dialogue are without limit. They extend into the deepest past and the most distant future. Even meaning born in dialogues of the remotest past will never be finally grasped once and for all, for they will always be renewed in later dialogue. At any present moment of the dialogue there are great masses of forgotten meanings, but these will be recalled again at a given moment in the dialogue's later course when it will be given new life.[72]

Thus, instead of a hermeneutic based on perfecting the repetition of interpretative stasis Gadamer introduces us to the notion of hermeneutic "recognition", a re-knowing that leads to what Gadamer identifies as the transformation into structure of understanding:

> . . . we do not understand . . . in its profoundest nature if we only regard it as knowing something again that we know already—ie; what is familiar is recognised again. The joy of recognition is rather the joy of knowing more than is already familiar. In recognition, what we know emerges as if illuminated from all the contingent and variable circumstances that condition it; it is grasped in its essence. It is known as something.[73]

Notes

1   For an analyisis of this hermeneutical tradition as it developed from Biblical exegesis to modern philosophy, see Richard Palmer, *Hermeneutics: Interpretation Theory in Schleiermacher, Dilthey, Heidegger and Gadamer* (Evanston: Northwestern University Press, 1969).

2   Peter Szondi, *An Introduction to Literary Hermeneutics* trans: by Martha Woodmansee (Cambridge: Cambridge University Press, 1995) p. 3.

3   Joel Weinsheimer in the Preface to Szondi's *Introduction to Literary Hermeneutics* p.xvii.

4   Gadamer, *TM* p. 100.

5   *Erlebnis* became popularised in the 1870's, and one of the earliest citations is found in one of Hegel's letters. Simmel [Georg Simmel *Lebensanschauung* (2nd ed., 1922) also refers to *Erlebnis* as the adventure of experience "which interrupts the customary course of events, but is positively and significantly related to the context which it interrupts." [*Truth and Method*, p.69] Gadamer relates the experience that is *Erlebnis* to aesthetic experience whereby the work of art not only tears the person out of the context of his life but also relates him back to the whole of his existence:

> An aesthetic Erlebnis always contains the experience of an infinite whole. [Truth and Method p. 70.]

It is posited in this discussion that the Rewrite is performative *Erlebnis* which through its performative re-reading tears the audience, by dint of occasionality wrought by historically effected consciousness, away from the received reception of the classic in order to relate us back to the whole of our existence, and with a more complete, but perpetually evolving, hermeneutic "understanding".

6   *Erfahrung* relates to the gathering of received knowledge and its retention, such as that passed down to us through tradition. However, this explanation should be balanced by the awareness that as Gadamer points out ". . . experience is always actually present only in the individual observation. It is not known in a previous universality. Here lies the fundamental openness of experience to new experience, not only in the general sense that errors are corrected, but that experience is essentially dependent on constant confirmation . . ." pp. 351–352. It is *Erlebnis*, the immediacy and vibrancy of experience in the present that interacts to transform our more empirically based grasp of experience that is *Erfahrung*.

7   See Chapter VI. Expanding on Nietzsche's observation that aesthetic theory and criticism has created in us an aesthetic consciousness that deprives us of the "effect" of art, Gadamer asserts that we are no longer constituted by our ability to "innocently" judge but rather, that after centuries of being subjected to the bias of aesthetic consciousness we are compelled to test our prejudices in order to hermeneutically "understand":

Whenever we say with an instinctive, even if perhaps erroneous, certainty (but a certainty that is initially valid for our consciousness) "this is classical; it will endure" what we are speaking of has already performed our possibility for aesthetic judgement. There are no purely formal criteria that can claim to judge and sanction the formative level simply on the basis of its artistic virtuosity. Rather, our sensitive-spiritual existence is an aesthetic resonance chamber that resonates with the voices that are constantly reaching us, preceding all explicit aesthetic judgement. [Gadamer, *Philosophical Hermeneutics*, 1977, p. 8. hereafter referred to as *PH*]

8   Gadamer, *TM* p. 4

9   The word "performative" is used here to emphasise the performance of drama, and by extension the performance of the Rewrite's *Erlebnis*-imbued interpretation. It should be noted that this use of the term "performative" is not an allusion or reference to J. L. Austin's speech act theory and its distinction between "performative" and "constative" language. (J. L. Austin, *How to do Things with Words*, 1962).

10   Weinsheimer, (a) p. 88.

11   Gadamer, *TM* p. 534.

12   Joel Weinsheimer, (a) p .8. Weinsheimer has coined the useful and less cumbersome term "hap" to convey Gadamer's concept of the situatedness and occasionality of the interpretative position and thus understanding. This term will be used throughout the study. A distinction should be noticed between *event* and *hap*. Hap is not synonomous with event because hap is the *consciousness of the event* for, as Camus observed, our consciousness is always lagging behind History. In this respect, I would argue that hap is an appropriate term to use when discussing our response to historical atrocities such as the Holocaust or Apartheid. Although these events were protracted, our consciousness of such events (as opposed to knowledge) is still taking shape, be it fifty years after the Holocaust or in the light of the post-Apartheid "Truth Commission".

13   Deborah Cook "Rereading Gadamer: A Response to James Risser" in *Gadamer and Hermeneutics* (London: Routledge, 1991) pp. 106–116.

14   Gadamer, *TM* p. 317.

15   Gadamer, *TM* p. 279.

16   See an illuminating article by Paul Abbott, "Authority" in *Screen* 20:2 (Summer 1979) 11–64.

17   Johnson, S "The Rambler" in *The Rambler: The Yale Edition of the Works of Samuel Johnson* Vol 3, (eds) W J Bate and Albrecht B Strauss, New Haven, Yale University Press, 1969, p.22. Also refer to Weinsheimer's discussion in "The Question of the Classic" in *Philosophical Hermeneutics and Literary Theory* (Yale and New Haven: Yale University Press, 1991) pp. 124–157.

18   *anspruchsvoll* is an important concept, and is particularly useful when considering the distinction between art and aesthetics [See Chapter VI]. The concept of

anspruchsvoll, according to Weinsheimer, translates into the "claim" that art, and especially traditionary art, exerts upon us, namely to take its effect seriously and specifically. Because art has greater specificity and definiteness it speaks to us [*uns anspricht*] in such a way as to make a determinate claim upon our attention [*bestimmter Anspruch*]. However, the claim exerted upon us by art is not to strive for a "correct" meaning through a rigorous, but ultimately subjective interpretative procedure; rather it is a correctness which derives from the work of art and what it has to say. Gadamer asserts that such responsibility or *anspruchsvoll* is even more in evidence with respect to traditionary art and the classics. Jauss argues that Gadamer is mistaken in contending that the work first speaks to us before we interrogate it. For Jauss, the work does not speak at all prior to the interpreter's question. See Jauss's "Literary History as a Challenge to Literary Theory" in *Toward an Aesthetic of Reception* trans. Timothy Bahti, Minneapolis, University of Minnesota Press, 1982.

Weinsheimer sees some similarities between Kant's definintion of *Urteil*, and the *Anspruch* behind Gadamer's notion of hermeneutic responsibility, but ". . . unlike *Urteil*, *Anspruch* is less something we do than something that first happens to us." (Weinsheimer, *Gadamer's Hermenuetics: A Reading of Truth and Method*, p. 86). For Gadamer, the conversation with a text only occurs only when the interpreter is drawn into a subject area (*Sache*) that says something interesting, something that concerns him too. Thus, although a conversation with a text, an historical text, is a responsibility and a task, it *cannot* be mechanized or the result of a premeditated methodological enterprise – the text must first hold a claim to the interpreter's interest and then the interpretative responsibility (or what Weinsheimer identifies as *anspruchsvoll*) is assumed. A more practical example of the way a text makes a claim on our interest and by extension how it demands our responsibility to engage in further conversation is provided in Chapter III dealing with *The Merchant of Venice* and Marowitz's negotiation with the source text with a post-Holocaust consciousness. It is the Shakespearean classic that has spoken to the post-Holocaust Marowitz – by dint of hap, or historically effected consciousness,a different, altered conversation has been initiated by the text, and thrown up a new focus, an altered subject matter – from which Marowitz presents the results of his intertextual and intratextual discussion, *Variations on The Merchant of Venice*. This is quite distinct from Marowitz (hypothetically) producing a completely "new" post-Holocaust play about anti-Semitism, for example.

19   Joel Weinsheimer, (a) p. 165.

20   Alan How, *The Habermas-Gadamer Debate and the Nature of the Social: Back to Bedrock* (Aldershot: Avebury, 1995). How has pointed out the similarity between Habermas and Ricoeur with respect to a hermeneutic of suspicion and mistrust which manifests itself as an opposition to the status quo, including authoritative texts like the classics. Gadamer however emphasises "good will" as the cornerstone of this dialogic hermeneutic.

21   David Linge, Introduction to *PH* p. xiii.

22   Pierre Maranda "The Dialectic of Metaphor: An Anthropological Essay on Herme-
     neutics" in *The Reader in the Text: Essays on Audience Interpretation* (eds)
     S. R. Suleiman and Inge Crosman (Princeton: Princeton University Press, 1980)
     p. 183.

23   Stanely Fish *Is there a Text in the Class?* p. 139.

24   Chladenius, as cited in Szondi p. 195.

25   Schott, R "Whose home is it anyway? A Feminist response to Gadamer's Herme-
     neutics" in *Gadamer and Hermeneutics: Science, Culture, Literature:
     Contintental Philosophy IV* (ed) Hugh J Silverman, (New York and London:
     Routledge 1991) pp. 202–209.

26   Patrocinio P. Schweickart, "Reading Ourselves Toward a Feminist Theory of Read-
     ing" *Gender and Reading: Essays on Readers, Texts and Contexts* (eds) A
     Flynn and P. P. Schweickart (Baltimore: The Johns Hopkins University Press,
     1984) p. 35.

27   Hans Georg Gadamer, "The Scope of Hermeneutical Reflection" in *PH* p. 32.

28   Leo Strauss develops the debate about exoteric and esoteric hermeneutics, par-
     ticularly with respect to works written under the threat of censorship in *Persecu-
     tion and the Art of Writing* (Glencoe: Free Press, 1952).

29   Wa Thiong'o Ngugi "Decolonising the Mind: The Politics of Language in African
     Literature" in *The Classics For Africa* (London: James Curry, 1987) p. 91.

30   Alan How, p. 33.

31   D. Linge, Introduction, *PH* p. xlvii.

32   Weinsheimer, (a) p. 170.

33   Schleiermacher's hermeneutic project is addressed at some length by Gadamer
     [*Truth and Method*, pp. 184–197]. Essentially Schleiermacher posits a recon-
     structive hermeneutic ". . . making intelligible what others have said in speech
     and text."[Gadamer, p. 185]. This is in sharp contradistinction to Gadamer, who
     deems reconstructive hermeneutics which attempts to recapture 'original' mean-
     ing as futile and moribund. Although Gadamer does applaud Schleiermacher as
     the first to focus on the general principles and conditions that make it possible to
     understand, as opposed to establishing practical guidelines for understanding, he
     considers Schleiermacher's hermeneutic theory to be historically limited and only
     directed at texts with an undisputed authority.

34   Dilthey, W. Like Schleiermacher, Dilthey identified the meaning of a text with the
     subjective intention of the author, and thus approached textual language as a
     cipher which if broken would yield hidden and difficult meanings:

        The more lax practice of the art of understanding proceeds on the assump-
        tion that understanding arises naturally . . . The more rigorous practice
        proceeds on the assumption that misunderstanding arises naturally, and

that understanding must be intended and sought at each point. [F Schleiermacher, *Hermeneutik* trans. H Kimmerle (Heidelberg: Karl Winter), 1959, p. 86.]

Although Gadamer acknowledges the contribution of both Schleiermacher and Dilthey in taking hermeneutics away from the limited pedagogical project to understand the previously not understood into an interpretative approach to avoid misunderstanding, he cites the failure of what he views as an essentially historicist reconstructive hermeneutic which does not take into account its own contingency, temporality and thus finitude.

35   Weinsheimer,(a) p. 168.

36   Dilthey developed the model of "the hermeneutic circle" which emphasises our inability to determine the meaning of separate words until we have grasped the meaning of the sentence as a whole. As a consequence, Dilthey's hermeneutic method is goal driven and derives its impetus from a desire to attain hermeneutic completion and closure. Gadamerian hermeneutics, however, places far more emphasis upon the hermeneutic journey and its interplay between anticipation and retrospection as opposed to arriving at a definitive hermeneutic destination or meaning.

37   Emilio Betti, *Teoria Generale della Interpretazione* 2 Vols (Milan: 1955) See Gadamer's citation and consideration of Betti's theories, *TM* pp. 510–512.

38   Joel Weinsheimer, *Philosophical Hermeneutics and Literary Theory* (New Haven and London: Yale University Press, 1991) p. 13. [hereafter referred to as (b)]

39   Gadamer, *TM* p. 290.

40   Gadamer usually refers to the classic as an 'eminent' text, which even more than other literary texts '. . . are governed by the fundamental hermeneutic structure of understanding something as something [so that] their constitutive form is nothing radically new." Gadamer retorts against what he views to be the 'pretensions' of novelty that supposedly supersede the need for artistic productions to be repeatable, identifiable and worth repeating. Of course he concedes that 'mere trick or legerdemain' can also be understood under the guise of art and ". . . it can be conceptualized; it can be imitated. It even tries to be adept and good. But its repetition, in Hegel's words, become "insipid, like a piece of legerdemain that has been seen through." Here, Gadamer attempts to define art as distinct from artifice and decoration, and he also points out how art can alter in practical contexts ". . . for example, in poster art and other forms of commerical and political advertisment." (*TM* p. 578). Also see Arthur C. Danto's *The Transfiguration of the Commonplace*. Benjamin also railed against what he considered to be the misplaced 'phantasmagoric' emphasis put on artistic novelty in his work *Charles Baudelaire: A Lyric Poet in the Era of High Capitalism* trans. by H. Zohn (London: New Left Books, 1973) p. 263:

Novelty is a quality which does not depend on the use-value of the commodity. It is the source to the illusion which belongs inalienably to the images which the collective unconscious engenders. It is the quintessence of false consciousness, of which fashion is the tireless agent. This illusion of novelty is reflected, like one mirror in another, in the illusion of infinite sameness.

41   Linda Hutcheon, *A Theory of Parody: The Teachings of Twentieth-Century Art Forms* (New York and London: Routledge, 1986) p. 22

42   Hutcheon, p. 38.

43   Hutcheon, p. 23.

44   Hutcheon pp. 43–49. Hutcheon draws the distinction between the intramural engagement of parody and the extramural impetus behind satire, which often alludes to social and moral issues outwith the text. However, she goes on to discuss instances when the two devices are conflated for aesthetic effect.

45   George Orwell, *The Collected Essays, Journalism and Letters*, vol. 2, Sonia Orwell and Ian Angus (eds) (Harmondsworth, Middlesex: Penguin, 1970) p. 152.

46   Terry Eagleton *Criticism and Ideology* (London: Verso, 1976) p. 18.

47   A.P. Foulkes *Literature and Propaganda* (London and New York: Methuen, 1983) p. 7.

48   Giuseppe Bottai, *La politica delle arti: Scritti 1918–1943* ed. Alessandro Masi (Rome: 1992) p. 122.

49   Richard Wolin, *Walter Benjamin: An Aesthetic of Redemption* (Berkeley: University of California Press, 1994) p. 93.

50   Walter Benjamin, *The Origin of German Tragic Drama* trans. by John Osborne (London: New Left Books, 1977) p. 36

51   Campbell Tatham "Mythotherapy and Postmodern Fictions: Magic is Afoot" in *Performance in Postmodern Culture* (eds) M. Benamou, Charles Carnello (Milwaukee, Wisconsin: Centre for Twentieth Century Studies, 1977) p. 146.

52   Gadamer, *TM* p. 357.

53   Weinsheimer, (a) p. 8.

54   Benjamin, *Illuminations* (ed) H. Arendt (New York: Schocken Books, 1969) p. 241. Benjamin states "All efforts to render politics aesthetic culminate in one thing: war." For an extremely informative and imaginative treatment of this particular aspect of Benjamin's work, and a further discussion of the limits of aestheticisation see Susan Buck-Morss's article "Aesthetics and Anaesthetics: Walter Benjamin's Artwork Essay Reconsidered" in *The Actuality of Walter Benjamin: New Formations* 20. Summer 1993, pp. 123–143.

55   Gadamer, "Plato and the Poets" in *Dialogue and Dialectic: Eight Hermeneutical Studies on Plato* trans. by P. Christopher Smith (New Haven: Yale University Press, 1980) p. 71. [hereafter referred to as *DD*]

56   Gadamer, *DD*, p. 81

57   Risser, J "The Two Faces of Socrates: Gadamer/Derrida" in *Dialogue and Deconstruction The Gadamer-Derrida Encounter* (eds) Diane P Michelfelder, Richard E Palmer (Albany: State University of New York Press, 1989) p. 177.

58   Gadamer, *TM* p. 395.

59   Gadamer, *TM* p. 85.

60   Gadamer, "The Universality of the Hermeneutical Problem" in *PH* p. 9.

61   Norris, C "Home Thoughts from Abroad: Derrida, Austin and the Oxford Connection" in *Philosophy and Literature*, Vol 10 No.1 April 1986 pp. 4–5. Norris points out that Derrida's emphasis that all language is inescapably metaphorical and thus operating through tropes and figures has ". . . erased the distinction between philosophy and literature treating the former as a purely textual phenomenon and thus effectively subjugating reason to rhetoric."

62   Risser, p. 184. Also refer to Risser's latest publication *Hermeneutics and the Voice of the Other: Rereading Gadamer's Philosophical Hermeneutics* (Albany: State University of New York Press, 1997)

63   Gadamer, *TM* p. 38.

64   Murray Krieger discusses the distinction between the plastic arts and literature in some depth, and in a similar vein to Gadamer

65   Heidegger, M "The Way to Language" in *Basic Writings* ed; David Farrell Krell, (London: Routledge, 1996) p. 411.

66   Gadamer, *TM* p. 417.

67   Jonathan Culler *Structuralist Poetics* (Ithaca: Cornell University Press, 1975) p. 31.

68   Jacques Derrida *Spurs: Nietzsche's Styles*, trans. by Barbara Harlow (Chicago: University of Chicago Press, 1978) p. 129.

69   Derrida, *Spurs*, p.129.

70   Walter Benjamin, *Gesammelte Schriften* (eds) R. Tiedemann, H. Schweppenhauser (Frankfurt am Main: 1974–1988) III p. 219.

71   Zygmunt Bauman, "Benjamin the Intellectual" in *The Actuality of Walter Benjamin: New Formations*, No. 20, Summer 1993, p. 51

72   M. Bakhtin, *Estetika* or *Author and Hero in Aesthetic Activity* (1979) cited by Michael Holquist in *Dialogism: Bakhtin and His World* (London: Routledge, 1991) p. 39.

73   Gadamer, *TM* p. 114

Chapter Three

The Merchant of Venice After The Holocaust: Wesker and Marowitz

Cynical Re-reading and Articulating the Inarticulable

The Merchant of Venice presents me with a problem unique in Shakespeare's work, for I have come to the conclusion that in the light of the twentieth century experience, Shakespeare would be likely to withdraw permission for the play to be performed in its present form.[1]

The Merchant of Venice (1599–1600) is often considered to be one of Shakespeare's "problem plays"[2] in part, because of the ostensibly stereotypical portrayal of its usurious and bitter Jewish moneylender, Shylock. In the shadow of the Holocaust many critics and directors consider Shakespeare's characterisation of Shylock as not only unacceptable but as contributing to the further promulgation of dangerous racial stereotypes:

Current criticism notwithstanding *The Merchant of Venice* seems to me a profoundly and crudely anti-Semitic play.[3]

and,

Hitler used it, Goebbels used it and it contributed directly to the extermination of the Jews, the 'final solution' of 1943. The Minister of Propaganda is quoted in the six files for the extermination of the Jewish people as ordering a performance of *The Merchant of Venice* . . . It is impossible in my view to play *The Merchant of Venice* in Germany after this example.[4]

Indeed, Arnold Wesker's opinion that the play fuelled "the word's astigmatic view of the murderous hatred of the Jew"[5] was to prompt him to set about writing his own version of *The Merchant of Venice*, subsequently followed by the first performance of his production of *Shylock* in

1976. Charles Marowitz also rewrote Shakespeare's play in the form of *Variations on The Merchant of Venice* (1976) for similar reasons to Wesker:

> It is difficult, almost impossible, to come to a play like *The Merchant of Venice* whose central character is an orthodox Jew, without bringing to the experience all one has learned and read about Jews in the last 2000 years; difficult to obliterate from the mind the last 75 years of Jewish history which includes the European pogroms, Hitler's 'death camps', the rise of Jewish Nationalism and the Arab-Israeli conflicts. Of course Shakespeare had no knowledge of any of these things and it is undeniable that none of these factors enter into *The Merchant of Venice*—and yet can they be excluded from the consciousness of the spectator who attends the play?[6]

Unlike John Russell Brown who states that ". . . in the theatre it is his [Shylock's] play"[7] and Leslie Fiedler who asserts that the play is ". . . undeniably, . . . about a Jew",[8] other critics, such as Marion Perret, have stated that *The Merchant of Venice* is not specifically concerned with Shylock, or even Jewry or anti-Semitism, an opinion that it is hard to concur with when one considers the frequency of references to Judaism and "the Jew" in the source text:

> The time is yet to come when performances of *The Merchant of Venice* shaped without reference to the audiences preconceptions about Jews can realise the text's painful richness.[9]

However, even when one directs one's attention away from the ritual humiliation with which the play ends, and towards, for example, the "love dimension" provided by the sub-plot between Bassanio and Portia, the play still exhibits a central concern with the persecution and control of minorities and the "other" in society, be it women, foreigners, the poor, Catholics or indeed "the Jew". In addition, even if the play's portrayal of victimisation and anti-Semitism was not searingly apparent and acute for earlier audiences[10], these facets of the play are unavoidably and unbearably foregrounded in any hermeneutically responsible and sensitive post-Holocaust interpretation, for as Gross astutely observes:

> Shylock is a special case. Not only does he stand out from his surroundings in peculiarly stark isolation; his myth has often flourished with very little reference to *The Merchant of Venice* as a whole, quite often with none at all.[11]

Regardless of unsubstantiated theses put forward as to authorial intention *The Merchant of Venice* has undeniably become enmeshed in the cyclical causation and production process of anti-Semitism, and as Michael Bristol has observed with reference to the play ". . . great literary works are more like complex and difficult memories that trouble the waking life of successor cultures."[12] In addition, *The Merchant of Venice* is a work that is particularly worthy of attention when reconsidering Benjamin's observation that "There is no document of civilisation which is not at the same time a document of barbarism."[13] However, as opposed to viewing such a charge as condemning all cultural activity as inescapably barbaric, Benjamin regarded such a socio-cultural indictment as a hermeneutic challenge, a hermeneutic challenge fulfilled by the Rewrite, whereby:

> . . . it is not a question of presenting works in the context of their time, but of articulating the time which grasps them—namely ours—in the time in which they originated.[14]

The Rewrite is a dramaturgical form, unlike the ideologically driven projects of appropriation, parody or recontextualisation, that rises to the hermeneutic endeavour to make as Marowitz observes, "creations in their own right: ideological extensions of the work from which they sprang."[15]. Such opinions are in keeping with Gadamer's hermeneutic approach that emphasises how the course of events bring out new aspects of meaning in historical material, including the classics.

Elie Wiesel has analysed the Midrashic tradition of bringing "new understanding to old stories"[16] and he concludes that biblical legends, (of which, by reference to Galations, it has been argued *The Merchant of Venice* is a literary derivation[17]) can be "understood" today only with and through an informed post-Holocaust consciousness. This view is echoed by Elizabeth Fiorenza and David Tracy's analysis of the relationship between Christian and Jew after the Holocaust, and is pertinent to any hermeneutically inspired approach to the source text:

> The theological fact is that Christian theology cannot fully return to history until it faces the Holocaust. It cannot face that interruption in history without facing as well the anti-Semitic effects of its own Christian history. It cannot face that interruption without realising that the return to history must now be the return through the radical negativity disclosed by the event. [18]

However, the articulation of the inarticulable that is the Holocaust, and in particular in a literary form, is often conceived to be insensitive and at the very least tasteless leaving us to ask, with Langer ". . . [h]ow do we verbalise the enigma of a language that alienates even as it struggles to connect?"[19]. Through the power of the representation of intratextual silence

elicited by the dramaturgical form of the Rewrite and its historical mediation, the post-Holocaust impurification of language which stifles a full
articulation of the source text, unlike the disinterestedness of mutism,
speaks to those of us who choose to listen with their historically effected
consciousness. Thus, although Marowitz does not make direct reference
to the Holocaust even once throughout his dramaturgical treatment of
The Merchant of Venice, his play, which is set in the immediate post-
Holocaust turmoil of the emergent State of Israel, is hermeneutically suffused with the reverberative echo of that unnameable event, that unspeakable subject matter, be it by way of the historical situatedness of the setting,
the fear and mistrust which pervades the play, or with references such as:

> SHYLOCK: . . . For cruelly we have toiled to inherit here
> And painful nights have been appointed me,
> Great injuries are not soon forgot.

Indeed, Marowitz engages the representation of silence, by way of our
historically effected consciousness of the Holocaust, to elicit the transformation into structure of *Variations*, whereby any "judgement" meted out
to, "the Jew", Shylock is no longer tenable and thus literally explosively
silenced. Blanchot's discussion of the limits of linguistic expression in *The
Writing of the Disaster* is pertinent in this respect:

> Another complaint of Nietzsche's, formulated in a surprising manner: "It might
> be said that we have words only for *extremes* of feeling"—joy, pain—and that we
> miss the greyish, scarcely felt underside of life which is its becoming. But the
> opposite may be the case: that we have no words for the extreme; that dazzling
> joy and great pain burn up every term and render them all mute. (An etymological
> paradox: if *éblouissement* ["bedazzlement"] is linked to the German *blöde* whose
> meaning is first "weak" and then "weak-sighted" it is surprising that an excess of
> light, which blinds, should be expressed in terms of a kind of myopia, a deficiency
> of the eye. What attracts us to etymology is its unreasonable part more than what
> it explains: we are interested by the form of enigma that it preserves or doubles as
> it deciphers). But is Nietzsche not simply noticing, as Bergson would later, that
> words are suitable only for the crude analysis of abstract understanding ("ex-
> treme," then would mean: what is unmistakable, schematic)? Here again, suspi-
> cion is not suspicious enough.[20]

The Rewrite, by its very form, emphasises that all interpretative 'understanding' is based on the temporal structure of re-cognition and is thus
intrinsically historical, enabling our historically effected consciousness about
the Holocaust to be engaged when considering *Variations* even without
specific reference to the unspeakable being made. This is in stark contrast

to the cumulative reiteration of our knowledge of the classic despite the vicissitudes of history, exemplified by Wesker's *Shylock*. Marowitz's Rewrite dramaturgically facilitates a hermeneutic re-cognition of *The Merchant of Venice* by temporarily mediating the hermeneutic trauma which the Holocaust has inescapably effected upon our reception of the text, and thus approximates something close to Lyotard's attempt:

> . . . to indicate the irreducible immemorial . . . responsibilities of all thought and writing, especially "after Auschwitz." It constitutes a demand for forms of thinking and writing that do not forget "the fact" of the forgotten and the unrepresentable.[21]

In this respect, the Rewrite of *The Merchant of Venice* not only addresses the anti-Semitic effect of the source text and its cultural implication in the atrocity of the Holocaust, but also it dramaturgically refuses to endorse Bloom's *aesthesis* or White's "poeticised" reality[22], and instead literally performs a hermeneutic mediation between our knowledge of the text and its place in our literary tradition as based on *poiesis* and *techne*, *and* our burgeoning awareness of the reality of the Holocaust, born of *praxis* and *phronesis*, so that we no longer "receive" the Shakespearean classic, but rather "re-cognize" it with a post-Holocaust understanding. Indeed, the limits of Bloom's *aesthesis* are revealed by his own comments about *The Merchant of Venice*:

> I'm well aware that my trouble in achieving any pleasure in reading or viewing Shylock is because other factors are getting in the way of apprehending the Shakespearean sublime.[23]

Western metaphysics' traditional distinction between *poiesis* and *praxis* is highlighted by the Heidegger affair and the subsequent debate over Heidegger's intellectual standing, and it is similar anomalies which Gadamer's formulation of performative *Erlebnis* attempts to resolve through his refusal to methodologise. Indeed, our propensity to seek out methods which have the effect of denying the historical consciousness of our own historicity, have contributed toward the sustained anomalous distinction between *poiesis* and *praxis* under the methodology of Western metaphysics, which, in turn, has given rise to the likes of the Heidegger Affair. As Bernasconi explains:

> The point is not simply that a thinker of Heidegger's stature was misled, so that we must draw some distinctions to protect our most cherished illusions about philosophy. It is no longer enough to separate person and work, or

Weltanschauung and work, or the realm of the thinker from the public realm. Heidegger's failings, which extend beyond the political and the moral to thinking itself, reflect not just on him, or on a school of philosophy, but on the very ideal of the Western philosophical tradition as a way of life. This ideal constitutes a conviction about philosophy so deeply held that only a philosopher's apparent blindness to events as cataclysmic as those witnessed in Europe in the middle of the century could destroy it. Here is an end of philosophy, of philosophy's self-conception. It was not the same end of philosophy that Heidegger envisaged in his works. Nor was it brought about in his works alone. He enacted it in his life and works by showing what for too long had gone unsuspected, that great thoughts under the mask of nobility can lead us astray. The task of thinking this end, the task of ploughing through the wreckage, not just to track down the diabolical, but to see what can be scavenged has barely begun.[24]

As a result of such a distinction our reception of texts has often become distorted, for our thoughts about a text (*poiesis*) have become divorced from our historically contingent experience (*praxis*) with the result, for example, of the sanitization of a text like *The Merchant of Venice* either through Kantian aesthetic distanciation or by way of faithful dramatic reconstructions of the past which serve to create a temporal and psychological gulf between the audience and the classic. Gadamer critiques the Kantian tradition of thought that was to split "aesthetic consciousness" from other forms of thought as one which led to an increasingly subjectivised aesthetic judgement of art as "personal opinion" and which created the possibility for all art to degenerate into either the merely decorative and uncommitted or, even more worryingly, covert propaganda.

The Rewrite, in keeping with Gadamerian hermeneutics, is based upon *Erlebnis* which, to put it in simple terms, amounts to the historically effected consciousness of our being in the world in the present. Such a hermeneutic guards against the distancing with which we unquestioningly yield to our cultural tradition's "eminence" or kudos, and through the application of hap compels us to experience the past of the classic in the present. The immediacy of such a hermeneutic project prevents us from assuming a disinterested lack of involvement with culture and its implication in the history of events, just as it prevails against the classics becoming closely guarded canonical museum pieces, and instead it makes those very texts which create a sense of unease or discomfort engage us in a hermeneutic dialogue with an historically effected consciousness. Our history, just like our understanding of the classics, cannot be designated as research into the past as "post"[25] because we are part of the ongoing historical process. As Gadamer states:

There is no such thing in fact as a point outside history from which the identity of a problem can be conceived within the vicissitudes of the history of attempts to solve it. The fact is that understanding philosophical texts always requires recognizing what is cognized in them. Without this we would understand nothing at all.[26]

Although Wesker and Marowitz put forward a similar rationale for revisiting Shakespeare's text, it is my intention to contrast both plays in order to further explain the political potential *pace* Gadamer, of performative *Erlebnis*, whereby a dramaturgical engagement with the past is facilitated, in this case with the classic, so that tradition is confronted as that through which we both question the past and feel addressed by it. As Alan How observes with respect to Gadamerian hermeneutics:

Gadamer reverses the normal assumptions of what successful interpretation consists of; instead of a brand new understanding emerging he claims that we amplify and extend what we already know, by disclosing more thoroughly the tradition in which we are immersed.[27]

Although we may think we empirically "know" the past, including our literary tradition, in a similar manner to an exercise in *techne* and *poiesis*, the contrast between Marowitz's mediation between the past and present imbued with historically effected consciousness of the Holocaust, and Wesker's attempt to control the past from the present, through selective amnesia and wish fulfilment is edifying. This analysis of the contrast between the two dramatists illustrates that true understanding can only arise when it is founded upon an acknowledgement of *praxis* and *phronesis*, that is, a cognizance of the process of *becoming* that constitutes our present perspective in its engagement with the past, in keeping with Larmore's observation that:

. . . the essential part is that we overcome the deep-seated notion that history and reason are like oil and water. The pursuit of objectivity is often assumed to require that we neutralise the effects of historical contingency on our thinking and strive to see the world from something like the standpoint of eternity.[28]

Wesker's *Shylock*, unlike the Marowitz play, does not address the ideological subtext and accretions which have attached themselves to *The Merchant of Venice*, in particular since the Holocaust, and as a result, he fails to acknowledge that all knowledge is woven into the historical situation of its production as well as into the historical situation of its reception.

Instead of performing an interpretative mediation with the representation of "the Jew" from Shakespeare's time to the present fully possessed of a post-Holocaust consciousness, Wesker merely 'replaces' Shylock in an unsatisfactorily apologetic manner, and as such reveals a rereading and subsequent rewriting similar to what Laclau and Mouffe identify as an unproductive interpretative "formula of antagonism"[29]. Thus, Wesker's *Shylock* does not engage with *The Merchant of Venice* with an historically effected consciousness, and merely attempts to dramaturgically replace Shakespeare's play with another play imbued with a spirit of determined amnesia. In this respect Wesker's play is similar to Gadamer's notion of alteration, as opposed to the transformation into structure that typifies "understanding", and which:

> . . . always means that what is altered also remains the same and is maintained. However totally it may change something changes in it. In terms of categories, all alteration (*aleosis*) belongs in the sphere of quality—i.e., of an accident of substance. But transformation means that something is suddenly and as a whole something else, that this other, transformed thing that it has become is its true being, in comparison with which its earlier being is nil. When we find someone transformed we mean precisely this, that he has become another person as it were. There cannot here be any gradual transition leading from one to the other since the one is the denial of the other. Thus transformation into structure means that what existed previously exists no longer. But also that what now exists, what represents itself in the play of art is lasting and true.[30]

Shapiro has observed *The Merchant of Venice* offers us one of the greatest opportunities to negotiate the relationship between "cultural myths and peoples' identities" and ". . . this is why censoring the play is *always* more dangerous than staging it."[31] However, as opposed to the dramaturgical engagement in the intratextual relationship between cultural myths and Jewish identity as exemplified by Marowitz's *Variations*, Wesker constructively censors the source text. By inverting what he considers to be the malevolent and mean-spirited stereotypical Jewish miser in Shakespeare's play into a "good" Jew, Wesker's approach is in accordance and thus complicitous with the evaluative parameters set out by Shylock's original victimisers, as exemplified by Shakespeare's Antonio who immediately equates Shylock's seemingly "good" faith with respect to the bond as evidence that the "Hebrew will turn Christian," (1.3.175). The tailored *replacement* of one Shylock with another precludes the productivity of hermeneutic play in favour of what is in effect interpretative stasis based on reiteration, and as such Wesker's treatment of the source text fails to exhibit the "ludic" re-reading espoused by Barthes:

Re-reading is here suggested at the outset, for it alone saves the text from repetition (those who fail to re-read are obliged to read the same story everywhere) and multiplies it in its variety and pluralities.[32]

On the other hand, Marowitz *Variations* is based, in part, on a very clear and acknowledged incorporative but highly cynical "received" re-reading of the source text which does not leave the audience with any "doubt" about the motivation behind the deeds perpetrated by various characters, whether it be Shylock's "revenge" or Bassanio's social aspirations. When the rereading of the source text upon which Marowitz's play is predicated is described as 'received' it is in the awareness that the almost mythical status of the interpretation of Shylock as duplicitous, mean and untrustworthy has been based on a biased but nonetheless sustained acceptance of what the Christians in the source text say about "the Jew" as opposed to being substantiated by his deeds and words. As Fiedler's summation of the effect of the play for a late twentieth century consciousness reveals, the cynicism engaged and foregrounded for the larger part of Marowitz's Rewrite is the only way we can hermeneutically cope with an unadulterated version of the source text:

It took three generations of nineteenth-century romantic actors to make the Jew seem sympathetic as well as central, so that the poet Heine, sitting in the audience, could feel free to weep at his discomfiture. The final and irrevocable redemption of Shylock, however, was the inadvertent achievement of the greatest anti-Semite of all time, who did not appear until the twentieth century was almost three decades old. Since Hitler's 'final solution' to the terror which cues the uneasy laughter of *The Merchant of Venice*, it has seemed immoral to question the process by which Shylock has been converted from a false-nosed, red-wigged monster, (his hair the colour of Judas's) half spook and half clown, into a sympathetic victim.[33]

There are numerous examples in the source text of the way in which our encounter with Shylock is coloured by negative and derogatory descriptions, most of which are directly linked to his creed, as put forward by the Christian characters:

ANTONIO [*Aside*]: Mark you this Bassanio
                    The Devil can cite Scripture for his purpose.
                    [Act I, Scene III l. 93–4]

and

BASSANIO: I like not fair terms and a villain's mind
           [Act I, Scene III, l. 173]

and

> LAUNCELOT GOBBO: . . . Certainly the Jew is the very devil
> incarnation . . .
> [Act II, Scene II, l.24]

and

> SOLANIO: The villain Jew with outcries rais'd the
> Duke . . .
> [Act II, Scene VIII, l. 4]

Indeed, despite all the slurs and abuse directed toward him, the textual evidence does not reveal Shylock as either duplicitous or dishonest, and even though Shakespeare does not, like Wesker, portray Shylock as an overtly sympathetic character Shylock most definitely is not implicated in any concerted form of deceit. The only examples of deceit either by way of physical or spiritual disguise are attributable to the Christian characters, most notably Portia and Bassanio, and to a lesser extent Jessica and Launcelot Gobbo, both of whom leave us with the impression that their deceit is shaped under the weight of religious persecution and the pressure to conform exerted upon them by the Christian hegemony. Indeed, with respect to the construction of the Jew as a projection of Christian self-hatred, and which in part gives rise to Launcelot Gobbo and Jessica's desertion, it is important to recall that until the relative relaxation of the usury laws, between 1571 and 1624, usury was once theologically vilified by the Christians, whilst also being, for a certain period, the only "profession" which Jews were conveniently allowed to practise. Thus as Adorno observes ". . . Commerce was not their [the Jews] vocation it was their fate."[34] and one is provided with yet another distressing aspect of emergent post-Holocaust meaning in the source text, when one takes into account what Blanchot has described as the deathly aspect that work was to assume for Jews with respect to the concentration camp motto which was raised above the entrances, "Work Liberates":

> For work has ceased to be his way of living and has become his way of dying.
> Work, death: equivalents. And the workplace is everywhere; work is all the time.[35]

Shylock is almost uncomfortably honest throughout the source text and this is emphasised by his plain and uncompromising use of language amidst the often florid and, one could venture to say, ambiguously misleading verbosity of the Venetians:

SHYLOCK: You'll ask me why I'd rather choose to have
          A weight of carrion flesh than to receive
          Three thousand ducats. I'll not answer that,
          But say it is my humour—is it answer'd?
          What if my house be troubled by a rat,
          And I be pleased to give ten thousand ducats
          To have it ban'd? What are you answered yet?
          Some men there are love not a gaping pig.
          Some that are mad if they behold a cat;
          And others, when the bagpipe sings I' th' nose,
          Cannot contain their urine; for affection
          Mistress of passion, sways it to the mood
          Of what it likes or loathes.
          [Act IV, Scene I, l. 34–51]

When we reread Shylock's plain speaking language in the source text, with an historically effected consciousness and as focused by Marowitz's Rewrite, the damagingly distorted effects of centuries of aesthetic distanciation are revealed. We "re-cognize" Shylock's language for what it is; plain, clear and, most importantly, honest, although admittedly far from beautiful language, especially when contrasted with the high-flown and poetic verbosity employed by the Venetians to duplicitously bamboozle and mislead others. Historically effected consciousness reveals to us how the aesthetic effect of language can promote in us a distorting aesthetic consciousness, similar to that espoused by Fichte and Schiller, which leads us not only to divest ourselves of discernment but which also allows us to be aesthetically duped by the effect of language rather than its meaning.[36] Gadamer refers to the cultivation of aesthetic consciousness, and its contribution to the harmful distanciation between our reception of art and our life "experience", whereby art as beautiful appearance is "seen" to be in sharp contrast to more prosaic and practical reality. According to Gadamer, one of the effects of aesthetic consciousness has been that art and nature are no longer considered to be the two complementary sides of one coin, but rather they are schismatically contrasted as appearance and reality. This divisive relationship means that nature no longer represents a comprehensive framework, and that "art" claims its own autonomous superior standpoint—an "ideal kingdom"[37] - distinct, distant and transcending reality, state and society. Indeed, the contrast between the less seductive but honest language used by Shylock, and the versified word-play which is employed by the Venetians to "mask, veil and transfigure" suggests the extent to which aesthetic consciousness has played a part in our centuries' long vilification and damnation of the less pleasurable and far from appealing, plain-speaking "Jew". In many respects, the Venetian hegemony in the play represent an "ideal kingdom" of aestheticisation[38] similar to the one outlined by Gadamer, not only with respect to matters of the heart being reduced to word-play but also with respect to the somewhat incongruous and contrived "show" of reconciliation at the end of the play. Other examples of the self-conscious artifice and aestheticisation practised by the Venetians, (effects which have cumulatively conspired toward our reception of Shylock as villain) include Gratiano's bombastic, but strangely ironic show of word-play, as well as the role-playing quality of Antonio as distracted melancholic and the stylised courtly love-suit on which Portia's future depends. Also, another interesting aspect to the self-conscious aestheticisation in the source text, which has dramaturgically effected a bias in our reception, is the thematized use of the language of legality and morality to mask gross barbarity, a technique which was to be appropriated through an "act of will" by the Nazis, with over 20 productions of the play during 1933 alone and at least 30 productions of the play being staged between 1934–9 (all of which carefully edited any reference to the inter-racial marriage between Jessica and Lorenzo).[39]

Marowitz incorporates and thus implicates the audience in the pervasive stealth, duplicity and deceit in his play as predicated not only on a performative rereading and "re-cognition" of the written source text, but also based on a re-cognition of the often unperceived dissembling "popular" source text which has been disguised and promulgated by centuries of intratextual appropriative productions and ideologically motivated criticism. In this respect, Marowitz cynically engages the audience in the received and reiterated rereading of *The Merchant of Venice* in order to highlight how institutionalised our perception of Shylock, 'the Jew" has become. Indeed, one is reminded of Antonio's words " I hold the world as but the world, Gratiano—A stage where every man must play a part" [Act I, Scene I, l. 77–8] and not only does Shylock appear to have been cast as the villain of the piece on the Venetian stage, but by extension this derogatory character "part" has been allotted to him down the centuries.

Kolodny's observation, although specifically directed at the way in which genre can circumscribe our hermeneutic horizons, is also pertinent to our received interpretation of character:

> Frequently, our reading habits become fixed, so that successive reading experience functions, in effect, normatively, with one particular kind of novel stylising our expectations of those to follow.[40]

Indeed, the intratextuality[41] of the source text, in the light of Kolodny's remarks, is of even more interest when we consider that the play has been successively designated over the centuries as "comical history", "romantic comedy" and "tragedy" until, post-Holocaust, I would argue, the play has come to defy generic classification and thus can only be painfully received with the aesthetic distanciation provided by cynicism. It is because we can no longer experience the play as "play" that *The Merchant of Venice* is such an apposite and worthy classic for the attentions of the rewriter, in keeping with Marowitz's emphasis on the organic complexity of cultural formation and our subsequent "understanding" of it:

> Our job is to retrace, rediscover, reconsider and re-angle the classics—not simply regurgitate them. 'I re-think therefore I am,' said Descartes, or at least he should have.[42]

Marowitz also highlights how rewriting the classics preempts the atrophying canonised reading practices which assume not only an indifferent or disinterested, but also a dangerous level of aesthetic distanciation:

> They (the audience) have certain fixed expectations as to what they are going to see when certain plays of Shakespeare are announced. They get what they expect and they expect what have been led to expect and it is only when they do not get what they have been led to expect that they are on the threshold of having an experience.[43]

By participatively including the audience in Shylock's cynical use of disguise and thus allowing us to know what other characters do not, Marowitz dramaturgically highlights the way in which we have adhered and thus become culturally implicated in the perpetuation of the defamatory image of the Jew as deceitful, duplicitous and untrustworthy. In this respect, as opposed to transposing one image for another, Marowtiz dramaturgically implicates us as being involved in the production, and not just the reception of an image of the Jew that has direct links with the scurrilous and hateful propaganda machine operated by the Nazis. Of course, as Cheyette has illustrated the image of the Jew has vacillated, in a manner akin to Wesker's dramaturgical "replacement", between the good and bad image of the Jew, but as any cursory knowledge of the mechanism of representation reveals, the artificially constructed "good" image can only be sustained by reference to the referential perpetuity of its inverse and "bad" counterpart.[44]

The intratextual disguise founded on the maintenance of the artificial construction of the image of the Jew, which has surrounded our proactive reception of the source text for centuries, and which has resulted in the text vacillating between being both an *apologia* for jewishness and a cultural purveyor of outright anti-Semitism, is symbolised in *Variations* by an abundance of examples of disguise, dissembling, feigning, duplicity and caricature in the text. However, as opposed to merely rewriting *The Merchant of Venice* as a recontextualised parody, which affords the audience a posture of aesthetic and cynical distanciation, Marowitz achieves a devastating dramaturgical coup, which refuses the audience their hitherto protected and unsatisfactory abdication from cultural guilt. Marowitz does this by re-presenting a transformed Shylock, who steps outside the centuries old representational bind which not only continues to suppress our understanding of *The Merchant of Venice*, but which, despite postures of sophisticated cynicism on the part of a modern audience, also condemns us to culturally endorse and thus perpetuate a proven dangerous and untenable post-Holocaust perception of the Jew. Thus although Marowitz places considerable emphasis on the past reception of the source text, he does not allow his interpretation to become thematic *in toto*, and thus he precludes the effect of the Rewrite resting wholly on a dramaturgical aesthetic distanciation, albeit for cynical ends, which forfeits the experience that is *Erlebnis*. Rather Marowitz engages his audience in the ruse of cynical rereading in order to elicit the transformation into structure of the source text, as centred on the transformation of the archetypal signification of the Jew. Indeed, Marowitz' articulation of the transformation into structure of the depleted and defeated Shylock is particularly powerful when one considers the final words uttered by Shylock in the source text, "I am content." (Act IV, Scene I, l. 380). Marowitz purposively does not transcribe these words, and as such he not only dispenses with the humiliating court "judgement", but also by extension he linguistically challenges Shylock's past intratextual representation and his treatment as an image which has been both produced and evaluated down the centuries as either tragic, loathsome, comical. By editing these words Marowitz draws attention to their alterity, so that by the final scenes of *Variations*, Shylock most definitely has been transformed into "content" as opposed to a one dimensional sign upon which centuries of interpretative "judgements" have imposed sentence.

Thus, although both dramatists consider the character as an unequivocally dangerous stereotype in the popular imagination, the crucial distinction between Marowitz's and Wesker's Shylock is that the latter does not negotiate with the subsequent intratextuality, as well as the source text, which has created him, and as opposed to liberating Shylock from the discursive bind that surrounds his characterisation Wesker operates within it, for as Stam and Spence have perspicaciously observed:

> The insistence on 'positive images' finally obscures the fact that 'nice' images might at times be as pernicious as overtly degrading ones, providing a bourgeois facade for paternalism, a more pervasive racism.[45]

Marowitz, on the other hand, utilises the intratextual representation of the Jew to mediate our past and present with a post-Holocaust consciousness, so that as opposed to reiterating the discursive parameters within which a certain image has been contained, an amplificatory effect akin to "transformation into structure" leads to completely different and new "understanding". To fully explain the effect of such a "transformation into structure" that liberates us from reiterating past discursivity by negotiating with it, it is useful to quote Gadamer's analysis in full:

> Transformation into structure is not simply transposition into another world. Certainly the play takes place in another, closed world. But inasmuch as it is a structure, it is, so to speak, its own measure and measures itself by nothing outside it. Thus the action of the drama—in this respect it still entirely resembles the religious act—exists as something that rests absolutely within itself. It no longer permits of any comparison with reality as the secret measure of all verisimilitude. It is raised above all such comparisons—and hence also above the question of whether it is all real—because a superior truth speaks from it. Even Plato, the most radical critic of the high estimation of art in the history of philosophy, speaks of the comedy and tragedy of life on the one hand and of the stage on the other without differentiating between them. For this difference is superseded if one knows how to see the meaning of the play that unfolds before one. The pleasure of drama is the same in both cases: it is the joy of knowledge.[46]

The intratextuality of *Variations* addresses not only empirically known historical facts, but also the way in which the Jew has been represented in literature over the centuries, be it as the assimilated "other" or the feared outsider, the servile peacemaker or the troublesome rebel, and in so doing Marowitz addresses the way in which literature is instrumental in the construction of stereotypes, archetypes and clichés in society at large. Bryan Cheyette's impressive study *Construction of "the jew" in English Literature* throws light on the promulgation of certain stock stereotypes of the Jew when he explains:

> . . . we have shown that writers do not passively draw on the eternal myth of 'the Jew' but actively construct them in relation to their own literary and political concerns. This active remaking of Jewish racial difference resulted in a bewilder-

ing variety of contradictory and over-determined representations of 'the Jew'
. . .⁴⁷

Unlike Marowitz, Wesker falls into the trap of what Cheyette identifies as "semitic discourse" whereby although the racial construction of the Jew is not fixed it vacillates within the controlled discursive parameters of assimilation, containment and demonisation as prescribed by Western liberal humanist attitudes at any given time.

James Shapiro discusses the disguises and dissembling practices adopted by jews to evade persecution and enforced conversion during the early modern period, a modus operandi which led to them being dubbed "the temporizing Jew", and as exemplified by the Barbary Jew, Nathanial Menda, who states in his own publication *Confession of Faith* that he had been conversant among the English for five years before his conversion under the supervision of John Foxe. Shapiro highlights that although jews were officially persona non grata in England between 1290 and 1656 many Marranos who had escaped persecution in Spain and Portugal, and other jews who did not leave after Edward I's edict continued to live in England, either by converting or by adopting disguises and dissembling, an aspect of society which did not go unnoticed by Montaigne who characterised ". . . dissimulation as the most notable quality of the age,"⁴⁸ :

> Some English writers [during the sixteenth century] struggled to invent new terms—such as *Christian Jew, false Jew,* and *counterfeit Christian*—to deal with these disturbing ambiguities which they found themselves confronting abroad and occasionally at home as well. Others like William Prynne, likened the performance of Marranos—individuals skilled at "playing the Jew in private"—to that of professional actors, expert at putting on and taking off disguises.⁴⁹

Undoubtedly Shakespeare would have been aware of the "temporising Jew", but no more than he would have been aware of the "temporising" Catholic, many of whom also suppressed their religious origins in order to escape persecution. As such the characteristic disguise and dissembling during the early modern period was very much linked to a pragmatic survival drive adopted by considerable numbers of the population rather than being attributable to an intrinsic racial trait of Jews or, for that matter any other persecuted group. However, Marowitz incorporates the general acceptance, albeit cynical, of the popular interpretation of the source text's representation of Shylock's duplicity and deceit, which, over the centuries, has been often transformed into an extratextual interpretative criterion when referring to the Jewish people, as exemplified not only by the relatively recent crude propaganda promulgated by the Nazis, but also as illustrated by this critique of Charles Macklin's "Shylock" penned by Georg Christoph Lichtenberg in December 1775:

> Picture to yourself a somewhat strong man, with a sallow, harsh face and a nose which is by no means lacking in any one of the three dimensions . . . slow, calm in his impenetrable cunning, and when he has the law on his side he is unflinching, even to the extreme of malice . . . the sight of this Jew suffices to awaken at once, in the best regulated mind, all the prejudices of childhood against this people.[50]

Thus Marowitz dramaturgically incorporates the cynicism which a post-Holocaust consciousness has engendered in us when viewing *The Merchant of Venice* into his own performative re-reading. The cynicism which necessarily shapes our reception of the source text and by extension the greater part of Marowitz's re-reading of the source text, before he dramaturgically accuses us of hermeneutic abdication in the final scene of his play, is powerfully displayed in the following scene which is replete with ostensibly unexplained dissembling, feigning, and thus "evil" action:

> SHYLOCK: My own flesh and blood.
> SALERIO: (*To* SOLANIO) There is more difference between his flesh and hers than between jet and ivory, more between their bloods, than there is between red wine and rhenish.
> SHYLOCK: Why there, there, there, there—a diamond gone, cost me two thousand ducats in Frankfort—the curse never fell upon my nation till now—two thousand ducats in that, and other precious, precious jewels. I would my daughter were dead at my foot, and the jewels in her ear! Would she were hearsed at my foot, and the ducats in her coffin. And I know not what's spent in the search. Why, thou loss upon loss. The thief gone with so much and so much to find the thief, and no satisfaction, no revenge, nor no ill luck stirring but what lights on my shoulders, no sighs but o' my breathing, no tears but o'my bidding. (*Feigns weeping*).

We unquestioningly "understand" the disguise in Marowitz's play not only by way of reference to the intratextual interpretation of the source text but in the acknowledgement of the centuries of persecution and fear culminating in the Holocaust which has punctuated the chronicle of Jewish survival, but which all too often has the dangerous propensity to be misconceived as racial characteristics which in turn lead to a constructive narrative about the redemptive power of suffering.

The cynicism elicited by Marowitz's Rewrite almost suggests that post-Holocaust, it is only by our assumption of a cynical posture akin to those characteristics that were once so despised and vilified in the character,

Shylock, that makes the source text bearable, an effect that performatively dispenses with the debatable and idealistic but most definitely naive "innocent" reading and interpretation espoused by Ingarden[51] and to a lesser extent critics like Bloom. Unlike Wesker's dramaturgical "replacement" that conveys an overwhelming interpretative amnesia about the source text's implication in the Holocaust, Marowitz's Rewrite at once performatively and silently emphasises the tragic levelling and corrupting effect wrought by the Holocaust on humanity, an effect, which in turn has denied interpretative stasis or a supposed "innocent" *aesthesis* with respect to a Shakespearean classic which undeniably contributed toward the anti-Semitism that was to culminate in the Holocaust. Thus, without resorting to offering a polarised example of previous representations of the Jew in order to convey his unease at the way the source text and our reading of it is implicated in the Holocaust, Marowitz's re-reading of *The Merchant of Venice* is silently suffused with the Holocaust without endorsing the representational discursivity that contributed to it, a point poignantly expressed by Lyotard's analysis of Claude Lanzmann's film *Shoah*:

> Whenever one represents, one inscribes in memory, and this might seem a good defence against forgetting. It is, I believe, just the opposite. Only that which has been inscribed can, in the current sense of the term, be forgotten, because it could be effaced. But what is not inscribed, through lack of inscribable surface, of duration and place for the inscription to be situated, what has no place in the space nor in the time of domination, in the geography and the diachrony of the self-assured spirit, because it is not synthesizable . . . One *must*, certainly, inscribe in words, in images. One cannot escape the necessity of representing. It would be sin itself to believe oneself safe and sound. But it is one thing to do it in view of saving the memory, and quite another to try to preserve the remainder, the unforgettable forgotten, in writing.[52]

Breaking the Mould

The post Holocaust consciousness that informs the cynicism with which we receive both Shakespeare's play and which, by extension, is articulated dramaturgically by *Variations*, is encapsulated by the play's abundance of disguise and play-acting. However, as opposed to Gadamer's notion of the engrossing play of play that elicits an experience of *Erlebnis* in the audience, such disguise is more concerned with revealing to the audience the superficial and misleading effect of image:

> A person who plays such a game denies, to all appearances, continuity with himself. But in truth that means that he holds on to this continuity with himself for himself and only withholds it from those before whom he is acting.[53]

The effect of Marowitz's incorporation of so many disguises and guises is to clearly polemicise, in contrast to Wesker, what Guillory has called the "politics of representation" which has surrounded the Jew in literature for centuries, in recognition of the fact that any reading imbued with historically effected consciousness must by necessity mean looking further than surface images. In this respect Marowitz emphasises the cynicism of image and the stories constructed around them, which we, like Portia in *Variations*, so often delusionally disregard in order to see what we want to see and to thus safely confirm our presuppositions and sense of knowledge, a point eloquently made by Shapiro:

> Dig deep enough and one discovers that the affirmation of cultural identity rests on the slippery foundations of prejudice and exclusion. Even as stories feed our hunger to imagine others as inferior, evil and dangerous, they succeed in masking the extent to which the storytellers' identities are formed (and often deformed) in the act of recounting such tales . . . One way of showing what stories can reveal about cultural prejudices is to turn those stories against the storytellers.[54]

Marowitz employs the cynicism of disguise in a manner akin to Brechtian alienation technique right up until the very last few moments of the play when the cynicism that facilitates our aesthetic distanciation is quite literally dropped like a hermeneutic bombshell. The reality that is Marowitz's Shylock as Irgun aggressor is exposed with the uncanny repetition of the words so often cited as an apologia for Jewishness being summoned up, but to very different effect:

SHYLOCK: He hath disgraced me and hindered half a million, laughed at my losses, mocked at my gains, scorned my nation, thwarted my bargains, cooled my friends, heated mine enemies—and what's his reason? I am a Jew. Hath not a Jew eyes? hath not a Jew hands, organs, dimensions, senses, affections, passions? Fed with the same food, hurt with the same weapons, subject to the same diseases, healed by the same means, warmed and cooled by the same winter and summer, as a Christian is? If you prick us do we not bleed? if you tickle us, do we not laugh? If you poison us, do we not die? and if you wrong us, shall we not revenge? If we are not like you in the rest, we shall resemble you in that. If a Jew wrong a Christian, what is his humility? Revenge. If a Christian wrong a Jew, what, should his sufferance be by Christian example? Why, revenge. The villainy you have taught me I will execute, and it shall go hard but I will better the instruction.

(SHYLOCK *turns on his heel and walks out of the courtroom.*)
(*Several of the guerillas force the* BRITISH GROUP *into a huddle, then step back to take aim. The weapons are raised and as the first shots are fired and the first bodies begin to fall, the* BLACKOUT *is immediate.*)

In this scene, Marowitz's ingenious reassembly of the source text presents the same words from the same character in a totally different light, but by placing the words prior to what proves to be the court's redundant judgement, he implicates those words, and that characterisation in the intratextuality which has taken place between his own play and the source text, including the Holocaust to which it contributed. Marowitz's explosive finale refuses his audience the luxury of continuing to maintain the aesthetic distanctiation proffered by a sophisticated and cynical re-reading of the source text, and instead he dramaturgically engages his audience in the transformation into structure that makes for a very different and unstereotypical Shylock, and in stark contrast to the one which their hermeneutic acquiescence has perpetuated.

Conversely, the concluding humiliation represented by Shylock's enforced submission to the assimilatory practices of the ruling hegemony, is absorbed and thus dissipated by Wesker's mono-dimensional re-characterisation of a "good" Shylock, with the effect that the painfully detailed study of persecution which has become increasingly 'uncomfortable' for a post-Holocaust audience to view, is replaced by a sanitised, anodyne and, ironically, Christianised 'version' of a classic. In a sense, Wesker's "Shylock" emerges as a post-*Merchant of Venice* reconstituted Christian, in a play which, although not a dramaturgical re-enactment and thus endorsement of the final "conversion" scene in the source text, is predicated upon an acquiescence to the subsequent repercussions and assimilatory "effect" of the "conversion", namely, that if you are a Jew, be a "good" Jew. By merely qualitatively altering one character from being, on the surface, "evil" to "good", Wesker operates within the very discursive parameters of stereotyping that he claims to dismantle, for as Bhabha has astutely observed:

> [The stereotype] . . . is a form of knowledge and identification that vacillates between what is always 'in place', already known, and something that must be anxiously repeated . . . [T]he point of intervention should shift from the *identification* of images as positive or negative, to an understanding of the *processes of subjectification* made possible (and plausible) through stereotypical discourse.[55]

The most often cited example of an inverted appropriation of our received interpretation of Shylock is Sheva, the "good" Jew, in Richard Cumberland's *The Jew* (1794). Cumberland sought to redress the way in which Georgian dramatists had wholeheartedly embraced the comic representation of the Jew, a representation which although ostensibly founded on an innocuous figure of fun and ridicule was nonetheless dangerously negative and simplistic. Indeed, in a series of essays penned ten years earlier, Cumberland created the persona of Abrahams—a vociferous mouthpiece for his own dissatisfaction with the continuing representation of the Jew, and in particular Shylock:

> I verily believe the odious character of Shylock has brought little less persecution upon us poor scattered sons of Abraham, than the Inquisition itself.[56]

Unlike Wesker, Marowitz confronts the necessity to avoid the perpetuation of stereotypical discourse which even when superficially sympathetic precludes any liberation from the discursive bind of the Jew as eternal victim, as suggested by Shylock's reference in *Variations* to a restless majority controlled by a minority of British colonisers in post-war Palestine:

> SHYLOCK: Why do we yield to their exploitation. We are a multitude and they
> but a few that now encompasseth what is our own.

Thus, as opposed to unproductively reiterating past oppression and thereby further consolidating the archetype of the Jew as eternal victim, Marowitz dramaturgically polemicises the discourse of the stereotype, in particular with his treatment of Bassanio's dissembling courtship which, in keeping with semiological analysis, questions the reduction of an image to a fixed relation between signifier and signified, something which Wesker fails to do in his simplistic inversion of what he perceives to be the "bad" Jew into the "good" Jew. By transforming the Venetian ghetto into the post-holocaust setting of Palestine, Marowitz addresses and contests the archetype of the Jew as the eternal victim, and as such he questions the perpetuation of the redemptive power of Jewish suffering. In contradistinction to such a transformation into structure Wesker maintains the Venetian ghettoized setting and indeed utilises Shylock as the mouthpiece for lengthy diatribes about Jewish suffering:

> SHYLOCK: They had God and Abraham had them. But—they were now cursed.
> For from that day moved they into a nationhood that had to be
> better than any other, and poor things all other nations found them
> unbearable to live with. What can I do? I'm chosen. I must be religious.

Philip Cohen's *Monstrous Images, Perverse Reasons* scrutinises the way in which events like the Holocaust, slavery, Apartheid and other "atrocity stories" may give rise to a humanistic tendency to invest suffering with redemptive power, similar to that represented by Wesker's *Shylock*.

Cohen suggests that such an approach to atrocity stories could be viewed as a ruse of Western reason and its imperialistic project of Enlightenment as:

> A humanity which is authenticated in the most extreme conditions of its denial, authorised when it is silenced, and which expresses itself in a series of triumphant epiphanies; for these are not just atrocity stories or survivor stories. They are narratives of human redemption.[57]

Indeed, Wesker's idealistic intention to present Shylock in as sympathetic guise as possible even leads him to edit the rebellious cynicism of Shakespeare's Shylock as conveyed in the following exchange between Antonio and Shylock:

> Signor Antonio many a time and oft
> In the Rialto you have rated me
> About my moneys and my usances:
> Still have I borne it with a patient shrug
> (For suff'rance is the badge of all our tribe)
> You call me a misbeliever, cut throat dog
> And spat upon my Jewish gaberdine,
> And all for use of that which is mine own.
> Well then it now appears you need my help:
> What should I say to you? Is it possible
> A cur can lend three thousand ducats?
> Shall I bend low and in a bondsman's key
> With bated breath, and whispering humbleness
> Say this:
> "Fair Sir you spet on me on Wednesday last,
> You spurned me such a day, another time
> You called me dog: and for these courtesies
> I'll lend you thus much moneys"?

In the light of such editing and alterations it would appear that Wesker is attempting to retrospectively present an ideal that did and does not exist, for by representing Shylock in an overtly favourable and "human" light Wesker is failing to address the unfortunate reality that the dehumanising caricatures and manufactured racial stereotypes which enable hegemonic groups to consolidate their might are still in evidence in today's post-Holocaust society.

Wesker has stated that by writing *Shylock* he is recreating the Jew he knows better, much more like the Jew he knows and that there is no doubt that Shylock in the Shakespearean version did contribute to the Holocaust. These reasons for his alteration of Shakespeare's play expose a fundamental failure on the part of Wesker to address the very issue of the anti-Semitism which he seeks to eradicate. Instead of engaging in a hermeneutic dialogue with the play he lambasts as a dramatic promulgation of anti-Semitism, Wesker merely invokes the classic on a superficial level in order to replace it with that he considers as a more positive and wholesome representation of the Jew or, to use his own oft cited words, "my Shylock". In this respect, Marowitz acknowledges what Wesker does not, namely, the danger of perpetuating a stereotype, a danger made manifest by the Nazis who actually employed the archetypal figurative Jew as eternal victim to create an acquiescent climate of stoic resignation amongst their victims, for as Roskies has observed:

> The Holocaust was the most demonic of conspiracies between literature and life. Designed as such by the Nazis (one of Hitler's professors had studied at the Hebrew University in Jerusalem) it was perceived by the Jews as a return to the hoary past.[58]

Indeed, Young has also commented on the way archetypal thinking was to foster a communal resignation amongst the Jews and which the Nazis exploited to encourage:

> . . . the victims to perceive their circumstances in the light of the past and the ancient stereotypes but also encouraged a paradigmatic response to and understanding of their predicament. By this lulling their victims into analogy, as it were, by recreating all previous persecutions, the Nazis were able to screen from view the difference of the present persecution until it was too late.[59]

However, the deference and resignation, albeit mock, displayed by Shylock at the end of Wesker's play compounds the opinion that he fails to transcend the discourse of the stereotype and this is emphasised further by the pathos aroused by the strains of a Sephardic song which accompanies Shylock's self-imposed exile:

> SHYLOCK [*sardonically and with finality*]: No. Take my books. The law must be observed. We have need of the law, what need do we have of books? Distressing, disturbing things, besides. Why, dear friend, they'd even make us question laws. Ha! And who in his right mind would want to do that? Certainly not old Shylock. Take my books. Take everything. I do not want the law departed from, not one letter departed from.
> [*Sound of song*]
> Perhaps now is the time to make that journey to Jerusalem. Join those other old men on the quayside, waiting to make a pilgrimage, to be buried there—ach! What do I care! My heart will not follow me, wherever it is. My appetites are dying, dear friend, for anything in this world. I am so tired of men.

[SHYLOCK *moves away, a bitter man. Everyone has left except* PORTIA. *The scene has changed to Belmont. We hear the distant sad singing of a woman. The song is 'Adios querida', a Sephardic song.*]

Although the injustice of Shylock's treatment at the hands of the Christian hegemony comes through in Wesker's play, it is little more than a pale reiterative, but sentimentalised, repetition of the "conversion" scene in the source text, although in the latter the stinging presentation of Shylock's humiliating demise has continued to engender an unsettling degree of unease amongst audiences throughout the centuries. However, Wesker ameliorates the tension and discomfort of Shakespeare's courtroom scene by the emotive inclusion of the incongruous and "conciliatory in defeat" effect of the musical strains which accompany Shylock's exit to "the promised land" lending a Hollywood quality to the scene which verges on descending to the level of a "spoof". The melodramatically pious manner of Shylock's exit leaves the audience, who may have prepared themselves to reach the hermeneutic horizons which Wesker's own paratextual writings have set for the play, with an unsatisfied sensation that the play is not so much about the way in which our cultural heritage is implicated in the anti-Semitism prior to the Holocaust, but rather is a sentimentalised and unproductive reiteration of the suffering of the Jewish people, regardless of the intratextual hap of the Holocaust which occurs between Shakespeare's play and his own version. In this respect, Wesker's apparent failure to negotiate with the historical intratextuality of the source text results in an anti-climactic desertion of his hermeneutic responsibility to reach the interpretative horizons which he himself set out in the paratextual explanation for writing the play:

> . . . I would passionately defend the right of anyone anywhere to present and teach this play. But nothing will make me admire it, nor has anyone persuaded me the Holocaust is irrelevant to my responses.[60]

Wesker confusingly lightens and sanitises the overall tone of the play and deterministically alters Shylock to such a degree that he unwittingly treats his own eponymous hero with the same condescension that Shylock uncompromisingly rails against:

> SHYLOCK: No, no, NO! I will not have it.[*Outraged but controlled.*] I do not want apologies for my humanity.

Although Wesker's play presents Shylock as no longer appealing to Christian humanism on the pragmatic, but palpably desperate level exhibited by Shakespeare's Shylock in the famous "Hath not a Jew . . ." scene of the source text, his re-characterisation of the 'good' Jew who has Christian friends is one which is fully absorbed by and operating within the discursive and moralistic parameters according to which the prevailing Christian ethos decides what is "good" and what is "evil":

> The more one attempts to identify with those who have labelled one as different, the more one accepts the values, social structures and attitudes of the determining group, the farther away from true acceptability one seems to be . . . In one's own eyes one becomes identical with the definition of acceptability and yet one is still not accepted.[61]

Wesker's overwhelming, and I would contend, misplaced desire to recreate Shylock in a more sympathetic surface light thus results in a dramaturgical forfeiture of the intensity with which Shakespeare's play, certainly through post-Holocaust eyes, has the potential to polemicise racial and religious persecution. Consequently, Wesker's approach to Shakespeare's play does not negotiate the composite experience of both *Erfahrung* and *Erlebnis* which typifies the hermeneutic endeavour of the Rewrite. As Gadamer points out:

> . . . understanding [the classical] will always involve more than merely historically reconstructing the past world to which the work belongs. Our understanding will always retain the consciousness that we too belong to that world and correlatively that the work too belongs to our world.[62]

Indeed, because Wesker does not negotiate with what he perceives to be the anti-Semitism in *The Merchant of Venice*, but rather merely replaces a supposedly "bad" representation of the Jew with a "good" one, *Shylock* overlooks a fundamental hermeneutic tenet to question one's own unexplained interpretative assumptions about the viewpoint held by one's textual interlocutor, the source text—namely whether Shakespeare's play is anti-Semitic. Thus, as opposed to engaging with the way in which our post-Holocaust sensibilities might now "re-cognize" more acutely an emergent and hitherto undisclosed anti-Semitism in the source text, Wesker appears to "unhistorically" proceed according to what he perceives to be the intrinsic anti-Semitism of *The Merchant of Venice* as predicated on unfounded notions about authorial psychologism and intention, despite the following paratextual explanation:

> It was not that Shakespeare's intentions were anti-semitic. His genius is a generous one. But the effects [of *The Merchant of Venice*] are anti-Semitic.[63]

Marion D. Perret has commented that today the audience at a performance of *The Merchant of Venice* possesses:

> Preconceptions about how Shylock should be treated [which] come from several sources; our own experience and belief; our reading of the play; our culture's acceptance of religious pluralism and rejection of the horrors of the Holocaust.[64]

However, she then laments that such "preconceptions" obscure our appreciation and enjoyment of the play for they encourage a "stubborn tendency to see this Jew as symbolic of all Jews". Even though Wesker rationalises his attempt to rewrite Shakespeare as being a response to the horrors of the Holocaust in which *The Merchant of Venice* is implicated, Perret's approach is a fair summation of Wesker's response to Shakespeare's play which treats the classic as exhibiting closure with self-contained fixed meanings and considers the themes and characterization within texts as separate and distinct from the history subsequent to their creation, which they have survived and of which they continue to form a part. Such a contention treats the text as existing independently of the reader, created at a specific historical moment and which continues to reference that specific moment as well as authorial intention, regardless of the conditions surrounding its subsequent readings. Undoubtedly, Wesker's "preconceptions" and "prejudices" have driven him to a rather one-dimensional attempt to replace Shakespeare's text, but when such "prejudice" is operating with an historically effected consciousness, as exhibited by Marowitz, the simple designs of the appropriation, alteration or adaptation transform into the dramaturgical Rewrite. As Gadamer explains, prejudice when incorporated with a textual reading directed by historically effected consciousness results in hermeneutic "understanding":

> The important thing is to be aware of one's own bias so that the text can present itself in all its otherness and thus assert its own truth against one's own foremeanings.[65]

Wesker's *Shylock* exhibits a rudimentary confusion as to whether *The Merchant of Venice* is a wholly and undiluted dramaturgical exercise in anti-semitism or whether it is a performative polemic *about* anti-Semitism and persecution, which, over the centuries subsequent to its production, has been appropriated for blatantly anti-Semitic purposes. Thus as opposed to negotiating with what he apodeictically stresses as being the anti-Semitic effect of Shakespeare's play with a post-Holocaust consciousness Wesker reveals a desire to disavow and thus replace the source text's incipient anti-Semitism in a spirit of determined amnesia, in stark contradistinction to Marowitz's opinions about rewriting the classics:

One should not back away from an idea which could not possibly have existed in Shakespeare's time if that idea has been inspired by Shakespeare's material. The resolution of what appear to be antithetical elements is often the first step towards the creation of a viable new form.[66]

After Appropriation and Parody: Rewriting Shakespeare

Throughout the centuries there have been numerous appropriations and adaptations of Shakespeare's plays, all of which have contributed to the glorification of Shakespeare, a phenomenon which was to be later dubbed "bardolatry" by George Bernard Shaw. Ironically, it was the abundance of contending political appropriations of Shakespeare carried out between the Restoration and the early decades of the eighteenth century, and their topically and contingent rewriting of his plays which contributed to the promotion of the Shakespearean corpus as one which was "above" politics, as the cultural purveyor of transcendent values.

The appropriation of Shakespeare began in earnest with the reopening of the theatres after the restoration of Charles II, as a new generation of playwrights rewrote Shakespeare's plays to please a new audience, adapting them to adjust to a changed political climate which witnessed amongst other things the appearance of actresses on the stage. However, by the 1730's there were hardly any dramatic appropriations of Shakespeare being produced, and instead there were to be far more strenuous efforts to emphasise and consolidate Shakespeare's canonical status through memorialization and by enthusiastic endeavours to authenticate the "original" works of the Bard, as exemplified by this anonymous letter which appeared in "The Weekly Register" on 26th January, 1734:

> I believe that everyone that visits this sacred repository of the illustrious dead (Westminster Abbey) cannot help looking round, like me, for the divine Milton and the immortal Shakespear; names which are the honour of their country and yet have received no honour from it.[67]

However, the late eighteenth and early nineteenth centuries marked the high point of Shakespeare's canonisation and were a time when Shakespeare was hailed as a hero of English culture to such an extent that the man became almost indistinguishable not only from his own works but also from works by other writers about the cultural icon "Shakespeare", as illustrated by this anecdote from Sir Walter Scott's journal:

> Funny thing at the theatre. Among the discourse in High Life below Stairs one of the Ladies asks who wrote Shakespeare. One says 'Ben Jonson' another 'Finis'. 'No' said Will Murray 'it is Sir Walter Scott; he confessed it at a publick meeting the other day.'[68]

Nicola Watson has drawn attention to John Philip Kemble's early nineteenth century venture to set about authenticating a number of Shakespeare "revivals" which by the use of meticulously researched period costumes and the promotion of the "History Plays" to the status of actual history, were intended to foster a sense that Shakespeare, the work and the man, represented far more than the production of a specific Renaissance art form but rather that he was intrinsic to the nation's sense of history. Watson concludes that many such enterprises were nationalistically inspired and greatly influenced by Burke's *Reflections on the Revolution in France* and that they illustrate a prevailing nineteenth century idealism about the organic State premised upon the conservation of past institutions.

Dramatic appropriations of Shakespeare have not only contributed to the canonisation of the Bard's plays, but perhaps more interestingly such appropriations may have had a distorting, historically contingent effect upon later interpretations of Shakespeare's works. Although later interpretations did not necessarily take the form of deterministic appropriations they were undoubtedly influenced by the emphases and editing wrought by previous adaptations. Indeed, with respect to *The Merchant of Venice* and in particular the representation of women in the play, Marowitz's Rewrite reasserts the feminine ambiguity and complexity which is undoubtedly apparent to contemporary readings of Shakespeare's play. However, the ambiguity and complexity of the female characters in Shakespeare's work have too frequently become obscured by earlier appropriative manoeuvres to subdue his heroines and these appropriations may have had the effect of shaping our subsequent readings. As Jean Marsden points out in her illuminating essay "Rewritten Women":

> Shakespeare's women are rarely meek and seldom passive. While many could qualify as monstrosities under Allestree's definition, the same is not true of female characters in the adaptations. Instead the plays recreate a patriarchal system in which women have no power beyond the masochistic ability to arouse sympathy by their suffering, an ability mirrored in the audience response to pathos.[69]

An example of the dramatic appropriations' distortion of the female characters in *The Merchant of Venice* is Gildon's *The Jew in Venice* (1701) in which Portia is depicted as a woman whose only reason to presume to be a man and deign to adorn male attire was in order to increase Bassanio's love for her. Such alterations are a reflection of the eighteenth century's preoccupation with the preservation of the impression of feminine meekness and modesty, which accounts for the rise in the publication of what were generally known as conduct books.[70] As

Marsden points out, these representations of Shakespeare's women were a reflection of eighteenth century mores and etiquette, but the effect that such popular representations of Shakespeare was to have on our subsequent reception of his plays should not be overlooked.

> Passive rather than active, meek rather than aggressive, these paragons of virtue cannot survive outside their narrowly defined sphere. Simultaneously elevated and exploited, they provide a spectacle of female suffering which underscores the contradictory nature of a world where chastity represents sexuality and pathos becomes a source of pleasure.[71]

For example, Marowitz's Jessica, as portrayed in his play *Variations on The Merchant of Venice* (1977) not only reasserts the independent free spirit, albeit subject to the coercive persuasions of the Venetian hegemony, which we find in Shakespeare's Jessica, but also she is presented as an amalgam of the roles which have been allotted to her over the centuries, including (albeit feigned) the meek, modest and subservient representations of the eighteenth and nineteenth centuries. The complexity of Jessica's characterisation in *Variations* as both an archetype of past dramatic representations and a personification of the struggle from colonial rule is captured in the scene in which she is instrumental in ensnaring the beguiled British soldiers into an Irgun terrorist trap. Jessica under the guidance of her father is tutored in the art of dissembling, something to which he has become accustomed:

```
SHYLOCK: Entertain Lorenzo as you will
              With all the courtesy you can afford
              Provided that you keep your maidenhead.
              Use him as if here a Philistine.
              Dissemble, swear, protest, vow to love him.
              In's company canst thou intercept
              Those fateful tidings which the governor's tongue
              Jealously would guard from others ears.
JESSICA:   What, shall I suffer him to be betrothed?
SHYLOCK: It's no sin to deceive a Christian
              For they themselves hold it a principle,
              Faith is not to be held with heretics,
              But all are heretics that are not Jews.
              This follows well and therefore fear it not
              [The Marowitz Shakespeare p 229]
```

Similar to Heidegger's project to uncover our Being-in-the-World, and thus get behind the ontic realm of empiricism which reason seeks to control through knowledge, the Rewrite according to this interpretation, is an example of performative *Erlebnis* whereby the distinction between understanding and knowledge, *poesis* and *praxis*, is dissolved into the actuality of the dramaturgical moment or monad. In this respect, the Rewrite does not conform to the project of dramatic appropriations whereby Shakespeare's works are assimilated to whatever ideology happens to be dominant at any given moment, and instead the *Erlebnis* of the Rewrite is born in part by its incorporation of acknowledged past *poiesis* within its own dramaturgical parameters. The Rewrite is not concerned to convey a message to the reader or audience which feeds off the cultural cachet of the classic; rather, it performatively "understands" the classic in its dramatic form at that moment in history. However, it is the determinism of appropriations and allegories that is in evidence in Wesker's play, *Shylock,* whereby his desire to alter the received characterisation of Shylock has led Wesker to merely replace Shakespeare's play with a new one. Examples of such deterministic appropriations are legion, like for example the appropriations of *Julius Ceasar* during the aftermath of the Glorious Revolution which not only served to bolster the Whig constitutionalist reform but which was also appropriated by those of a more aristocratic and Jacobite persuasion in the form of works such as *The Tragedy of Julius Caesar* and *The Tragedy of Marcus* by John Sheffield, Earl of Musgrave and Duke of Buckingham. The political determinism of such appropriations is quite distinct from the project of the Rewrite which is founded upon intratextual dialogue as opposed to an appropriative "act of will". Appropriations, like allegorical art, are motivated by deterministically utlilising the cultural cachet and kudos of Shakespeare for their own political concerns in the present, and are far removed from the intratextual dialogue founded upon "historically effected consciousness" that typifies the Rewrite. The Rewrite's excursion into cultural tradition is neither politically determined, oppositional or decorative; rather it is the result of an historically effected consciousness of our tradition for the present.

Of course not all earlier attempts to negotiate with the difficulties of Shakespeare's play have been overtly or covertly anti-Semitic or even appropriatively propagandist. Indeed, in 1796, Richard Hole was to uncannily anticipate Marowitz's twentieth century project with respect to *The Merchant of Venice* when he published an article entitled "An Apology for the Character and Conduct of Shylock", under the guise of a Jewish theatre critic domiciled in Palestine, some two hundred years later:

> On examining Shakespeare's numerous commentators, and other records of the times, it appears that no censure was ever cast, no unfavourable sentiment entertained of the unjust judge, the injurious merchant, the undutiful daughter and

prodigal lover. What an idea does this give of the English nation when such sentiments could be applauded![72]

An early example of what could well constitute a Rewrite, according to this interpretative Gadamerian interpretation, is Francis Talfourd's burlesque treatment of *The Merchant of Venice*.(1848)[73] Talfourd alludes to the source text's canonical status, and its intratextual history, in what appears to be a jocular tone but which under closer scrutiny betrays a scathing critique of the hypocrisy and cruelty of his own society, in which only the assimilating, albeit temporising, Jew can be the recipient of a grudgingly dispensed form of justice:

> ANTONIO: There are two points though that I must insist on,
> You'll shave your face and look more like a Christian,
> And take your daughter to your arms again.

Talfourd mocks the way canonicity and the elevation of authorial "genius" can subsume the incipient interpretative dangers and bias to which certain texts are subjected, and he emphasises this by drawing attention to the "correct" interpretation of his own text by way of the title and frontispiece:

Shylock
or the
Merchant of Venice
Preserved
AN ENTIRELY NEW READING OF
SHAKESPEARE,

From an edition hitherto undiscovered by modern authorities, and
which it is hoped may be received as the stray leaves of a
JERUSALEM HEARTY-JOKE
BY
FRANCIS TALFOURD

Unlike the intratextually alluded to "Old Fagin", Talfourd's Shylock is ultimately accepted, but only in open accordance with the discursive parameters of the Victorian establishment, a "bargain" to which Shylock only "openly" and thus, mockingly, agrees:

> DUKE: Then we're all friends?
> SHYLOCK: I trust so.
>   (*aside to audience*) It is clear
>   That I have diddled this Tribunal here,
>   *That's* t'wixt ourselves, not very hard to do,

> But how shall I contrive to diddle you?
> I'll touch your pity—bear to mind the fact,
> If we have sinned—'tis but *one trifling act.*
> Forgive us that—nay more—if you will deign
> To look in on old Shylock e'er again,
> Although reformed at present, you perhaps
> May find him not unwilling to relapse.

Shylock's acceptance of the judgement meted out by the Venetian court could suggest a greater spirit of "humanity" on the part of the oft played Jewish "villain", but as his aside to the audience reveals it is founded on a cynical pragmatism which negotiates with a rereading of his precursor's ultimate demise in the source text. Talfourd's "new" Shylock submits to the power wielded by the Venetian hegemony on the best terms he can, and in the acknowledgement that he, a mid-nineteenth century Shylock, is never foreseeably going to be freed from the intratextually enforced and "preserved" representational bind of "Shylock" and the negative connotations thereof. However, the poignant irony of the closing choric words for a post-Holocaust reception of Talfourd's play anticipatively reaffirm Marowitz's dramaturgical quest—to unchain Shylock from the interpretative shackles that bind him to a negative and, as proven, murderous archetypal and intratextually sedimented representation of "the Jew":

> CHORUS: Then why your feelings throw away
>   On a fictitious sorrow,
>   Nor weep for fancied woes to day
>   You may be real to-morrow.

Liberating the Interpretative Ghetto

Shakespeare wrote his play during a period which witnessed extreme persecution of Catholics and at the height of the enforcement of a draconian Elizabethan penal code, following on from the Act of Uniformity (1559) and the Act of Supremacy (1563). During the mid 1580's, recusancy had become a political offence in the eyes of the civil courts, as opposed to being an affair dealt by the ecclesiastical courts and the mere presence of priests in England was considered an act of treason. Such laws led to numerous court cases based upon religious allegiance and it is not unreasonable to forge a link between Shakespeare's sectarian England and the Venetian Doge's Court which sees fit to pass judgement upon the Jew, Shylock.

The research into Shakespeare's textual response to the sources he used when writing *The Merchant of Venice* is illuminating, such as his deliberate emphasis on the religious dimension of the bond by altering the words in *Il Pecerone* (1378) from "If thou dost shed one drop of blood" to "If thou dost shed one drop of *Christian* blood" (II 305–6). Also the translation of *Il Pecerone* has revealed that there was little doubt about a "Jew of Mestri's" intent to murder Ansaldo in the original story:

> Many merchants joined together in offering to pay the money, but the Jew would not have it for he wished to commit this homicide in order to be able to say that he put to death the greatest of Christian merchants.[74]

Although Shylock does not exhibit such a clear resolve to kill the Christian, the symbolism of "flesh and blood", contained within the terms of the bond, echo the death which wrought the fundamental separation between Jew and Christian. Indeed the religious significance of Shakespeare's reference to flesh and blood as represented by the bond forged between Shylock and Antonio is heightened by the fact that the only specific mention of the time of year in *The Merchant of Venice* is to Easter, when Launcelot alludes to the Crucifixion as symbolised by Eucharist:

> . . . was not for nothing that my nose fell a bleeding on Black Monday last at six o clock 'I th' morning, falling out that year on Ash Wednesday was four years in th' afternoon. (Act II, V, 23–24)

A further interesting alteration which Shakespeare has made with respect to the immediate sources for his play is with respect to Shylock's "conversion" which he portrays (albeit ironically) as an act of mercy on the part of the Christian Venetians as opposed to its presentation in Marlowe's *The Jew of Malta* (first performed in 1592, published 1633) as an unequivocal act of punishment. Such examples of the subtle but fundamental adaptations of source material within *The Merchant of Venice* would suggest that Shakespeare was concerned to polemicise the issues of racial and religious victimhood within Elizabethan society, although Wesker persists in viewing the play as one of many works within a long tradition of dangerous anti-Semitic comedies.

Although it is often cited that all Jews were expelled from England in 1290 and that they were not readmitted until 1655, it has been argued that Shakespeare would have come into contact with Jews and would have been aware of them as a persecuted minority for as Shapiro reveals:

Perhaps a hundred or more Jews might have jostled Shakespeare in the crowded streets of London and we know from Spanish Inquisition Records and the complaints of various Catholic ambassadors that Jewish holidays like Passover and Yom Kippur were celebrated (in secret) in England in the late sixteenth century.[75]

The Domus Conversorum in Chancery Lane, London, founded by Henry III in 1232 as a home for poor Jewish converts to Christianity was also present during Shakespeare's lifetime and could have influenced his depiction of the "merciful" conversion in *The Merchant of Venice* as presented by the Duke's sanctimonious gesture toward Shylock:

> That thou shalt see the difference of our spirit
> I pardon thee thy life before thou ask it (Act IV,I)

These facts alongside the much publicised case of Elizabeth's Jewish physician, Dr Roderigo Lopez, who was put to death in 1594 for allegedly conspiring to poison the Queen, serve to further the argument that Shakespeare did not necessarily write *The Merchant of Venice* simply to contribute to the anti-Semitic mythology which existed in England. Irrespective of authorial intent however, it has been the hap of subsequent events, most noticeably the Holocaust which has drawn out the questions raised by the classic about victimhood, whether the victims be persecuted and marginalized for race, religion or gender, like the Moroccan, women, homosexuals, Jews and as I have suggested the "symbolic" Catholic. Indeed, although the historical knowledge of the circumstances in which a text was produced may enhance our knowledge, such historical data is always restricted by the contingencies of our research and therefore such an approach does not supplant the "understanding" of *Erlebnis*, a point Gadamer emphasises in his critique of Chladenius' "naive" historicism:

> Every age has to understand a transmitted text in its own way, for the text belongs to the whole tradition whose content interests the age and in which it seeks to understand itself. The real meaning of a text, as it speaks to the interpreter, does not depend on the contingencies of the author and his original audience. It certainly is not identical to them for it is always co-determined also by the historical situation of the interpreter and hence by the totality of the objective course of history.[76]

The repressive atmosphere of Elizabethan England may well have prompted Shakespeare to dramatically polemicise the issue of religious persecution in his play, although rather than delve into the vagaries of authorial intent, it is suffice to say that the Holocaust has compelled the reader in possession of historically effected consciousness of looking more intently at the issue of religious persecution and victimhood in *The Merchant of Venice*.[77] Indeed, the plight of the Jews in Venice is analogous with the demise of Catholics in Elizabethan England and clear comparisons include the introduction of The Five Mile Act (1593) which restricted the movement of Catholics within a radius of five miles in designated areas, echoing the ghettoization of jews like Shylock in Venice, and more recently the Warsaw Ghetto. Also the practice of requisitioning recusants' estates as described by the Jesuit, Robert Southwell is a further similarity between the English Catholics and Shylock who is warned that:

> One drop of Christian blood, thy lands and goods
> Are (by the laws of Venice) confiscate
> Unto the state of Venice. (Act IV, I)

and

> Where poor farmers and husbandmen had but one cow for themselves and many children to live upon that for their recusancy hath been taken from them. And where both kine and cattle were wanting they have taken their coverlets, sheets and blankets from their beds, their victuals and poor provision, not sparing so much as the very glass of their windows.[78]

Despite reports of enforced "conversions" during the Elizabethan period such legislation and repression did not remove Catholicism from England, because as Edward Norman explains:

> The distinction between Catholics and non-Catholics was still in many cases unclear. Enormous numbers of people who retained Catholic inclinations conformed to the law by attendance on Sundays at parish churches in order to avoid the fines.[79]

A similar confusion over religion is alluded to in Shakespeare's play with Portia's question, "Which is the merchant here, which is the Jew? (Act IV,I). Thus, regardless of Shakespeare's intent it would appear that what Strauss refers to as a potential "esoteric" meaning of *The Merchant of Venice* has undoubtedly emerged, or has been foregrounded through the hap of historical circumstance, specifically the Holocaust. Such historically situated emergent meanings also place a question mark over the idea that Shakespeare's play is a comedy at the expense of the suffering of the Jew, prompting the suggestion that as opposed to unquestioningly accepting the play as "A Comical History" the original drama was, or at least has become, a scathingly ironic attempt to implicate an audience who saw fit to laugh at the humiliation and persecution of other men.

A central issue that fuelled the sectarianism of Elizabethan England was the debate about transubstantiation and the Eucharist, a fact that Goldberg expounds in his article "Remnants of the Sacred in Early Modern England":

> There is a link between the Eucharistic wafers that obsessed Renaissance subjects and the object that most exemplifies postmodernity, what Slavoj Zizek calls "the sublime object of ideology"[80].

The symbolic representation of Christ's blood and flesh, the wine and the wafer in the Eucharist, is most obviously alluded to in *The Merchant of Venice* with the bond and its legal proviso for the extraction of a pound of flesh without a drop of blood spilt. Catholics and Protestants during the Renaissance had fundamental theological rifts over the importance of the Eucharist which is the paramount ritual of Catholic mass, a historical fact which further consolidates the argument that, for contemporary readers, Shakespeare's play is polemicising religious persecution and victimhood rather than merely ridiculing the victimisation of a particular Jew in an almost mythical Mediterranean setting. The Eucharistic dimension to our understanding of the play is brought out even more when the hap of the Holocaust is attended to, for the very belief in the sacrificed body of Christ is one of the fundamental theological divisions between Jew and Christian, Old and New Testament. However, after Auschwitz such theological differences have, by necessity, assumed less important dimensions for as Metz observes;

> Christian theology after Auschwitz must—at long last—be guided by the insight that Christians can form and sufficiently understand their identity only in the face of the Jews.[81]

Lyotard has also observed the fundamental theological rupture left by the horror and destruction of the Holocaust when he identifies "the interminable anamnesis" with which "the unpayable debt Western thought owes to 'the jews'", a view elaborated on by Caroll:

> In a sense it [Lyotard's thesis] attempts to make 'jews' of all of us, that is what Lyotard refers to as a 'non-people of survivors, Jews and non-Jews' called here 'the jews' whose being together does not depend on the authenticity of any primary roots but on that singular debt of an interminable anamnesis"[82]

Rebecca Chopp has identified the "interruptive character" of the Holocaust which has irrevocably changed our understanding of history as being an ongoing process of evolution into the event of rupture and fragmentation. This interruptive character imbues our reception of *The Merchant of Venice*, and Marowitz's play addresses this interruption by situating Shylock in a position of rootedness and domicility as opposed to the archetypal eternal wandering and marginality of the Jew. In contrast to assuming postures within Western designated parameters of assimilation and persecution, Marowitz's representation of Shylock is one which ousts the Christian from the Jewish homeland, the final act of violence which overshadows the Eucharistic symbolism of "the bond" which has for centuries divided, and ironically, linked Jew and Christian.

In a sense, Marowitz's play exhibits a post-Holocaust sensibility that asserts that theological and doctrinal differences no longer have the power to subdue, placate and mislead the contemporary Shylock into accepting the burden of redemptive suffering. The symbolism of "the bond" has thus transformed into structure in the Marowitz play as the ruse by which the Christian hegemony has always contained the Jew, and which the contemporary Shylock parodically and mockingly colludes with right up until the final and destructive bomb explosion. Far from rewriting *The Merchant of Venice* with a view to reconciliation or pacification, Marowitz's play concludes with a tone of wrath and vengeance against the anti-Semitic part *The Merchant of Venice* has played over the centuries. In this respect the Holocaust is the event or hap which transforms the socio-historical symbolism of the Eucharist from that of religious divide and persecution, be it between Protestant and Catholic or Jew and Christian, into the *praxis* of historical reality. In a sense the overwhelming horror and destruction of the Holocaust is for the historically effected consciousness, the hap which constitutes the disturbing praxis of reality that overshadows and subsumes the *poesis* of all literary and theological symbolism in *The Merchant of Venice*, and I would argue that the Rewrite articulates this hermeneutic "truth", a process referred to by Langer:

> Before 1939 imagination was always in advance of reality, but after 1945 reality had outdistanced the imagination so that nothing the artist conjured could equal in intensity or scope the improbability of l'univers concentrationaire.[83]

By rereading and rewriting Shakespeare's play with an historically effected consciousness of the Holocaust the Eucharistic symbolism of "the bond" in Shakespeare's text *has* been made flesh, *has* been made blood, and the *poiesis* of the text has become one and the same with the *praxis* of our historical contingency. Indeed, Bassanio's words about the bond to which Antonio is bound have assumed larger and far more disturbing implicatory proportions for our post-Holocaust reception of *The Merchant of Venice*:

> BASSANIO: .... Here is a letter, lady,
> The paper as the body of my friend,
> And every word in it a gaping wound
> Issuing life-blood.
> [Act III, Scene II, 1.265–269]

It is such a conflation of *poiesis* and *praxis* through application (*Anwendung*) and not the appropriative "will to power" (*Aneignung*) that is the foundation for the disclosure of a transitory and ephemeral "truth" or hermeneutic *aletheia* for, as Gadamer states:

> The human good is something to be encountered in human praxis and is indeterminable without the concrete situation in which one thing is preferred to another. This alone and not a counterfactual agreement is the critical experience of good.[84]

Cascading Classic, Palatial Ruin

Michael Riffaterre has highlighted how, in the ninth century, John Scottus Eriugena's observation of a fountain led him to conclude that distortions are inherent in our perception, for it is not at the outlet of the fountain that water comes into being, rather it originates elsewhere out of sight and further away in hidden springs.[85] Similarly, the classic is not an aesthetic object which we receive aperspectivally, but is the present flourishing of many different, hidden and emergent sources. However, Riffaterre's conclusion that all "narrative truth is thus a linguistic phenomenon . . . it is a performative event,"[86] fails to adequately attend to historically effected consciousness which does not only concentrate on the way the source text linguistically 'alters' as language usage transforms but which also highlights how historical hap can alter our perspective of the truth of the past as represented by the classic, by changing the significance of the subject-content of the source text. In this respect, to take the previous analogy further, just as the fountain's effect is contingent on the springs divined beneath its artifice, so too a historically effected consciousness will be aware that over the course of history certain of the springs will dry up and others may become reinvigorated to provide a more plentiful store of water for the effect of the fountain. In this respect, Riffaterre's analysis is here supplemented by historically effected consciousness to embrace more fully the complex temporality of rereading, so that as Calinescu observes, ". . . priority and posteriority have lost the absolute character they have in our inner time-consciousness."[87] In *The Semiotic Challenge*, Barthes also draws attention to the necessarily temporal nature of rereading, which like the altered states of the springs which nourish the perceived artifice of the fountain, must acknowledge that ". . . the sources of a text are not only before it, they are also after it."[88]

Philosophical inquiry guided by an historically effected consciousness is an essential component of Gadamer's notion of the ideal political community but as Hoy points out such an approach should be carefully distinguished from the 'interpretative communities' espoused by Fish:[89]

> Whereas a consensus theory suggests that agreeing to something makes it true, Gadamer's sense is that we agree to something because it is true. So truth is not the result of agreement but agreement the result of truth.[90]

Gadamer adamantly upholds the opinion that truth cannot be objectively possessed but rather has the properties of an event, transitory, ephemeral and most importantly historical, and thus he avoids the notion of consensus politics which may fall prey to manipulation, fashion and coercion and become rigidly and institutionally entrenched. In terms of hermeneutic truth, therefore, Gadamer presents an argument to counter the stultifying canonised reading practices with which we are encouraged to approach the classics. As opposed to perpetuating the distinction between understanding and interpretation, Gadamer's hermeneutic emphasises the need to be continuously historically aware in our interpretation of texts, so that understanding of texts is not confused with and superseded by received ahistorical interpretative techniques. Just like political consensus, interpretative consensus of the classics can become a self-serving and self-justifying methodology which mutates from representative creativity to coercive sterility with imperceptible ease. In much the same way that Gadamer draws attention to the damaging artificial divide between interpretation and understanding, so too his hermeneutic project highlights the need to address and dissolve the normatively accepted distinctions which continue to persist between *poiesis* and *praxis*, truth and knowledge. The distinction between understanding and interpretation, truth and knowledge which Gadamerian hermeneutics attempts to bridge leads him to his theory of transformation into structure which contests the classical Aristotelian distinction between *praxis* and *poiesis* that has dominated Western metaphysics for centuries. Through performative *Erlebnis* (as exemplified, I would argue, by the Rewrite) one witnesses and participates in the experiential conflation of *praxis* and *poiesis*. The Gadamerian hermeneutic which informs this interpretation of the Rewrite is not founded upon the mythology of natural essentialism which astute interpretative techniques will reveal to anyone who attempts to find it, rather the Rewrite dramaturgically presents us with the choice to either accept or reject the performative *Erlebnis* offered by its specific negotiation of history. In this respect the Rewrite is not an inherently political form, but rather it is conjectural; that is, the political possibilities of performative *Erlebnis* depends on their significance according to hap. Indeed such an approach accords with that which Graff has identified as "anti-essentialist essentialism", but not one borne of a coercive and appropriative "will to power", rather the essence of historical hap:

> To be sure, essentialism (like any other ism) always has some political effect, but what that effect is cannot be deduced from the idea itself, but only from an examination of how the idea operates in a particular social conjuncture. Appealing to essences (or to the natural, the objective, etc.) is often a way of rationalizing coercive social practices, but not necessarily always. In the recent American and South African racial struggles, to take just one example, the idea that there is an essential human nature that racist regimes violate has had an important "oppositional" effect.[91]

The Rewrite therefore is not the simplistic labelling of that which is oppositional or complicitous within existing structures, nor does it embody Rorty's belief that because no theory or practice implies a particular politics, any attempt to make political judgements about forms of culture is necessarily pointless. In this respect, Gadamer's hermeneutic project in *Truth and Method* may well be considered a counter to the classical metaphysical distinction between *poiesis* and *praxis*, which has led to what Lévinas identified as the possibility and the uneasy accommodation for "human failure" as observed with particular reference to the infamous Heidegger Affair, a debate of singular significance when considering "understanding" after the Holocaust:

> Can we be assured, however, that there was never any echo of Evil in it? [*Being and Time*]. The diabolical is not limited to the wickedness popular wisdom ascribes to it, and whose malice, based on guile, is familiar and predictable in an adult culture. The diabolical is endowed with intelligence and enters where it will. To reject it, it is first necessary to refute it. Intellectual effort is needed to recognise it. Who can boast of having done so? Say what you will, the diabolical gives food for thought.[92]

Hayden White has pointed out, "many kinds of truth even in history could be presented to the reader only by means of fictional techniques of representation."[93]—a point which is particularly pertinent to a post-Holocaust re-reading and rewriting of *The Merchant of Venice*. Many critics have remarked upon the difficulty of forming an aesthetic articulation of issues concerned with the Holocaust, a problem eloquently expressed by Rosenfeld:

> Holocaust literature . . . extends so far as to force us to contemplate what may be fundamental changes in our modes of perception and expression, our altered way of being-in-the-world . . . we begin to see that Holocaust literature is an attempt to express a new order of consciousness, a recognisable shift in being . . . Stunned by the awesomeness and pressure of event, the imagination comes to one of its periodic endings; undoubtedly, it also stands at the threshold of new and more difficult beginnings.[94]

The Rewrite of *The Merchant of Venice* is, I would argue, a hermeneutic application which is appropriate to an endeavour to meet the demand for a post-Holocaust articulation of the Holocaust. Marowitz's *Variations* facilitates an historically effected consciousness of such events without demeaning or undermining their awesome proportions by naming them, but with the hermeneutic efficacy to elicit *aletheia*. As Steiner has stated one of the distinguishing features of the Nazi preparation for the Holocaust was its verbosity, which has had the effect of making verbal response to the aftermath of the Holocaust such an agonising task:

> Not silence or evasion, but an immense outpouring of precise, serviceable words. It was one of the peculiar horrors of the Nazi era that all that happened was recorded, catalogued, chronicled, set down; that words were committed to saying things no human mouth should ever have said and no paper made by man should ever have been inscribed with.[95]

The Rewrite is a dramaturgical form which, according to this Gadamerian interpretation does offer a way "to express and convey the experience of a radically negating event that has shattered the very convention of speech and discourse", but "without employing those conventions and thereby domesticating that radical negativity."[96]

Marowitz's play, unlike Wesker's *Shylock*, does fulfil, if we borrow the Benjaminian metaphor for cultural "afterlife", the dramaturgical transformation into the structure of the "ruin" of *The Merchant of Venice*. For Benjamin the ruin is not a pejorative or demeaning state of decay, it is vibrant testimony to the historical process which stands as a witness against any of the mythical or picturesque notions of the past with which we delude ourselves. Similarly the ruin is a visual metaphor for the historically effected consciousness with which we read the classics as opposed to the ahistorical interpretative reconstruction required of a literary museum piece:

> The object of philosophical criticism is to show that the function of artistic form is as follows: to make historical content such as provides the basis of every important work of art, into a philosophical truth. The transformation of material content into truth content makes the loss of effect, whereby the attractiveness of the earlier charms diminishes decade by decade into the basis for a rebirth in which all ephemeral beauty is completely stripped off and the work stands as a ruin. [97]

As opposed to the dramatic adaptation or alteration which merely adopts an ahistorical intertextual relationship with the past, thus denoting repetition, and which therefore continues to be the mythical result of an unredeemed historical life, the Rewrite dramaturgically represents what Benjamin identified as "now-time which is shot through with chips of Messianic time."[98] This is not to suggest any quasi-religious or timeless notion of history; rather, it is a secular and systematic history, that acknowledges that remembrance cannot take place without a sense of hope.

Benjamin's celebration of a historically effected consciousness created out of the ruins of time is peculiarly pertinent to our post-Holocaust reception of *The Merchant of Venice*. Not only is it impossible to read or view the play without being conscious of the legacy of anti-Semitism which contributed to the Holocaust, but consciousness of the Holocaust also actually alters and reshapes our reception of the play—a transformation into structure dramaturgically presented as performative *Erlebnis* by Marowitz. Shakespeare's play has been transformed into a weather-beaten, battle stormed and desolate ruin over the centuries, but since the Holocaust it has become decidedly uninhabitable and uninviting. Despite such ravages of time, it is precisely when the classic is at its most bare, stripped of all ephemerality that the transformation into structure will elicit what Benjamin refers to as the "monad" of truth. Benjamin asserts it is ruins and not palaces that bear testimony to truth, it is not the historicist's victors but history's victims who bear witness, and indeed after Auschwitz any attempt to portray historical narrative focused on historical "victors" or any teleological schema would merely reduce victims to being the means to an end. It is for these reasons that *The Merchant of Venice*, oft cited as both a cause and a product of anti-Semitism and thus a cultural artefact implicated in the Holocaust, is such a powerful literary ruin to explore and excavate.

The Rewrite dramaturgically asserts that *The Merchant of Venice* cannot be consigned to Tillyard's Elizabethan World Picture, but rather that it has been and continues to be implicated in subsequent historical realities like Auschwitz and by extension our post-Holocaust consciousness. The particular demise of Shylock in Shakespeare's play is thus rewritten to encompass the subsequent history of "the Jew" in which Shylock has played and continues to play a part. However, far from rewriting the classic merely to highlight the way in which culture is implicated in the social injustices of daily *praxis* Marowitz revisits Shylock so that the character might give voice to his opinions about the intervening centuries as well as the present, so that he might step out from the ruin of his fictional ghetto and from the archetypal victimhood which he has simultaneously fought against and contributed to. The Rewrite enables Shylock whom *we*, and not merely the abstraction which we refer to as culture have created, to be released from the deeper recesses of our consciousness into the immediacy of our post-Holocaust experience.

Notes

1 David Thacker, Director of RSC in *The Guardian*, October 1993

2 The original use of the term "problem plays" in relation to Shakespeare's corpus of work can be found in Tillyard's book, *Shakespeare's Problem Plays: Hamlet, Troilus and Cressida, All's Well That Ends Well and Measure for Measure*. According to Tillyard the aforementioned plays are "problem plays" because they do not have the unity of effect presented in his other works. However, following the aftermath of the anti-semitism that culminated in the Holocaust, I consider *The Merchant of Venice* to have become problematic because of the ahistorical unity with which the play continues to be produced and received today.

3 D. M. Cohen, "The Jew and Shylock", *Shakespeare Quarterly*, 31 (1980), pp. 53–63, p. 53.

4 Ernst Schumacher cited in *Is Shakespeare Still Our Contemporary?* ed. John Elsom (London: Routledge, 1990) pp. 143–4.

5 Arnold Wesker, Preface to "Shylock" *Arnold Wesker: Volume Four* (London: Penguin, 1990) p. 178.

6 Charles Marowitz, Preface to *The Marowitz Shakespeare* (New York: Marion Boyars, 1990) p. 22.

7 John Russell Brown, *Shakespeare's Plays in Performance* (London: 1966), p. 71.

8 Leslie Fiedler, *The Stranger in Shakespeare* (London: 1973), p. 86.

9 Marion Perret, *Shakespeare Studies XX* p. 267.

10 John Gross, *Shylock: Four Hundred Years in the Life of a Legend* (London: Vintage, 1994) discusses the Elizabethans' attitude toward jews and he confirms that for most christians at the time the Jew was not only an almost pantomime figure of fun onto which they would vent all their anxieties and neuroses, but also associated with the diabolic and satanism, often portrayed as the original "Christ-killer". On one level Shakespeare's play could be viewed as playing to this anti-semitic gallery, but as my later discussion elucidates I consider the play to be a polemic of persecution whereby Shakespeare focusses on the painful ritual humiliation of the Jew exoterically in order to esoterically allude to the persecution of other religious groups in his own society, namely the Catholics. For an interesting insight into the exoteric/esoteric dimension of Renaissance texts see Annabel Patterson's *Reading Between the Lines* (London: Routledge, 1993). For further information about those who wrote and published in censoring societies, see Annabel Patterson's *Censorship and Interpretation* (Madison, 1990). Also for a more general consideration about the often hidden sceptical subtext within the text see, Leo Strauss's *Persecution and the Art of Writing* (Chicago: University of Chicago Press, 1952).

11   John Gross, *Shylock* (London: Vintage, 1994) pp.1–2.

12   Michael Bristol, *Big Time Shakespeare* (London: Routledge, 1996) p. 138.

13   Walter Benjamin, 'Theses on the Philosophy of History' in *Illuminations*, ed., Hannah Arendt, trans. by Harry Zohn (London: Jonathon Cape, 1973) p. 258.

14   Walter Benjamin, cited by Irving Wohlfarth "The Measure of the Possible, . . ." in *The Actuality of Walter Benjamin: New Formations* Vol. 20, Summer 1993 p.6. [from Walter Benjamin's *Gesammelte Schriften* eds., R. Tiedemann and H. Schweppenhauser (Frankfurt am Main) 1974–1988, Vol. III, p. 290.]

15   Charles Marowitz, *The Marowitz Shakespeare* (New York and London: Marion Boyars, 1990) p. 25.

16   From Elie Wiesel's *Messengers of God: Biblical Portraits and Legends* as cited in Young's *Writing and Rewriting the Holocaust: Narrative and the Consequences of Interpretation* (Bloomington: Indiana University Press, 1990) pp.94–95, and refer to "The Holocaust as Literary Inspiration" in *Dimensions of the Holocaust*, ed., Lacey Baldwin Smith (Evanston, 1977) p. 7

17   Galations 6:13 *"For they themselves which are circumcised keep not the Law, but desire to have you circumcised that they might rejoice in your flesh."* and St. Paul in Thessalonians 2:15–16 *"The Jews, who killed the Lord Jesus and the prophets and drove us out . . ."*

18   Elizabeth Schussler Fiorenza, David Tracy, "The Holocaust as Interruption and the Christian Return into History" cited in *The Holocaust as Interruption* eds., E.S. Fiorenza, Tracy, David (Edinburgh: T. and T. Clark, 1985) p. 85.

19   Lawrence Langer, "History in Holocaust Literature", *Reflections of the Holocaust in Art and Literature* ed., R. L Braham (Holocaust Studies Series, 1990) p.119.

20   Maurice Blanchot, *The Writing of the Disaster* trans. by Anne Smock (Lincoln and London: University of Nebraska Press, 1995) p. 106.

21   David Carroll, Preface to Lyotard's *Heidegger and "the jews"*, trans. by Andreas Michel and Mark S. Roberts (Minneapolis: University of Minnesota Press, 1990) p. xiii

22   Hayden White's "politics of interpretation" emphasises the need to abstain from 'extra worldly' extrapolation when confronted with a text, because it too often descends into extratextual or politically motivated determinism:

   . . . the politics of interpretation must find the means either to effect this repression or to sublimate the impulse to appeal to political authority as to transform it into an instrument of interpretation itself.

23   Harold Bloom "Interview Conducted by Antonio Weis" *Writers at Work: The Paris Review Interviews* 9th Series (ed) George Plimpton (New York: Penguin Books, 1990) p. 225.

24   Robert Bernasconi, *Heidegger in Question: The Art of Existing* (New Jersey: Humanities Press, 1996) p. 73.

25   Central to Gadamerian hermeneutics is the tenet that we cannot objectively survey the 'past', and we cannot chronologically compartmentalize history because it is only formed and being continually formed through the present. Thus, a concept like, for example, postmodernism which constitutes itself against the passing of a previous period does not heed this simultaneous relationship between past and present. However, it will become apparent that the phrase "post" Holocaust is used with some frequency throughout this chapter, but it should be noted that this is for the sake of brevity and it is not to suggest in anyway that the effects of the Holocaust are not very much with us in the present and thus essentially inform our present 'understanding'.

26   Gadamer, *TM* pp. 375–376.

27   Alan How, *The Habermas-Gadamer Debate and the Nature of the Social* (Aldershot: Avebury Series in Philosophy, 1995) p. 9.

28   Charles Larmore, *The Morals of Modernity* (Cambridge: Cambridge University Press, 1996) p. 11.

29   Ernesto Laclau and Chantal Mouffe *Hegemony and Socialist Strategy: Toward a Radical Democratic Politics* (London: Verso, 1985) p. 127–128.

30   Gadamer *TM*, p. 111.

31   James Shapiro, *Shakespeare and the Jews* (New York: Columbia University Press, 1996) p. 228.

32   Roland Barthes, *S/Z*, trans. by Richard Miller (New York: Hill and Wang, 1974) p. 16.

33   Leslie Fiedler *The Stranger in Shakespeare* (St. Albans: Frogmore, 1974) p. 81–82.

34   Theodor Adorno and Max Horkheimer, "Elements of Anti-Semitism" in *Dialectic of Enlightenment* trans. by John Cumming, (New York: Continuum, 1994) p. 175

35   Maurice Blanchot, *The Writing of the Disaster* p. 81.

36   Gadamer distinguishes between Kant's "disinterestedness" based on taste and Schiller's aesthetic consciousness which "precludes any criterion of content." See, *TM* pp. 81–88.

37   Gadamer, *TM*, p. 82–83

38   Within the context of this study the term *aestheticisation* refers to the way the work of art can become distanced from our experience or everyday *praxis* through the false claim put forward for the objectification of our reception of art. As Gadamer states the objectifying attempt at "pure seeing" and "pure hearing" is merely recourse to "dogmatic abstractions that artificially reduce phenomena."

[*TM* p.92] Indeed, the supposed claim for an objective reception of art often results in the evaluation of art becoming little more than the invocation of a self-gratifying and self-aggrandising "feel good" factor. [See Chapter VI for a more detailed analysis of the effects of aestheticisation as polemicised by Tony Harrison's *The Trackers of Oxyrynchus*.] Aestheticisation and cognate notions such as "taste" not only precipitate the distancing of art from experience, but also lend themselves to the promulgation of divisive and elitist social attitudes. [See Chapter III for a discussion of the distorted reception created by the poetic form and aesthetic *affect* of the Venetian hegemony's language in *The Merchant of Venice*.] Also refer to Nietzsche's observations concerning the way the *effect* of art has been supplanted by the *affect* of the aesthetic in *The Birth of Tragedy*.

39   Peter Smith gives a comprehensive historiography of the productions of *The Merchant of Venice* in his illuminating work *Social Shakespeare: Aspects of Renaissance Dramaturgy and Contemporary Society* (London and New York: Macmillan Press, 1995). Also see James Bulman's study *The Merchant of Venice* for more information about productions and specific directors' interpretations of the play in *Shakespeare in Performance: The Merchant of Venice* (Manchester: Manchester University Press, 1991)

40   Annette Kolodny "Dancing Through the Minefield: Some Observations on the Theory, Practice and Politics of Feminist Literary Criticism" in *Feminist Studies* 6 (1980) p. 11.

41   The term *intratextuality* is used throughout this study to emphasise not only the relationship between texts or *intertextuality* but also the way in which those texts have been received, adapted, distorted, appropriated in the light of historical mores, attitudes or indeed specific events. Undoubtedly, the Holocaust is perhaps one of most devastating inratextual events upon our reception of literature produced before the Holocaust, but as argued and as observed by both Wesker and Marowitz, the Holocaust is a particularly pertinent intratextual event with respect to any subsequent reception of *The Merchant of Venice*. Indeed the *intertextuality* between *Variations* and *The Merchant of Venice* is inextricably bound up with the consciousness of, or hap, of the *intratextual* event that is the Holocaust. The term *intratextuality* encapsulates most effectively the way the Rewrite negotiates not only with a source text, but also with the intervening historical events that have shaped its particular dramaturgical interpretation of the source text. Likewise, *intratextuality* need not manifest itself in the form of intervening appropriations, parodies or events, but may be, as discussed in Chapter VI, an intratextual void between two texts. Such an intratextual void however is distinct from the almost mechanistic relationship between two texts created by *intertextuality*, because the void is in itself an historical event that precipitates further and subsequent historical activity, such as the cultural imperialism of Grenfell and Hunt in *The Trackers of Oxyrynchus*.

      Besides being aware of the difference between *intertextuality* and *intratextuality* in this discussion of the Rewrite, attention should be drawn to the clear distinction between *intratextuality* and *extratextuality*. The discussion of Freud's extratextual imposition of the Oedipal Complex onto the source text,

Oedipus Rex, elucidates the distinction between *intratextual* and *extratextual,* although as explained the *extratextual* Oedipal Complex as imposed upon the source text by Freud has subsequently assumed an *intratextual* significance that is addressed by Berkoff's Rewrite, *Greek.* [See Chapter V]

For a discussion of the relationship between the work of art and *intratextuality* see J. Goodwin's *Akira Kurosawa and Intertextual Cinema* (Baltimore and London: The Johns Hopkins Press, 1994) and for related work on this topic see Linda Hutcheon's discussion of the intramural and extramural aspect of parody in *A Theory of Parody* (London: Routledge, 1991). In addition Edward Said's *The World, the Text and the Critic* (London: Vintage, 1983) is a seminal work about the text's relationship with history and the effect this has on interpretation.

42   Charles Marowitz, *Recycling Shakespeare* (London: Macmillan, 1991) p. 24.

43   Marowitz, *Recycling Shakespeare* pp. 26–27.

44   See B. Cheyette's *Construction of 'the jew' In English Literature: Racial Representation 1875–1945* (Cambridge: Cambridge University Press, 1995). Bryan Cheyette has carried out some illuminating research into the way in which polarised categorisations of either the "good" or "bad" Jew have been presented in literature, and he argues that such polarised representations of the Jew are not symptomatic of an impetus toward anti-racism but rather a nationalistic endeavour to contain the alien. Indeed, Shapiro also points out that post-Reformation the negative representation of the Jew became less focussed on the Christian-Jew divide and became more concerned with the perceived antithesis between the English and subsequently the British and the Jew. Indeed, nineteenth century literature abounds with the literary alternation between the presentation of a "good" Jew as one who seeks to assimilate into British society, (like Mr Riah in *Our Mutual Friend*) or one endeavouring to reach his homeland in Palestine (such as Daniel Deronda and Mordecai in Eliot's *Daniel Deronda*) is in clear contrast to the "bad" Jewish counterpart (Fagin in *Oliver Twist*) or the "denationalised" Cohen family. Cheyette's argument that the depiction of either the "good" or "bad" Jew in literature can be considered contingent upon the political attitudes to foreigners and the "other" at any given time serves to illustrate the unsatisfactory simplicity of Wesker's approach toward the complex and ambiguous Shakespearean character, Shylock. Literary representations of the Jew perceived within the ambivalent discourse of "good" or "bad" are not validated on the grounds of their Jewish identity but as Cheyette points out ". . . on the basis of their conformity to the values and manners of bourgeois English society (at any given time) . . ." In a similar vein, Wesker's representation of Shylock as the "good" Jew works within similar polarities and thus fails to address the far more challenging theme of how the ruling Venetian hegemony compels such role-playing from those they persecute.

45   Robert Stam and Louise Spence "Colonialism, Racism and Representation" Introduction to *Screen* 24:2 (March-April 1983) p. 3

46   Gadamer, *TM* pp. 111–112.

47   Cheyette, *Construction of 'the jew'* p. 268.

48 Montaigne, "De Dementir: 'Car la Dissimulation Est de Plus Notable Qualitez de Ce Siecle,'" as cited in Perez Zagorin's *Ways of Lying, Dissimulation, Persecution and Conformity in Early Modern Europe*, (Cambridge, Mass: Harvard University Press, 1990) p. xi.

49 James Shapiro, *Shakespeare and the Jews* (New York: Columbia University Press, 1996) p. 6. Shapiro's impressive study incorporates detailed reference to primary sources and literature during the early modern period to show how, amongst other things, although Edward I expelled the Jews from England in 1290 many jews continued to live and work in urban areas of England up until and after Cromwell officially readmitted them into the country.

50 Georg Christoph Lichtenberg's critique of Charles Macklin's performance as Shylock in December 1775 as cited in H.H. Furness, ed., *The Merchant of Venice: A New Variorum Edition* (Philadelphia: J. P. Lippincott, 1888) p. 322.

51 Ingarden emphasises the freedom of literary interpretation to the point of what Gadamer identifies as the "free and arbitrary" (Gadamer, p.118.) *aesthesis* which refuses the historical contextualisation of any act of reading. [R. S. Ingarden, *Ontology of the Work of Art, the Musical Work, the Picture, the Architectural Work* trans. by Raymond Meyer, John Goldthwait (Athens: Ohio University Press, 1989)]. In effect, there is no such thing as an "innocent reading", although this does not entail necessary hermeneutic reiteration, rather a process summed up by Calvino:

   Every re-reading of a classic is as much a voyage of discovery as the first reading. [Italo Calvino *The Uses of Literature*, trans: by Patrick Creagh (San Diego: Harcourt Brace Jovanovich, 1986) p. 127.

52 Jean-Francois Lyotard, *Heidegger and "the jews"* , trans: by Andreas Michel (Minneapolis: University of Minnesota Press, 1990) p. 26.

53 Gadamer, *TM* p. 111.

54 Shapiro, *Shakespeare and the Jews* p. 227.

55 Homi Bhabha, "The Other Question . . ." *Screen* 24:6 (Nov-Dec 1983) 18–36, p. 18.

56 Richard Cumberland quoted by Stanley Thomas Williams *Richard Cumberland: His Life and Dramatic Works* (New Haven: Yale University Press, 1917) p. 215.

57 Philip Cohen, "Monstrous Images, Perverse Reasons" Cultural Studies in Anti-Racist Education Working Paper No.11, Centre for Multicultural Education, Institute of Education, University of London, p. 2.

58 David Roskies, *Apocalypse: Response to Catastrophe in Modern Jewish Culture* (Cambridge, Mass. and London: Harvard University Press, 1984) p. 13

59 James Young, *Writing and Rewriting the Holocaust: Narrative and the Consequences of Interpretation* (Bloomington: Indiana University Press, 1990) p. 94.

60   Arnold Wesker, Preface to "Shylock" *Arnold Wesker: Volume Four* (London: Penguin, 1990) p. 177.

61   Sander L. Gilman in *Jewish Self Hatred: Anti-Semitism and the Hidden Language of the Jews* (Baltimore and London: The Johns Hopkins Press, 1986) pp.2–3.

62   Gadamer, *TM*, p. 290.

63   Arnold Wesker "The Birth of a Play" from a public paper given at the Hay-on-Wye Music and Literature Festival, (May 1995) 1–27, p. 3

64   Marion Perret, *Shakespeare Studies XX* (1989) p. 268.

65   Gadamer, *TM* p. 269.

66   Charles Marowitz, *The Marowitz Shakespeare: Adaptations and Collages of Hamlet, Macbeth, The Taming of the Shrew, Measure for Measure and The Merchant of Venice* (New York and London: Marion Boyars, 1990) p. 24.

67   Anonymous, first appearing in "The Weekly Register" 26 January, 1734 and later reprinted in the January issue of "The London Magazine", 3, 1734, p. 30.

68   Walter Scott, *The Journal of Sir Walter Scott* 2, March 1827, p284, ed: W E K Anderson, (Oxford: Clarendon Press, 1972)

69   Jean Marsden, "Rewritten Women: Shakespeare's Heroines in the Restoration", *The Appropriation of Shakespeare: Post Renaissance Reconstructions of the Work and the Myth* (New York and London: Harvester Wheatsheaf, 1991) pp. 43–54, p. 46.

70   Conduct books were popular during the seventeenth century, many of which stressed that a woman's strongest weapon was to perfect a show of meekness and modesty, such as the code of conduct proposed in R Allestree's "Of Wives" in *The Ladies Calling* (Oxford: 1673)

71   Marsden pp. 53–54

72   Richard Hole, "An Apology for the Character and Conduct of Shylock" in *Essays by a Society of Gentlemen at Exeter* (Exeter, 1796)

73   Francis Talfourd wrote a number of burlesque versions of Shakespeare's plays, including *Mabeth* and *The Merchant of Venice. Shylock or the Merchant of Venice Preserved: An Entirely New Reading of Shakespeare* (London: Thomas Hailes Lacey, 1848) was first produced at the Royal Olympic Theatre, London on Monday, July 4th, 1853.

74   Fiorentino, *Il Pecerone* (1378)

75   Shapiro, J., *The Jews: The Parkes Lecture* (University of Southampton, 1992) p. 3.

76   Gadamer, *TM* p. 296.

77 Bill Alexander's "Catholic" version of *The Merchant of Venice* dramaturgically suggests through the use of set, costume and "popish" regalia that there is an esoteric 'Catholic dimension' to a play which is not merely the stylised persecution of "the Jew", Shylock but actually a detailed and sensitive consideration about religious and racial persecution, be it between Jew and Christian, Catholic and Protestant.

Indeed throughout the sixteenth century there were heated debates between Protestant and Catholic theologians about transubstantiation and the Eucharist, most notably the Jewel-Harding ecclesiastical debate in 1558. Also B. D. Fulke, "Maister of Pembroke Hall in Cambridge" wrote a diatribe against the Catholics which links what he deems to be their religious heresy with the Jews and the Jewish place of worship:

> Heskins Parleament Repealed" in D. Heskins, D. Sanders and M. Rastel accounted (among their faction) three pillars and arch patriarches of the Popish Synagogue (utter enemies to the truth of Christes Gospell, and all that syncerely professe the same) overthrowne and detected of their severall blasphemous heresies. [B. D. Fulke *Catalogue of Popish Books*, 1579]

Also the same year, 1579 Edmund Tilney was made Master of the Revels, the centralised autonomous censor of publications and theatrical productions. Elizabeth I's reign is punctuated with her attempt to keep religous subversion at bay, and indeed in her very first year as Queen she issued a proclamation "Prohibiting Unlicensed Interludes and Plays Especially on Religion or Policy."

78 Robert Southwell, *An Humble Supplication to her Majestie*, (ed) R. C. Bald (Cambridge: Cambridge University Press, 1953) p. 45. Devlin also points out just how repressive society had become during the sixteenth century, and how 'the temporizing' of the Jew was most definitely carried over into other sections of the community, as revealed by Lord Chief Justice Coke's remarks about the 'misappropriation of texts' at the trial of the Jesuit poet Robert Southwell:

> And them likewise we met withal, and made it a felony to publish them and a felony to keep them. A good point my masters, to be observed. Beware how you read them! [C. Devlin, *The Life of Robert Southwell* (London: 1967) p. 309.

79 Edward Norman, *Roman Catholicism in England from the Elizabethan Settlement to the Second Vatican Council* (Oxford: Oxford University Press, 1985) p. 14.

80 Stephan Goldberg, "Remnants of the Sacred in Early Modern England" in *James I and the Politics of Literature* (Baltimore: Johns Hopkins University Press, 1986) p. 338.

81 Metz, J-B., "Facing the Jews: Christian Theology After Auschwitz" in *The Holocaust as Interruption* (Edinburgh: T. and T. Clarke, 1985) p. 26.

82 David Carroll, Preface to Lyotard's *Heidegger and the 'jews'* p. xii.

83   Lawrence Langer, *The Holocaust and the Literary Imagination*, (New Haven and London: Yale University Press, 1976) p. 35.

84   Gadamer, H. G., *Replik* trans. by G. H. Leiner (Ormiston & Schrift, 1990) p. 293

85   Michael Riffaterre, *Fictional Truth* (Baltimore, Maryland: The Johns Hopkins University Press, 1990) p. xiv.

86   Riffaterre, p.xiv.

87   Mattei Calinescu, *Rereading* (London: Yale University Press, 1993) p. 53.

88   Roland Barthes, *The Semiotic Challenge* trans. by Richard Howard, (New York: Hill and Wang, 1988) p. 231.

89   Stanley Fish, see *Is there a text in this class? The Authority of Interpretive Communities* (Cambridge, Mass: Harvard University Press, 1980)

90   David Hoy, *The Critical Theory: Literature, History and Philosophical Hermeneutics* (Berkeley and Los Angeles: University of California, 1978) p. 189.

91   Gerald Graff, "Co-optation" in *The New Historicism* (ed Veseer, H A) , 1989 p. 174.

92   Emanuel Levinas, "As if Consenting to the Horror" *Critical Inquiry* 15, (1989) p. 488.

93   Hayden White, "The Politics of Historical Interpretation: Discipline and Desublimation" *Critical Inquiry* 9/1 (1982) p. 113.

94   Alvin. H. Rosenfeld, *A Double Dying: Reflections on Holocaust Literature* (Bloomington and London: 1980) pp. 60–61. See also Lucy Davidowicz *A Holocaust Reader* (New York: Indiana University Press, 1976) Introduction.

95   George Steiner, "The Hollow Miracle" in *Language and Silence* (London:Faber and Faber, 1992) p. 122.

96   Susan Shapiro, "Hearing Testimony of Radical Negation" in *The Holocaust as Interruption* (Edinburgh: T. and T. Clark, 1984) p. 6. Also see Zygmunt Bauman's *Modernity and The Holocaust* and Horkheimmer and Adorno's "After Auschwitz" in which they state that Auschwitz has given visibility to the inbuilt violence of the technological society, and is a judgement on positivistic society.

97   Richard Wolin, *Walter Benjamin: An Aesthetic of Redemption* (Berkeley, Los Angeles: University of California Press, 1994) p. 53.

98   Walter Benjamin, "Theses on the Philosophy of History" in *Illuminations* trans. by Harry Zohn, preface by Hannah Arendt (London: Cape, 1970) p. 265.

Chapter Four

Antigone, Fugard and "The Tradition of the Oppressed"[1]

The Judeo-Christian Absorption of the *Pharmakon*[2]

The Island (1973) is an example of what Walter Benjamin identified as "revolutionary nostalgia"[3] in that Fugard et al. return to the Western liberal humanist literary tradition in order to articulate a critique of dominant conceptual and ideological notions about the "tradition of the oppressed". George Steiner's work on the mythological roots and literary appropriations of *Antigone* clearly delineates the way in which Christianity and its separative cosmology which has traditionally adhered to clear distinctions between "good" and "evil" came to be superimposed upon our reception of the source text:

> Why did Barthelemy choose just this tragedy for seminal reference? Why did Shelley, Hegel, Hebbel see in the mythical persona of Antigone the 'highest presence' to have entered the world of men? What intention attaches to the repeated hints (in de Quincey, in Kierkegaard, they are more than hints) that Antigone is to be understood as a counterpart to Christ, as God's child and messenger before Revelation? Complete answers elude us. Only the judgement of supremacy is clear. From it arise some of the most radically transformative interpretations and 're-experiencings' ever elicited by a literary text.[4]

It was from the legacy of such radically transformative and Christian interpretations that "Antigone" was to become a dramaturgical re-experience of the "good" conscience against the state, of the lone warrior battling against all odds, the symbolic hero of "the tradition of the oppressed". Thus, over the centuries the ambiguity of the fifth century concept of 'the *pharmakon*'[5] has been supplanted by the rigid demarcations between "good" and "evil" which constitute the separative cosmology of the Judeo-

Christian tradition. The tragic ambiguity of fifth century drama was presented through lexical complexity and characterisation[6] but over the centuries, with for example, Robert Garnier's *Antigone* (1580),[7] and later appropriations by, amongst others, Hegel[8] and Goethe[9], such ambiguity was to be replaced with the interpretative transformation of the play into a dramaturgical icon for the constancy of human suffering. Cohen has identified the imposition of such interpretations as a "teleology of the oppressed"[10] which produces comforting, stable narratives whereby the meaning of any conjuncture from any point in time is seen to represent a stage in the dynamic unfolding of some ultimate and pre-defined goal. Such triumphalist narratives, like "the tradition of the oppressed":

> . . . ease the pain of lived contradictions, furnishing missing links between origins and destinies, stitching together scattered histories into a singular totalising consciousness.[11]

Thus, Steiner's assertion that "no artifice of transfer is required as between the classical and the biblical"[12] appears to overlook the fundamental distinction between the *pharmakon* which peculiarly imbued the production and reception of fifth century tragedy and the later Christian separative cosmological reception of such plays, and so Steiner's easy application of the didactic moralism of the Judeo-Christian tradition to Sophoclean tragedy is questionable:

> Humanist tragedy, whether classical or biblical, is a sustained analogy, unifying time through an invariance of exemplum and moral meaning. For Garnier this meaning is naturally Christian. The paganism of the Sophoclean or Senecan sources is to sixteenth century humanists (the elusive guarded exception being Montaigne) of ornamental accident.[13]

Vernant and Vidal-Naquet have pointed out how tragedy in fifth century Athens presented man as a problem or a riddle whose double meanings could never be pinned down or exhausted, but which subsequent Christian translations have invariably transformed into a work concerned with human salvation and the 'tradition of the oppressed':

> In Sophocles' *Oedipus Rex*, Laius' servant realises that the man before him, the now sovereign of Thebes, is that self-same child with pierced feet whom he handed over to the shepherd of the King of Corinth. In the French translation by Jean and Mayotte Bollack what he says to Oedipus at this point is: "Si tu es cet homme que lui [le berger de Corinth] il dit que tu es, sache que tu es né damné [If you are the man whom he (the shepherd from Corinth) says you are know that you were born damned]." What the Greek text says is: "Know that you were born for fatal

destiny." What does the use of the word "damned," with all its Christian over-
tones, contribute? Nothing, apart from an immediacy that is "disturbing" not
because it transmits a tragic anxiety, but because it replaces that with the idea of
Augustinian or Calvinistic predestination. The dialogue with the ancient poet is
shattered. [14]

When surveying the rise and decay of Attic tragedy during the course
of the fifth century one can clearly see the centrality which the concept of
the *pharmakon* played at that time. Fifth century Athens witnessed a
period of crisis in which transformation and abrupt change became sufficiently interwoven with elements of continuity for there to be a clash
between the ancient forms of religious thought and the new ideas relating
to the development of the law and new political practices. Indeed, as
Vernant observes the later tragedians, like Euripides, exhibit a tendency
to background divine agency in favour of delineating the vicissitudes of
human life, in an attempt to escape and thus resolve the *pharmakon*
which had dominated the great tragedies of Aeschylus and Sophocles.
However, as Vernant concludes, such an attempt to "humanise" tragedy,
"cut off from the general order of the world governed by the gods appears
so indeterminate and confused that it leaves no room for responsible
action."[15] With the subsequent imposition of the moralism of the Judeo-
Christian tradition upon Sophoclean tragedy, tragic heroes, like Antigone,
were provided with a new and radically different ethos in which to operate, an ethos which provided the piety of the precepts of Faith, Hope and
Charity which constitute received notions about "the tradition of the oppressed". As Oudemans observes:

> At the same time the cosmology of *Antigone* is familiar to us, not merely because
> this tragedy touches emotional chords in the modern European mind, but prima-
> rily because it tries to cope with the cosmological problems with which we are
> confronted as well, although its solutions and ours are mutually exclusive. In this
> sense, *Antigone* is a thorn in the flesh of modern European cosmology, small
> wonder that a range of interpretative efforts have been made.[16]

Thus, *Antigone* has assumed an almost elegiac status as an icon for
the "tradition of the oppressed", far removed from the representation of
the almost utilitarian *pharmakon* which lends tragic ambiguity to fifth
century drama. Indeed Shelley, writing to John Gisborne in October 1821
exemplifies the popular tendency to view Antigone as the downtrodden,
saintly victim, the martyr to conscience:

> You are right about Antigone . . . how sublime a picture of woman and what
> think you of the choruses, and especially the lyrical complaint of the godlike

victim? And the menaces of Tiresias and their rapid fulfilment? Some of us have
in a prior existence been in love with an Antigone, and that makes us find no full
content in any moral tie.[17]

Later, in 1846, De Quincey's rhapsodic summation of the play made
clear links with Antigone and Christian precepts, casting the heroine as a
figura of Christ:

Holy heathen, daughter of God before God was known, flower from Paradise
after Paradise was closed . . . idolatrous yet Christian lady, that in the spirit of
martyrdom trodst alone the yawning billows of the grave, flying from earthly
hopes, lest everlasting despair should settle upon the grave of thy brother.[18]

Indeed, De Quincey's writings reveal the view, as represented by other
critics of his age, that the superimposition of Christian precepts onto
Sophocles' source text was a necessary sophistication and embellishment
to what was generally considered to be a rather crude simplification of the
human condition. For example in his essay "Theory of Greek Tragedy"
De Quincey states:

. . . the Greek poet used simply that faint outline of character, in its gross distinctions of good and bad which the situation itself implied. For example, the
Creon of Thebes is pretty uniformly exhibited as tyrannical and cruel . . .[19]

Steiner has also made the observation that following the French Revolution "Sophocles' text and the figure of Antigone [became] talismanic to
the European spirit"[20], and one can see Antigone as the oppressed rebel,
the struggling underdog and the champion of the disempowered as potentially analogous with the spirit of the French Revolution. Additionally
as Steiner asserts "The rights of man, as 1789 voiced them, are, em-
phatically, the rights of women"[21] and the politically iconographic power
of Antigone as the lone, single and vulnerable heroic feminine agent against
evil is not difficult to understand. Indeed, Matthew Arnold's condemna-
tion of Sophocles' Antigone (1853) is telling in the light of the writer's
Christianising moralism and perhaps such a response belies Arnold's perception of the play's inherent and dangerous ambiguity:

An action like the action of Antigone of Sophocles which turns upon the conflict
between the heroine's duty to her brother's corpse and that to the laws of her
country is no longer one in which it is possible that we should have a deep
interest.[22]

Thus, one can chart, most notably after 1789, the way in which Sophocles'
play was to transmute from a fifth century city-state polemic about the

unresolvable and ambiguous complexities of the *pharmakon* into the separative cosmological poles of Christian precepts of "good" and "evil" which, in turn, nourished the ritualised pietism of "the tradition of the oppressed". In this sense, after 1789, the *pharmakon* of Attic tragedy was supplanted with the monodimensional representation of the "remedy" of idealistic utopianism, the representation of the power of the spirit of good to overcome evil through suffering, a transmutation which Oudemans comments upon:

[It is unlikely the Greeks] . . . would have recognised the essentially romantic problem of the individual in revolt against the state.[23]

The Iconoclastic Rewrite: "Antigone" as Ritual and Conformism Confronted

Fugard's approach to Sophocles' *Antigone* is one which invokes active remembrance of the archetypal and iconographical "tradition of the oppressed" as represented by "Antigone" and to situate this in violent opposition to the political present he was experiencing in South Africa. Fugard's Rewrite engages not only our socio-historical consciousness in much the same way Marowitz reinvokes *The Merchant of Venice* for a post-Holocaust reception, but also he is confronting our geopolitical consciousness about the incongruities of our eurocentric, ritualised and canonised reading practices in and for another part of the world. Fugard is not ridiculing the canon per se, but rather he harnesses the cultural cachet of the classic for the political present, and as a result he ironically mocks the highly selective and edited perceptions we possess of "civilised" Western liberal humanist traditions to which we defer for our present moral, political and aesthetic presuppositions and justifications. *The Island* serves to actively deconstruct one of the *grands recits* enshrined in the Western liberal humanist tradition in order to draw our attention to the limits of such narratives and thus one could say that it dramaturgically imposes upon a Western eurocentric audience a process which Spivak describes as "unlearning privileged discourse"[24]. The coloniser's consciousness is thus assaulted by re-presenting his self referential traditions, including canonical texts, through the eyes of the colonised, transforming the powerless voice against the status quo from white ethnocentric and aristocratic into black, African and oppressed.

Fugard's dramaturgical reinvocation of the Sophoclean tragedy breaks open the closure represented by Western eurocentric interpretative discourse and thereby the totalisation of Western iconography is contested, heeding Gadamer's dictum that making any form of history, including the classics, into an object depends on methodological sterility because:

> The very idea of a situation means that we are not standing outside it and hence are unable to have any objective knowledge of it. We always find ourselves within a situation, and throwing light on it is a task that is never entirely finished..[25]

The radicality of recontextualisation presented by *The Island* is so emphatic that the Christian interpretative stasis[26], which for centuries has dominated the Sophoclean tragedy and which through interpretative sophistry has simplified *Antigone* into an iconographic solution and "remedy" of pietism is transformed by Fugard's Rewrite into a dialogue with the past for the present 'living' moment. Achebe, Dhlomo and others have commented on the necessity of addressing the near past in order to forge and reclaim a cultural history and have advocated the productively liberating power of negotiating with the colonial past for the independent present:

> It is clear to me that an African creative writer who tries to avoid the big social and political issues of the contemporary Africa will end up being completely irrelevant like that absurd man in the proverb who leaves the house burning to pursue a rat fleeing from the flames.[27]

Similarly, *The Island* dramaturgically negotiates with the past for the present to highlight the way in which our reading of "high" culture and the classics has colluded to create and perpetuate oppression in the present in the form of Apartheid. Fugard's play, through the use of dialogue and testimony, demonstrates how we may iconoclastically escape the bind of an essentially colonialist interpretative stasis for the present and the future.

The Rewrite as Platonic Dialogue

The hermeneutic complexity of dialogue whereby the interpreter confronts lexical ambiguity to reach an interpretative understanding has been supplanted over the centuries by a pleasure principle to reveal the stasis of knowledge of good, as presented through the canonised and Christianised reading practices of Sophocles' *Antigone*. Indeed, many documents and policy papers about the white settlers' mission in Africa bear the hallmark of moralism, paternalism and colonialism based upon adherence to interpretative stasis, clearly exemplifying how the textuality of history is often complicit with placing power, in the guise of a biased sense of "good", in ascendancy over truth. The superimposition of the Christian 'remedy' of interpretative stasis with respect to Sophocles' play is implicitly alluded to throughout *The Island* whereby the real "Antigones", John and Winston, as opposed to the representational metadramatic "Antigone", have no opportunity for dialogue with their judge and jury, the State. The silencing of dialogue for the modern day "Antigones" on Robben Island is reflected in the discussion between John and Winston about their fellow prisoner, Sipho, who has been sent to solitary confinement as a punishment for speaking::

John: What was it this time?
Winston: Complained about the food I think. Demanded to see the book of
          Prison Regulations. [Scene I, p. 204]

Fugard's Rewrite clearly exposes the inadequacy of the interpretative stasis which has silenced "Antigone", and he dramaturgically critiques the simplistic and Eurocentric notion that the resolution proffered by the "remedy" is the path to "good" for as Zuckert points out, the Platonic conversations:

> . . . not only demonstrate the inadequacy of pleasure as a definition for good; they also illustrate the need for philosophy. Socrates' signal discovery (which distinguished him from the "pre-Socratics") was not merely that human beings claimed to have knowledge they did not possess, but that they recognised their ignorance only when asked to justify themselves. Forced to defend their chosen way of life, they saw such a defence rested on a claim about what is good.[28]

Fugard's *The Island* elicits a "transformation into structure" of *Antigone* which has the effect of presenting a re-emergence of the *pharmakon*, or something approaching it, for twentieth century South Africa, a context in which the palliative "remedy" of Christian separative cosmology, as it has been traditionally re-presented with *Antigone,* is exposed as unsatisfactory and ineffectual. Indeed, Derrida has pointed out how the *pharmakon* has been devalued and misrepresented by later translations, and it is clear to see how translations which have overlooked the ambiguity of this central concept in Greek culture and art, in preference for interpretative closure, contributed to the ease of its disappearance from later Christianising interpretations:

> The common translation of the *pharmakon* by remedy—a beneficent drug—is not of course inaccurate. Not only can *pharmakon* really mean remedy and thus erase, on a certain surface of its functioning, the ambiguity of its meaning . . . Its translation by "remedy" nonetheless erases, in going outside the Greek language, the other pole reserved in the word *pharmakon*. It cancels out the resources of ambiguity and makes more difficult, if not impossible, an understanding of the context.[29]

Fugard's play highlights how the totalising interpretative "remedies" offered up by the Judeo-Christian tradition can become at the least ineffective and at the worst hypocritical, and one can discover elements of the tragic ambiguity and complexity of the *Pharmakon* as presented in the Sophoclean "Antigone" re-emerging in *The Island*. One moving example of this is displayed when John's "reported" new release date evokes in him a great rush of elation followed by depressive deflation when he realises that his "remedy" will constitute the "poison" of loss of comradeship and support for Winston. In this way, Fugard juxtaposes the easy gratification and redemptive 'remedy' of the triumphalist narrative of "the tradition of the oppressed" with the base and cruel reality of incarceration on Robben Island, and thereby John's "exemplum" release is starkly revealed to be a Pyrrhic victory over his oppressors:

> John: Remember your words when we jumped off onto the jetty?
> [*Pause. The two men look at each other.*]
>   Heavy words, Winston. You looked back at the mountains . . . 'Farewell Africa.' I've never forgotten them. That was three years ago.
> Winston: And now, for you, it's three months to go.
> [*Pause. The mood of innocent celebration has passed. John realises what his good news means to the other man.*]
> John: To hell with everything. Let's go to bed.
> [*Winston doesn't move. John finds Antigone's wig.*]
>   We'll talk about Antigone tomorrow.
> [*John prepares for bed.*]
>   Hey Winston. I just realised. My family. Princess and the children. Do you think they've been told? Jesus, man, maybe they're also saying . . . three months. Those three months are going to feel as long as the three years. Time passes slowly when you've got something . . . to wait for . . .
> [*Pause. Winston still hasn't moved. John changes his tone.*]
>   Look, in this cell we're going to forget those three months. The whole bloody thing is probably a trick anyway. So let's just forget about it. We run to the quarry tomorrow. Together. So let's sleep. [Scene 2, pp. 215–6]

The reference made to the sadistic practice of the prison guards of playing a trick on prisoners by conjuring up the fabricated expectation of release metaphorically conveys the oppressive power of triumphalist narratives like "the tradition of the oppressed". As opposed to such totalising strategies prompting productive dialogue, Fugard dramaturgically exposes how they merely encourage in those who are oppressed the unresponsive stasis of hope.

Central to the effect of Fugard's Rewrite is its dialogic structure, the dramaturgical conversation between the past and the present, and as such it is a dramaturgical riposte to the opportunistic interpretative stasis of Sophistry. Undoubtedly, Plato's diatribe against the Sophists' oratorical persuasion lies at the heart of his assault against writing, including speech writing, which he deems a lowlier and potentially subversive substitute for the honesty and spontaneity of speaking together, especially through dialogue, a point raised by Socrates in Plato's *Gorgias*:

> Socrates: And the orator does not teach juries and other bodies about right and wrong—he merely persuades them; he could hardly teach so large a number of people matters of such importance in a short time. [455]

and later,

> Socrates: I'm speaking to you now Polus—because it makes pleasure its aim instead of good, and I maintain that it is merely a knack and not an art because it has no rational account to give of the nature of the various things it offers. [465][30]

Plato, through the voice of Socrates, describes oratory, the premeditated and essentially written vehicle of the Sophists, as possessing no more claim to be a genuine art than cookery, as both aim at the immediate gratification of the consumer without any regard for his welfare, and indeed he makes the corollary between sophistry and propaganda with:

> In my view oratory is a spurious counterfeit of a branch of the art of government. [463][31]

Indeed, the "oratory" by John *as* 'Creon' towards the end of *The Island* dramaturgically exemplifies the superficiality and exhaustiveness of oratorical and sophistic messages, and indeed "Creon's" cliché-ridden tirade hardly summons up one's confidence in his powers to disclose the truth. [Scene 4] The use of parody to trivialise Creon's message enables us, the audience, to sense that the metadramatic "play" is an uneasy and disconcerting experience for John and Winston, and that "Creon's" words are hollow, deceitful and literally dead to their ears. Also, the interpretative bias of contempt and derision with respect to the metadrama's underdeveloped characterisation of "Creon" belies the inherent inequality and thus injustice of the Manichaean contest between "good" and "evil" espoused by what is shown to be the redundant and defunct Christian interpretative stasis which has appropriated the Sophoclean tragedy. In this sense, the tragic dimension of the Sophoclean tragedy as well as the redemptive teleology provided by Judeo-Christian moralism are both exposed as being redundant explanations for the horror of Apartheid, which is nothing more nor less than political oppression *in extremis*. This redressing of interpretative balance is powerfully suggested by the parodic manner in which the metadramatic "Creon" is presented as being on a par with an unsophisticated and patronising touring evangelist or a canvassing opportunistic politician, as exemplified by the hollow tone of his register which is contrasted with the eloquence with which "Antigone" speaks afterwards.

> John [as Creon]: . . . . What's that I hear? You, good man, speak up. Did I hear
> 'Hail the King'? You, good man, speak up . . . Creon's crown is as
> simple and I hope as clean as the apron Nanny wears. . . . The law is
> no more or less than a shield in your faithful servant's hand to protect
> YOU. [Scene 4, pp. 223–4]

Additionally, a sense of unease and discontent with the constancy of human suffering as represented by "Antigone" is also suggested by the recurring reference to Antigone's "necklace of nails" [Scene 4 p225] "necklace" [Scene I p 202] "necklace" [Scene I p198]. Despite providing a distorted allusion to Christ's crown of thorns, the necklace is particularly pertinent as an image of black South African punishment crime against those who are deemed to be traitors to their struggle, perhaps alluding to the perceived treachery and complicity of endorsing the mantle of the archetypal Western icon of redemptive suffering.[32] Indeed, one has only to recall Winston's difficulty in grasping the details and characterisation of the play which he is to perform to confirm that the play is little more than another prison chore for him. In this way Fugard appears to convey that Sophocles' *Antigone* can no longer summon up the experience, which according to Gadamerian hermeneutics leads to *Erlebnis*, for as opposed to the "play" of *Erlebnis*, the metadramatic play has become a self-conscious and self-referential parody:

> According to all that we have observed concerning the nature of play, this subjective distinction between oneself and the play implicit in putting up a show is not the true nature of play. Rather play itself is a transformation of such a kind that the identity of the player does not continue to exist for anybody. Everybody asks instead what is supposed to be represented, what is "meant." The players or (playwright) no longer exist, only what they are playing.[33]

Conversely, the "play" which John and Winston indulge in to wile away the tedium of prison life and to imaginatively escape their imposed silence, such as the dialogic telephone-game, does exhibit the self absorption of *Erlebnis* which typifies child's play:

> [*He is now seated on his bed-roll. After a moment's thought he holds up an empty mug as a telephone receiver and starts to dial. Winston watches him with puzzlement.*]
>
> John: Operator put me through to New Brighton, please . . . yes, New Brighton, Port Elizabeth. The number is 414624 . . . Yes, mine is local . . . local . . .
>
> Winston: The Shop.
>
> [*He sits upright with excitement as John launches into the telephone conversation.*]
>
> John: That you. Scott? Hello, man . . . how things with you? No, still inside. Give me the news man . . . you don't say. No, we don't hear anything here . . . not a word . . . What's that? Business is bad? . . . You bloody undertaker. People aren't dying fast enough. No, things are fine here . . .
>
> [*Winston, squirming with excitement, has been trying unsuccessfully to interrupt John's torrent of words and laughter. He finally succeeds in drawing John's attention.*]
>
> Winston: Who else is there? Who's with Scott?
>
> John: Hey, Scott, who's there with you? . . . On no. . . . call him to the phone, man . . .
>
> Winston: Who's it?
>
> John: [*ignoring Winston*]. Just for a minute, man, please Scott . . .
>
> [*Ecstatic response from John as another voice comes over the phone.*]
>
> [Scene 1, p. 204–205]

In "Play as the Clue to Ontological Explanation" Gadamer sees play as basic to the experience of *Erlebnis*, as opposed to play as the result of the aesthetic consciousness which confronts an object. Unlike the play with *Antigone* undertaken by Winston, whereby there is a clear distinction between the material of play and what Winston makes of it, the telephone-game exemplifies play as true self-absorption, for as Gadamer explains:

> Play fulfils its purpose only if the player loses himself in play. . . . The player experiences the game as a reality that surpasses. This is all the more the case where the game is itself "intended" as such a reality—for instance, the play which appears as *presentation for an audience*.[34]

Fugard's Rewrite alludes to the ritualisation and aesthetic distanciation thereof which has become synonymous with our reception of Sophocle's *Antigone* by juxtaposing Winston's uncomfortable pretence at playing the part of "Antigone", with the *Erlebnis* of the telephone-game in which

John and Winston participate. By extension, *The Island* makes a distinction between the stultification and conformism of interpretative stasis, as represented by the almost rote-like way John as "Creon" delivers words, and the creative productivity and *Erlebnis* of dialogue as represented by the imaginative conversation of the telephone-game.

The reworking of a classic inevitably provokes the historical consciousness of the audience by presenting two accounts of the same event, one ancient and one modern, but Fugard further engages our political consciousness by invoking and reinscribing the other binary configurations of white/black, ethnocentric/African, canonical/minority discourse, aristocratic/enslaved, myth/reality. Indeed, when one considers that one of the most outrageous and controversial laws invoked by the South African authorities during the 1950's included The Population Registration Act which forbade "mixed race" relationships, it is a supreme irony that Fugard's play should represent, as based on fact, a black African man who is cast to play for his captors one of the most feted Christian heroines of the white, bourgeois Western humanist literary tradition. In this respect Fugard's play recodes Sophocles' classic with the effect of establishing difference at the heart of similarity, and thus prompting us to interrogate the validity of our ideological assumptions, for as Linda Hutcheon points out:

> . . . double-voiced parodic forms play on the tensions created by historical awareness.[35]

This is not to suggest that *The Island* is a parody of Sophocles' play, but rather it employs parodic devices such as metadrama for its overall effect of transformation into structure. Indeed, Fugard's use of the play-within-a-play device does not constitute the Gadamerian transformation into structure; rather it is the parodic dramaturgical vehicle which prompts the transformation into structure that occurs in the enveloping play, *The Island*. Parody cannot by necessity elicit a Gadamerian transformation into structure because its intrinsic artifice is such that it does not fulfil Gadamer's criterion that ". . . Play fulfils its purpose only if the player loses himself in play."[36] Parody represents what Gadamer refers to as aesthetic differentiation whereby ". . . [W]hen a distinction is made, it is between the material and what the poet makes of it, between the poem and the conception".[37] Thus, Fugard utilises the parodic metadrama to prompt and elicit the effect of a transformation into structure which Gadamer describes with:

This gives what we called transformation into structure its full meaning. The transformation is a transformation into the true. It is not enchantment in the sense of bewitchment that waits for the redeeming word that will transform things back to what they were; rather, it is itself redemption and transformation back into true being. In being presented in play, what is emerges. It produces and brings to light what is otherwise constantly hidden and withdrawn.[38]

Rather than the re-presentation of *Antigone* and the archetype of 'the tradition of the oppressed', which is half-heartedly portrayed by John and Winston, constituting the Rewrite, it is John and Winston, the central characters of *The Island* that are the rewritten "Antigones" within the Apartheid-riven context of 1970's South Africa. Unlike the blatantly reductionist representation of the Jew in *The Merchant of Venice*[39] which from the hap of the Holocaust and its inherent historical anti-Semitic roots has subsequently elicited a transformation into structure as represented by Marowitz's *Variations*, *Antigone* is not immediately accessible as a transformation into structure by the hap of Apartheid. Rather, Fugard prompts this transformation into structure with his use of metadrama, and the subsequent radicality of metadramatic recontextualization, so that John and Winston are the rewritten "Antigones" of Apartheid, for as Gadamer points out:

To investigate the origin of the plot on which it is based is to move out of the real experience of the play if the spectator reflects about the conception behind a performance or about the proficiency of the actors. Already implicit in this kind of reflection is the aesthetic differentiation of the work itself from its representation. [*The process which is inherent to our reception of parody*] But for the content of the experience as such, as we have seen, it is not even important whether the tragic or the comic scene playing before one is taking place on the stage or in life—when one is only a spectator. What we have called a structure is one insofar as it presents itself as a meaningful whole. It does not exist in itself, nor is it encountered in a mediation (*Vermittlung*) accidental to it; rather it acquires its proper being in being mediated.[40]

The rewritten "Antigones" of *The Island* not only represent the transformation into structure of *Antigone* for the Apartheid context, but also they emphasise the autobiographical *Erlebnis* of the Rewrite, whereby the historical precursors to the production of Fugard's play are incorporated into its dramaturgy. This autobiographical *Erlebnis* concerns the dramaturgical acknowledgement of the way in which the South African regime silenced (by incarceration on Robben Island) a member of the Serpent Players drama troupe, Norman Ntshinga, during a season of

Antigone in which he was playing the part of Haemon. Ntshinga was charged with being a member of the ANC in June 1965, and it is interesting to note that Fugard's 1973 reworking of *Antigone* defiantly deletes the Haemon character as if to dramatically emasculate the efforts of the South African regime almost ten years earlier, when they brought Ntshinga/ Haemon to an abrupt silence. Indeed, as this historical anecdote reveals even when black actors attempted to play the role of "Antigone" who has come to iconographically represent the never-ending procession of 'the tradition of the oppressed' they were silenced as being potentially subversive.[41] Such testimony bears witness to the measure of the limits and boundaries which Western eurocentric cultural paternalism imposes when under threat, a fact alluded to by Fugard's dramaturgical presentation of the staging of *Antigone* by John and Winston for the 'entertainment' of their captors within the confines of the state prison walls.

Thus, to merely parody the "tradition of the oppressed" through the recontextualised re-presentation of *Antigone* would not elicit the intratextual experience of *Erlebnis*, and "transformation into structure", and would fail to invoke the consciousness of the audience about the play's legacy of appropriative Christian complacency. The aesthetic distanciation provided by parody would not convey the Benjaminian dictum that "the tradition of the oppressed" "teaches us that the state of emergency in which we live is not the exception but the rule"[42]—a view echoed by the character, Rieux, in Camus's *The Plague* when he reflects on the fact that survival does not ensure immunity of future plague:

> He knew what those jubilant crowds did not know but could have learnt from books; that the plague bacillus never dies or disappears for good; that it can lie dormant for years and years . . . and that perhaps the day would come when, for the bane and the enlightenment of men, it would rouse up its rats again and send them forth to die in a happy city.[43]

However by *incorporating the parodic device* of metadrama Fugard focuses our attention not only toward the intratextual unity which typifies *Erlebnis*, but also this Brechtian-like alienation technique preempts the danger of slipping into an unconscious, subjectivist and empathetic mode of reception, so that the play:

> . . . suggests the immediacy with which something real is grasped—unlike something which one presumes to know but which is unattested by one's own experience . . . What is experienced is always what one has experienced oneself.[44]

In this way, "Antigone" is transformed from the archetypal but mythologically distanced representation or reified souvenir (*Andenken*) of the "tradition of the oppressed" to be realised, through a fusion of conscious *Erlebnis* and *Erfahrung*, as a living part of our cultural tradition. In this respect, Fugard's reference to "Antigone" produces the obverse effect of being a dramaturgical device to arouse the empathetic abstraction of sentimentalism rooted in conformism, or to quote Blanchot as an:

> . . . ephemeral character who is born and dies each evening in order to make himself [herself] extravagantly seen, killed by the performance that makes him invisible.[45]

Indeed, Fugard reworks *Antigone* in order that we might recognise how outmoded our frames of cognitive reference can become, and how they can serve to indict us in the perpetuation and tacit endorsement of atrocities like Apartheid. In this respect, the notion of textuality as history becomes even more complicated, for just as *The Merchant of Venice* is a text which, as discussed, is inextricably linked to the promulgation of the anti-Semitic discourse which helped to contribute to the Holocaust, so too, comforting and anodyne readings of the classics, like *Antigone* perpetuate artificial frames of reference which culturally sanction suffering and oppression. As Felman astutely observes:

> We blind ourselves to the historical reality of that past by reducing its obscurity to a paradigm of readability—an easily intelligible and safely remote Manichaean allegory of good and evil.[46]

Like canonised reading practices, ritual as historical repetition subsumes history by becoming historical, and our knowledge as opposed to an understanding of 'the tradition of the oppressed' is akin to this process. An uncanny effect of Fugard's dramaturgical release of "the tradition of the oppressed" for the moment and for the oppressed in the present-day South Africa, as opposed to repeating a methodological response to that which has been deemed a representation of "the tradition of the oppressed", is that the *pharmakon* of the original fifth century tragedy has reappeared once again, and it is useful to revert back to Plato's *Phaedrus* to elaborate this point. King Thadmus, having been presented with the new phenomenon of writing, the *pharmakon* of writing which might be at once an aid and an obstacle to learning, a remedy and a poison, is deprecating and critical whilst simultaneously providing Plato with a dialogic vehicle to critique Sophistry:

> But the king said "Theuth, my master of arts, to one man it is given to create the elements of an art, to another to judge the extent of harm and usefulness it will

have for those who are going to employ it. And now, since you are father of written letters your paternal good will has led you to pronounce that this invention will produce forgetfulness in the souls of those that have learned it because they will not need to exercise their memories, being able to rely on what is written using the stimulus of external marks that are alien to themselves rather than from within, their own unaided powers to call things to mind. So it's not a remedy for memory, but for reminding, that you have discovered. And as for wisdom you're equipping your pupils with only a semblance of it, not with truth. Thanks to you and your invention, your pupils will be widely read without benefit of a teacher's instruction; in consequence they'll entertain the delusion that they have wide knowledge, while they are, in fact for the most part incapable of real judgement. They will also be difficult to get on with since they will be men filled with the conceit of wisdom, not men of wisdom.[47]

King Thadmus' words fittingly convey the way in which canonisation and subsequent ritualisation of reading practices are not representative of truth, but merely repeated knowledge. The "tradition of the oppressed" too often becomes conformist and even a ritualised form of empathy in our consciousness, a stultification which Benjamin warned against in his "Theses on the Philosophy of History":

For every image of the past that is not recognised by the present as one of its own concerns threatens to disappear irretrievably . . . In every era the attempt must be made anew to wrest tradition away from a conformism that is about to overpower it.[48]

Derrida's work on the *pharmakon* of writing emphasises the way in which writing as *pharmakon* can have the effect of making the logoi the orphan, abandoned by its life force, its father, or to revert back to Gadamerian terminology, the immediacy of *Erlebnis*:

All translations into languages that are the heirs and depositories of Western metaphysics thus produce on the *pharmakon* an effect of analysis that violently destroys it, reduces it to one of its simple elements by interpreting it, paradoxically enough, in the light of the ulterior developments it itself has made possible. Such an interpretative translation is thus as violent as it is impotent: it destroys the *pharmakon* but at the same time forbids itself access to it, leaving it untouched in its reserve.[49]

Like Derrida's "orphans" *Antigone* has been adopted by interpretative Christian separative cosmological moralism and thus deprived of the inherent, innate and dynamic power, which the ambiguity of the *pharmakon* can present, if the *pharmakon* is not silenced by either one of its poles, for as Derrida states: "There is no such thing as a harmless remedy. The *pharmakon* can never be simply beneficial."[50] King Thadmus' critique of writing is thus directed at writing's potentially stultifying and embalming effect in the name of knowledge (particularly when placed in the hands of the *doxosophoi*) with its corresponding loss of spontaneity, life and understanding, so that the logoi become orphans as opposed to filial offspring of *Erlebnis* who are as Derrida points out:

> Alive enough to protest on occasion and to let themselves be questioned; capable too in contrast to written things, of responding when their father is there. They are their father's responsible presence.[51]

Once abandoned, the "orphan" texts subjected to appropriative interpretative stasis lose all filial continuity, and in a sense lose their power to react against their precursors, their tradition. In this way interpretative repetition sets in, and tradition degenerates into conformism and ritual, ignoring the truth of the dictum that there cannot be tradition without change, and there cannot be change without tradition.

The Rewrite, by virtue of its very name would suggest the attempt to deprive the logoi of its life force or *zoon*, for as shown, writing may have the effect that ambiguity becomes eroded and structured for sophistic ends, although as Plato concedes writing possesses the double edged properties of both remedy and poison. However, because of the dialogic nature of the Rewrite, that is its conversation with tradition through the classic, the lifeforce of speech is enabled once more to be heard over the centuries within the context of performative *Erlebnis*. The dialogic nature of the Rewrite, the dramaturgical dialogue between past and present, prevents memory from becoming a memorial, like the Judeo-Christian interpretative separative cosmology with which *Antigone* has been appropriated over the centuries. In this respect, the Rewrite is dialogically distinct from the project of the Sophists:

> What Plato is attacking in Sophistics, therefore, is not simply recourse to memory but, within such recourse, the substitution of the mnemonic device for live memory, of the prosthesis for the organ; the perversion that consists of replacing a limb by a thing here, substituting the passive, mechanical "by-heart" for the active reanimation of knowledge for its reproduction in the present. The boundary (between inside and outside, living and non-living) separates not only speech from writing but also memory as an unveiling (re-)producing a presence from re-memoriation as the mere repetition of a monument; truth is distinct from its sign, being as distinct from types. The outside does not begin at the point where what we now call the psychic and physical meet, but at the point where the *mneme*, instead of being present to itself in its life as a movement of truth, is supplanted by the archive, evicted by a sign of re-memoration or of com-memoration.[52]

Such sterile ritualisation is founded upon the erroneous notion that tradition binds us, when in fact it can be a source of all change and rupture, and can be the *zoon* which nourishes the hermeneutic "offspring" of the present, a fact dramaturgically emphasised by *The Island*. As Benjamin pointed out a true tradition of the oppressed must be vibrant, and must not be allowed to fall into the sterility of ritual and conformism. It is the aporia between the two notions of 'the tradition of the oppressed', as ritual or as experience, that is explored by Fugard's play, not merely to emphasise the cultural guilt of the Western liberal humanist "ritualised" tradition, but in order to awaken our consciousness to oppression and the often ostensibly anodyne and comforting way in which it operates in the present.

Hap and Testimony in *The Island*

Camus acknowledged that "consciousness is always lagging behind history"[53] —a point that illustrates the way the 'hap' of history can often be the devastating outcome of a denial of the way in which our outmoded frames of reference may assume ridiculous, and more importantly, dangerous and inhumane proportions. Camus was to expound his view that the artist must be alert to the way that ". . . history rushes onwards and thought reflects . . . [and] this inevitable backwardness becomes even more pronounced the faster History speeds up . . ."[54] when he stated:

> Indeed, history's amphitheatre has always contained the martyr and the lion. The former relied on eternal consciousness and the latter on raw historical meat. But until now the artist was on the sidelines. He used to sing purposely . . . to encourage the martyr and make the lion forget his appetite. But now the artist is in the amphitheatre. Of necessity his voice is not quite the same; it is not nearly so firm.
> . . . To create today is to create dangerously. *Any publication is an act, and that act exposes one to the passions of an age that forgives nothing* . . . The questioning of art by the artist has many reasons . . . Among the best explanations is the feeling the contemporary artist has of lying or indulging in useless words if he pays no attention to history.[55]

The interpretative stasis which typifies the perpetuation of the myth of the 'tradition of the oppressed', the everlasting battle between the "martyr" and the "lion", is what Fugard seeks to expose and eradicate, because he, like Camus, considers it to be the residual effect of a lack of artistic commitment to disclose socio-historical "truth".[56] One way to capture the *Erlebnis* of art, devoid of subjectified aesthetic distance, is through the use of testimony, which as Felman points out, has the power to elicit:

. . . a performative engagement between consciousness and history, [to make] a readjustment between the integrative scope of words and the unintegrated impact of events.[57]

The testimonial dimension of *The Island* brings an immediacy and contemporanaeity which compels the audience to question his aesthetic and political assumptions in a similar way to the process employed by Camus in *L'Etranger*. However, as opposed to presenting and re-presenting a day in the life of Meursault within one text and thus enforcing the reader to engage in a purposive re-evaluation of the protagonist's guilt or innocence, Fugard intratextually juxtaposes Sophocles' *Antigone* with *The Island* in order to engage *our* socio-historical consciousness and thus arouse a self-awareness of *our* own "cultural" culpability and collusion in the perpetration of Apartheid. The dramaturgical testimony represented by Fugard's play does not lapse into propaganda or crass oratory because through prompting historically effected consciousness our complicity is emphasised, that is our complicity in perpetuating triumphalist and redemptive narratives like the "tradition of the oppressed" which in turn have served, through aesthetic distanciation, to cushion us from and even justify harsh social realities. In this respect, Fugard textualises the event of Apartheid as being inextricably textually interwoven with our cultural heritage, such as the classic *Antigone*, and in so doing he dramaturgically implicates us in the testimony of the silenced "John" and "Winston", in order to make us:

. . . apprehend . . . the ways in which our cultural frames of reference and our pre-existing categories which delimit and determine our perception of reality have failed, essentially, both to contain and to account for the scale of what has happened in contemporary history.[58]

To refer back to the Gadamerian hermeneutic, which serves as the interpretative "model" here, Fugard thus engages our Eurocentric assumptions and prejudice in order to elicit new meanings and understanding, for as Gadamer states:

Just as the recipient of a letter understands the news that it contains and first sees things with the eyes of the person who wrote the letter—i.e., considers what he writes as true, and is not trying to understand the writer's peculiar opinions as such—so also do we understand traditionary texts on the basis of expectations of meaning drawn from our own prior relation to the subject matter. And just as we believe the news reported by a correspondent because he was present or is better informed, so too we are fundamentally open to the possibility that the writer of a transmitted text is better informed than we are, with our prior opinion. It is only when the attempt to accept what is said as true fails that we try to "understand" the text, psychologically or historically, as another's opinion. The prejudice of completeness, then, implies not only this formal element—that a text should completely express its meaning—but also that what it says should be the complete truth. Here again we see that understanding means, primarily, to understand the content of what is said, and only secondarily to isolate and understand another's meaning as such.[59]

Felman has pointed out how the dialogic properties of testimony, which by necessity are made on the assumption that somebody is being spoken to and addressed, represent a discursive strategy that shatters the solipsistic insularity of a culture of narcissism whereby the audience and indeed the artist can assume a comfortable and unthreatened distance from the issues confronted in art. Similarly, Fugard's Rewrite provides a vehicle for testimony for the long-silenced and oppressed black population of South Africa by ironically reinvoking one of the iconographic figures of the 'tradition of the oppressed' as enshrined in the self-same Western liberal humanist tradition that is implicated in the atrocity of Apartheid. It is the testimonial dimension of Fugard's Rewrite that elicits *Erlebnis*, and thus refuses the audience the opportunity to escape implication in the present day events to which John and Winston bear witness, events which are, as the play discloses, inextricably linked to the interpretative stasis with which we insulate the classics. Felman, with particular reference to the literature of the Holocaust, but which, I would suggest is equally as relevant to the "silenced" voice of those who lived for decades under the oppression of Apartheid, has identified the compelling necessity of the narrative of testimony when negotiating in the present with the past:

> The specific task of literary testimony is . . . to open up in the belated witness, which the reader now historically becomes, the imaginative capability of perceiving history—what is happening to others—*in one's own body*, with the power of sight (of insight) usually afforded by one's own immediate physical involvement.[60]

Antigone is revivified, *not repeated,* through the life story of John and Winston as shaped by the historical hap of Apartheid, an atrocity contained by the frame of reference which has been perpetuated by the sterile consciousness produced by the promulgation of a canonised reading practice and discourse like the "tradition of the oppressed". Fugard incorporates the metadramatic *Antigone* into the enveloping play in order to invite, by contrast, the reader/audience to reconsider the appropriatively silenced "Antigone" of the past in and for the present. Thus, we are compelled to a "response-ability"[61] by the inclusionist dramaturgical device of testimony, unlike the unseen audience of captors and prison guards who only witness the production of Antigone by John and Winston and who by extension do not hear or have any "immediate physical involvement" in the testimony. John and Winston testify to the plight of many poor, uneducated and deprived black South Africans, but also by way of the theatrical theme running through the play they testify to the plight of Fugard's co-authors, John Kani and Winston Ntshona, and also Norman Ntshinga, the black actor who was arrested during a production of Antigone in 1965. In this sense Fugard's Rewrite emphasises the reality of all the "Antigones" who have been and continue to be silenced in the theatre and in society, and in so doing he prompts the audience to confront their own, very real, implication in the perpetuation of such oppression, as opposed to acquiring the comfortable aesthetic distanciation afforded to the classics by ritualised and canonised reading practices. Thus, testimony, and by extension the act of witnessing the testimony, are forms of action or *Erlebnis* which are themselves modes not merely of accounting for, but of going through, a change, or to use Gadamer's terminology "transformation into structure."

Fugard's use of metadrama is essential to the effect of testimony because it creates a sense of getting behind-the-scenes realism to the experience represented on stage which in turn reminds the audience of their role as witness to the testimony, unlike the 'unseen' audience of captors and prison guards who view *Antigone* according to the ritualised monodimensional interpretative stasis which has contributed to the frame of reference with which we rationalise suffering. In this sense, the audience is immediately implicated in responding to the testimony, for to avoid such responsiblity would be to cast themselves in the role of the unseen mass that forms the audience within the play within the play.

Fugard's reinvocation of the Christianising myth of 'the tradition of the oppressed' as represented by "Antigone" is akin to Camus' allegorisation of the horrors of the Second World War and the Holocaust with "the Plague" in the novel of the same name, because as Felman states,

> ". . . the Plague designates not simply a metaphorically substitutive event, but an event that is *historically impossible: an event without referent.* "It is impossible," say the doctors at the first signs of the plague, "everybody knows that it has vanished from the Western world."[62]

Because the "tradition of the oppressed" has become canonised and ritualised, in part by the stultifying and moribund manner in which our cultural heritage and its reception has been appropriated, Fugard's allusion to the teleological tale's mythical qualities is similar to the way in which Camus' allegorises the Holocaust with "the Plague". The Plague, a horrific, but almost mythical manifestation of the unhygenic and "uncivilised" past, is presented by Camus to convey the way in which the hangover from the erroneous Enlightenment belief in progress may often make us blind and deaf to the realities of the present, just as stultifying mythologies like the 'tradition of the oppressed' can contribute and even sanction complacency in the face of atrocities. As Felman points out:

> The Plague [the Holocaust] is disbelieved [by the protagonists in the novel] because it does not enter and cannot be framed by any existing frame of reference (be it of knowledge or belief). Because our perception of reality is moulded by frames of reference, what is outside them, however imminent and otherwise conspicuous remains historically invisible, unreal, and can only be encountered by a systematic disbelief.[63]

Fugard reverts to the classic, *Antigone*, to highlight our cultural implication in the complacency about, if not the actual construction of, subsequent historical atrocities, but also by doing so his work dramaturgically exemplifies the way in which historical hap is intrinsic to our historically effected consciousness according to the Gadamerian interpretative model. The historical hap of Apartheid, like the Holocaust, is such that the historical imperative to bear witness could essentially not be met during the actual occurrences (the former because of draconian cultural oppression and the latter because of the Nazis' concerted efforts to cover up the evidence) and it is for this very reason that testimonial art is of such importance to bear witness to these atrocities after the event. Indeed, with respect to the power of testimony and its particular pertinence for the late twentieth century, Elie Wiesel has stated:

> If the Greeks invented tragedy, the Romans the epistle, and the Renaissance the sonnet, our generation invented a new literature, that of testimony.[64]

Admittedly, *The Island* was produced and staged during the Apartheid regime and did manage to convey a political message to a limited audience in South Africa, but in a sense the very danger of producing the play and its subsequent improvisational and unscripted form, is a dramaturgical testimony to the horror that was Apartheid that is itself intrinsic to the play but which can only be disclosed after the event or hap. The very dramaturgical history of the play, (and by *play* I am referring to the source text as well as the Rewrite) is part of the subsequent dramaturgical effect of *The Island*—it has literally broken free of the silence not only of the South African censorship laws, but more importantly the iconography of the "tradition of the oppressed":

. . . repossessing one's life story through giving testimony is itself a form of action, of change, which has to actually pass through, in order to continue and complete the process of survival after liberation. The event must be reclaimed because even if successfully repressed, it nevertheless invariably plays a decisive formative role in who one comes to be and how one comes to live one's life.[65]

The Rewrite and Translating as *Erlebnis*

In the course of their research into testimony Felman and Laub have referred to Paul de Man's work on the role of the translator in response to Benjamin's "The Task of the Translator".[66] The translator's task, I would suggest, can be viewed as a similar project to that of the Rewrite, and it is illuminating in the context of considering the afterlife of a source text and the way in which historical hap can disclose truth after the textual event. De Man's reflections on Shelley's work in the light of his accidental death by drowning are pertinent to our understanding of not only the way Apartheid has rewritten *Antigone*, but also how the more localised and biographical hap during the conception and subsequent performance of Fugard's play have not only shaped the play's production, but are also unconscious forces which have rearticulated our understanding of Fugard's text as the Rewrite of *Antigone*:

> [The] defaced body is present in the margin of the last manuscript page and has become an inseparable part of the poem. At this point, figuration and cognition are actually interrupted by an event which shapes the text but which is not present in its represented or articulated meaning. It may seem a freak of chance to have a text thus moulded by an actual occurrence, yet the reading of The Triumph of Life establishes that this mutilated textual model exposes the wound of a fracture that lies hidden in all texts . . . In Shelley's absence the task of . . . reinscribing the disfiguration now devolves entirely on the reader. The final test of reading, in The Triumph of Life depends on how one reads the textuality of this event, how one disposes of Shelley's body . . . For what we have done with the dead Shelley and with all the other dead bodies . . . is simply to bury them in their own texts, made into epitaphs and monumental graves . . . They have transformed into historical and aesthetic objects.[67]

Paul de Man's notion of the role of the translator as being one which, if successful, denies the apocalyptic or apologetic discourse which typifies textual closure is in many ways similar to the project of the Rewrite, according to this Gadamerian interpretation:

> Reading as disfiguration to the very extent that it resists historicism, turns out to be more reliable than the products of historical archaeology . . . To monumentalize this observation into a *method* of reading would be to regress from the rigour exhibited by Shelley which is exemplary reading because it refuses to be generalised into a system.[68]

Thus, just as de Man emphasises that the translation should not seek to overthrow the original, the Rewrite does not seek to eradicate the source text, for to do so is to efface history, or to use Felman's words to evade "articulation of a radical inarticulateness of contemporary history."[69] Indeed, as discussed in Chapter III such effacement of history by replacing the source text, is precisely what Wesker's *Shylock* attempts with *The Merchant of Venice*, and in so doing the very anti-Semitism which Wesker finds abhorrent in the source text is not addressed but apologetically effaced. It is the articulation of history, to bear witness in total perfectibility, that is at once attempted and failed by the Rewrite, for it dramaturgically exposes how history which is always in the process of becoming precludes us from reaching such interpretative closure and totalisation. Conversely, if we choose to efface history or hap from our consciousness we are left with the blind sterility and potential injustice of interpretative stasis—a demise highlighted in Fugard's play when Winston throws down his makeshift "Antigone" persona with disgust and abjection:

> Winston: There he goes. Serves him right. I just hope Hodoshe teaches him a lesson. Antigone is important. Antigone this. Antigone that. Shit, man. Nobody can sleep in this bloody cell because of all that bullshit. Polynices. Eteocles. The other prisoners too. Antigone. I hope Hodoshe gives it to him.
> [He is now at the cell door. He listens, then moves over to the wig on the floor and circles it. He finally picks it up. Moves back to the cell door to make sure no one is coming. The water bucket gives him an idea. He puts on the wig, and after some difficulty, manages to see his reflection in the water. A good laugh, which he cuts off abruptly. He moves around the cell trying out a few of Antigone's poses. None of them work. He feels a fool. He finally tears off the wig and throws it down on the floor with disgust.] (Scene 2 p211)

In this scene Fugard powerfully exposes the limits of the iconography of the "tradition of the oppressed" for the realities of John and Winston, for by highlighting Winston's humiliation at having to assume a female role he poignantly conveys the inadequacy of such totalising triumphalist narratives for John and Winston, even though we know that neither character fully appreciates the message their actions disclose. Thus Fugard does not make his characters preach or proselytise about the inadequacy and injustice of Western Enlightenment narratives, (to do so would be merely using drama to crudely espouse political opinion and dogma) rather he ironically presents their unembellished testimony to the sheer horror and degradation of their existence to further emphasise the inherent cruelty and barbarism of the Western liberal humanist interpretative stasis of the source text, and its insidious implication in the dangerous perpetuation of complacent and canonised forms of cultural consciousness. In this sense testimony is quite distinct from a sermon or confession, because it is not complete and discrete; rather it is inherently fragmentary and unfinished. Testimony has the potential to artistically bear witness to what we do not know of our lived historical relation to events of our times, just as it is our retrospective witnessing of *Antigone* after the hap of Apartheid that compels us to acknowledge ourselves as being accomplices to barbarism.

Thus, just as the translator should strive for a continuous disarticulation of any illusory historical closure or totalisation, so too, the Rewrite dramaturgically exemplifies the process that makes, as Benjamin stated:

> . . . both the original and translation recognisable as fragments of a greater language . . . [70]

In this respect, the Rewrite dramaturgically "testifies" and bears witness to history in the form of the classic, not by the effacement of imitation but through the creativity of *Erlebnis* in the present, the *Erlebnis* of a singular, transitory and ephemeral monadic truth. Through historically effected consciousness the Rewrite evolves from the after-life of the source text, not as repetition but as historically effected recognition, just as Benjamin's "fragments" become recognisable or re-known. Such hermeneutic recognition is quite distinct from an interpretative striving to be faithful to the letter of the source text and the source text's context, for to do so is merely to strive to copy itself into disappearance, for as Gadamer observes:

> The essence of a copy is to have no other task but to resemble the original. The measure of its success is that one recognises the original in the copy. This means that its nature is to lose its own independent existence and serve entirely to mediate what is copied . . . A copy tries to be nothing but the reproduction of something and has its only function in identifying it (e.g., as a passport photo or a picture in a sales catalogue). A copy effaces itself in the sense that it functions as a means and, like all means, loses its function when it achieves its end. It exists by itself in order to efface itself in this way . . . Thus it fulfils itself in its self-effacement. [71]

The Rewrite neither attempts the self-effacement of the faithful "copy" nor the imposition of a discourse of readability which leads to discrete interpretative closure. Instead, like de Man's perception of the translation, the Rewrite is a performative engagement with the afterlife which subsequent history shapes for the "historical" classic:

> [Translation] is associated with another word that Benjamin constantly uses, the word *uberleben*, to live beyond your own death in a sense. The translation belongs

not to the life of the original, the original is already dead, but the translation
belongs to the afterlife of the original, thus assuming and confirming the death of
the original.[72]

Erlebnis and Praise Poetry—Antigone
as Apartheid's Anti-Hero

Unlike Freudian, Marxist and other critical approaches to texts which are
driven by the method and principle that there must always be an end-
point to the process of textual or rhetorical decoding, Fugard's play exemplifies the Gadamerian hermeneutic of *Erlebnis* which through historical
and totally serendipitous hap may result in an ephemeral transient sense
of end-meaning or awakened consciousness, but which is not motivated
by it. In a sense, the Rewrite revisits the paradigmatic source text for its
own syntagmatic, albeit transitory, purposes. In this sense Fugard's play
clearly illustrates the transitory and ephemeral constraints within which
the Rewrite operates, which sacrifices notions of aesthetic autonomy
(which, as shown are implicated in the continuation of dangerously outmoded traditions) for a new, historically effected consciousness of understanding and contingent truth. Thus the lack of methodology which typifies the Rewrite exemplifies many of the critical precepts of
deconstructionism, but with the important distinction that historical consciousness of 'hap' is its unintentional impetus. The Rewrite, in an even
less methodological manner than deconstructionism, does not adhere to
Hillis Miller's dictum to submit to the law of the text and adamantly refuse
to be seduced into treating textuality as somehow giving access to a realm
of extra textual themes; rather, it deconstructs the source text because
and in spite of historically effected consciousness. The Rewrite conforms
to Norris's description of deconstructionist technique, but not in order to
release all texts from all other wordly and supposedly logocentric concerns, but to awaken our consciousness of the world and the part culture
plays in perpetuating sterile and defunct notions of static logocentricism:

> What occurs in the text, as distinct from its reading by hoodwinked or 'mystified'
> interpreters, is a complicated process of figural exchange which on the one hand
> openly solicits such a reading, while on the other it provides all the necessary
> materials for its own rhetorical deconstruction.[73]

Undoubtedly, the Nietzschean notion of "will to power" is the motivating impetus behind much word-play and sophistry and other approaches
which allow the text and the word to supersede any other worldly attempts
we might have to understanding or wisdom, in contradistinction to the

dialogic route of philosophical inquiry to *aletheia*—a practice exemplified by the Rewrite. Like cookery, the sophistic roots of interpretative persuasion rest on offering pleasure, a resolution and a "remedy", an uncomplicated effect elicited and echoed by the interpretative stasis based on pietism and conformism that ritualises notions about "Antigone" as icon of 'the tradition of the oppressed'. Interpretation which is based upon the pleasure principle or remedy, that is, based upon pandering to the recipient's desire to make up a deficiency or lack, is analogous to slaking one's thirst when parched or sating one's hunger when famished, a point expanded by Gadamer:

> But is all longing really of such a nature that it depends upon a deficiency, upon what I lack? If such were the case that which is longed for would cease to be good once my need were fulfilled. And is there not something dear which remains when the bad thing, the privation, is gone? Is all longing a need which has passed when it is satisfied in the way that thirst is quenched when one has drunk something? Is it really sufficient to say that one values something to drink only when one is thirsty? Or is it not much more the case that one enjoys something which is not to be washed down with water and the goodness of which does not depend on my being thirsty and having nothing else around to drink. This trivial example can easily be carried over into the realm of friendship. Does the proper attraction which brings and holds friends together consist in a person's being for another what the other lacks? Or is there a mode of attraction which is not governed by the law of self-termination but which of itself nourishes and augments itself, as it were, so that we can say of friends that they are always becoming more for each other? [74]

In this respect, Plato, and in turn Gadamer, refute what they perceive as the dangerous tradition of education which had always presented the moral truths of any given time using models taken from the Homeric myths, received through interpretative stasis or, to pursue the previous analogy, through imbibing an expeditious ancient 'remedy' for a present vitamin deficiency:

> The real object of Plato's criticism is not the degenerate forms of contemporary art and the perception of the older, classical poetry which the contemporary taste in art had defined. Rather it is the contemporary morality and moral education which had established itself upon the basis of poetic formulations of the older morality and which, in adhering to ageing moral forms found itself defenceless against arbitrary perversions of those forms brought on by the spirit of sophism. Accordingly Socrates rejects the current interpretations of poetry and questions whether we still understand the wisdom of the ancient poets at all. It may be that in a world defined by binding actions and definitely prescribed morals the words of these "divine men" were the most noble and powerful statement of the moral world edification. But in a time of decline a message which could stop the advancing

corruption of the political spirit was not to be found in even the loftiest poetry of the past.[75]

Fugard's play is replete with images and symbols which highlight the dangers of psychological ritualisation, like the interpretative stasis of "the tradition of the oppressed", which through the power of repetition ceases to be questioned or challenged. Fugard makes a sinister and symbolic reference to the soul-destroying aspects of ritualised interpretation by describing, in some detail, the ritualised Sisyphian prison regime which John and Winston play out every day:

> Their heads are shaven. It is an image of back breaking and grotesquely futile labour. Each in turns fills a wheelbarrow and then with great effort pushes it to where the other man is digging and empties it. As a result the piles of sand never diminish. Their labour is interminable. The only sounds are their grunts as they dig, the squeal of the wheelbarrows as they circle the cell, and the hum of the Hodoshe, the green carrion fly. [Scene I, p. 195]

Through descriptions like the above Fugard is making an implicit criticism of the futility of triumphalist narratives, which through the ossifying power of ritual may transform themselves into psychological living deaths as precipitated by the dehumanising "grunts" and the waiting, "circling", almost vulture-like, wheelbarrows and hodoshe. It would appear, that in reality, the only redemption offered by ritualised triumphalist narratives is the long-anticipated grave and death. Additionally Fugard reinvokes the traditions and rituals of childhood throughout the play, but not to analogise the carefree and unburdened existence of Africa's mythical infancy, rather to dramaturgically suggest the potentially formative period of development and growth for the blacks in the South African context which could result in the tranquilising obedience to mindless rules set by the Nanny state or become the initiation of the rites of passage into freedom and independence. Fugard's references to childhood present the re-emergence of the *pharmakon* of *Antigone*, as being either the interpretation of the orphan text according to the wilful appropriation of ritualised tradition, or to be the child which questions the tradition from which it attempts to assert its independence, prefiguring the final struggle before the dismantling of Apartheid and the institution of a nascent multicultural South African republic. The abjection scene in the play is a turning point because it dramaturgically reflects the *pharmakon* of Antigone's possible adherence to the role of martyrdom which interpretative stasis has allotted to her, and on the other hand, her strength to break through the silent suffering which has been imposed upon her by a textual living death down the centuries. Winston's disgust and abjection at the mirror-image as "Antigone" confronting him dramaturgically captures the ambiguity of *Antigone* during the Apartheid regime, as well as implicitly suggesting the birth of independent subjectivity as defined by Kristeva's abjection theory.[76] Unlike Lacan's mirror-stage, that he identifies as heralding the conception of a sense of self-unity that it does not actually experience itself, Kristeva identifies a primal repression of undifferentiated being called the *chora*, prior to the mirror stage. Before abjection, when the child is immersed in the chora, being is *undifferentiated*, and it is only through a process of abjection—that is expelling the mother's body from its own self, that the child begins to form personal boundaries and then can experience mirror identification with alien images:

> If it be true that the abject simultaneously beseeches and pulverises the subject, one can understand that it is experienced at the peak of its strength when that subject, weary of fruitless attempts to identify with something on the outside, finds the impossible within; when it finds that the impossible constitutes its very being, that it is none other than abject. The abjection of self would be the culminating form that experience of the subject to which it is revealed that all its objects are based merely on the inaugural loss that laid the foundations of its own being.[77]

Similarly, Winston's abjection at assuming the disguise of "Antigone" is clearly illustrated throughout the play, either symbolically or directly with for example:

> Winston: . . . Everytime I run to the quarry . . . Nyah . . . nyah . . . Here comes Antigone. . . . Help the poor lady . . . Well, you can go to hell with your Antigone. [Scene 2, p 208]

However, by the time Winston attempts to differentiate himself from identification through the mirror-stage as represented in the water bucket scene his sense of abjection is so great that he rejects the disguise offered to him by the Nanny state, the teleology of the oppressed. This scene symbolically represents the nascent free South Africa in evolution, and it ironically affirms the words used by John when he was attempting to persuade Winston to don the disguise of martyrdom:

> John: . . . But just remember this brother, nobody laughs forever. There'll come a time when they'll stop laughing, and that will be the time our Antigone hits them with her words. [Scene 2, p209]

In effect, the disguise of Antigone is understood for what it is by Winston, to such an extent that his new-found sense of identity is revealed to us by his failure to "play" the part at the end of the play. In this respect the self-effacement represented by the mirror image in the cell water bucket has reasserted in Winston a new sense of identity and selfhood, almost like a rebirth in the face of imminent disappearance through assimilation, for as Gadamer states:

> . . . the ideal copy would be a mirror image, for its being really does disappear; it exists only for someone looking into the mirror, and is nothing beyond its appearance. But in fact it is not a picture or a copy at all, for it has not separate existence.[78]

Winston's claim for a "separate existence" releases the *pharmakon* of "Antigone" who, as opposed to the role of martyr promulgated by Christian interpretative stasis, re-emerges, and gives voice to the liberated and independent "Antigone" that Winston has become:

> [*Tearing off his wig and confronting the audience as Winston, not Antigone.*]
> Winston: Gods of our Fathers. My Land. My Home
> Time waits no longer. I go now to my living death, because I honoured those things to which honour belongs. [Scene 4, p. 227]

Plato, and Gadamer after him, point out the deleterious effects of the promulgation of aesthetic consciousness and the subjectification of art which ultimately considers the experience of art "to be the discontinuity of experiences"[79] in much the same way that interpretative stasis can lead to the disassociation of consciousness:

> Pure seeing and pure hearing are dogmatic abstractions that artificially reduce phenomena. Perception always includes meaning. Thus to seek the unity of the work of art solely in its form as opposed to its content is a perverse formalism.[80]

Similarly, Fugard dramaturgically explores the dangers of the practice of subjectifying art, whereby aesthetic distanciation reduces the classics to the ritualised interpretative stasis which, for example, has condemned *Antigone* to be an icon of "the tradition of the oppressed". Indeed, the rigidity of interpretation exhibited by John and Winston with respect to their staging of *Antigone* for their captors, expresses the sense of sterility and lifelessness which the dramaturgical motif for "the tradition of the oppressed" called "Antigone" has for these persecuted actors:

Winston: Only last night you tell me that this Antigone is a bloody . . . what
you call it . . . legend. A Greek one at that. Bloody thing never even
happened. Not even history. Look, brother, I got no time for bullshit.
Fuck legends. Me? I live my life here. I know why I'm here, and it's
history, not legends. I had my chat with a magistrate in Cradock and
now I'm here. Your Antigone is a child's play, man. [Scene 2, p210]

and

Winston [as Antigone to the audience]: Brothers and Sisters of the Land. I go
now on my last journey . I must leave the light of day forever, for the
Island, strange and cold, to be lost between life and death. So, to my
grave, my everlasting prison, condemned alive to solitary death.
[Tearing off his wig and confronting the audience as Winston, not Antigone]
[Scene 4, p227]

Winston's gesture of frustration at the end of the play, "tearing" off the
emblematic dress of "the tradition of the oppressed" reveals to us the
inappropriateness of such an icon for Apartheid-riven South Africa and
just how distant it is from the life experience or *Erlebnis* of the two pro-
tagonists. The ending of *The Island* dramaturgically exemplifies the finite
nature of redemptive and triumphalist narratives, as well as suggesting
the way in which racism often operates by a process of the projection of
values by those in power upon those who are powerless, in the guise of
virtue, for as Cohen points out:

Every time a literary critic claims a universal ethical, moral or emotional instance
in a piece of English literature, he or she colludes in the violence of the colonial
legacy in which the European value or truth is defined as the universal one.[81]

Indeed, Peterson has commented upon the process of cultural projection
onto the indigenous population in South Africa during the early years of
the separatist and Apartheid regime:

The pedagogic appeal of performance for missionaries and liberal whites was
that it seemed amenable to the transmission of Christian 'civilised' ideals and
values. Furthermore, theatre could be locked into their political and social projects.
The stock themes of Theatre-in-Education in mission schools were those of re-
pentance, character training, habits of industry, diligence, thrift and obedience.[82]

Aesthetic distanciation, promulgated by interpretative stasis, fails to
capture the honesty, spontaneity and consciousness of dialogue, or to
invoke Gadamer, *Erlebnis*. [Of course, it is essential to differentiate
Gadamer's notion of *Erlebnis* here from the subjectivist instantaneous

flash of genius which cannot withstand the claim of human existence to continuity and unity of self understanding. Rather, Gadamer's notion of the heightened consciousness of *Erlebnis* is one which is closely married to the binding quality of experience represented by *Erfahrung*.] Indeed, it is the dangerous and ritualised self-estrangement perpetuated by mimetic theory which accommodates distance between *praxis* and *poiesis*, that compels Plato to announce his belief that all poets, powerful prey to sophists and who in turn have the power to elicit unhealthy empathetic responses, should be banished from the Republic. However, Fugard's *The Island,* based on dialogue with the source text, and testimony which includes the audience as witness, escapes the self-estrangement which one finds, for example, in Hegel's appropriation and Anouilh's recontextualisation of *Antigone* and, as such, the immediacy of *Erlebnis* which prevents aesthetic distanciation, is in evidence. The immediacy of *Erlebnis* is even more present in Fugard's play if one considers its improvisatory mode of production, inevitable during the State of Emergency in South Africa during the 1970's, which censored all artistic activity and forbade black people to participate in any cultural production. *The Island* was produced under the draconian censorship laws in operation in South Africa during the 1970's whereby all cultural expression not sanctioned by the ruling powers was outlawed, and which led Fugard with his black co-authors, Kani and Ntshona to produce the play through a non scripted and thus non confiscatory process of improvisation. By the time *The Island* came to the stage black people were not permitted to be actors, a job category which was not recognised by the South African authorities when producing the obligatory passes for black people, and this was to severely restrict the collaboration of John Kani and Winston Ntshona with Athol Fugard. Thus, under the guise of "servants" to Fugard, Kani and Ntshona devised plays including *The Island* and produced improvisations without proper seating, lighting, props of backstage facilities. Such an approach not only made it easier for the dramatic collaborators to evade the censure of the South African authorities but also it ironically reflected Fugard's firm belief that actors, (particularly within a highly politically charged milieu) should be more than mere interpretative artists. As Fugard explains:

> . . . instead of first putting words on paper in order to arrive eventually at the stage and a live performance, I was able to write directly into its space and silence via the actor.[83]

In this respect the mode of production of *The Island*, just like the sorrow-ful inspiration provided by Ntshinga's imprisonment, is in keeping with the vibrancy and immediacy of speaking, be it through improvisation or by way of dialogue over the centuries with the source text. Fugard's play reflects the vibrancy and life-force of his dramaturgy by maintaining the names of the "actors" for the "characters", whereby the blurred and fad-ing antithesis between *poiesis* and *praxis* is emphasised, as encapsulated by the following programme note to *The Island* written by Kani:

> It is for the audience to call a play political not for the artist to intend it so. These plays are political because they show our lives not because we are politicians.[84]

Kani and Ntshona presented their lives on stage, unscripted, as blacks who were at that very moment politically and culturally oppressed and not merely participating in a stage managed representation of their lives, which however naturalistic, entails aesthetic distanciation and the effect of the subjectivication of art. Such a production one could say was 'life' theatre as opposed to 'live' theatre, and exemplifies the return to tradition (*Erfahrung*) in the spirit of *Erlebnis*. Additionally, the inverted allusion to the South African oral tradition of praise poetry in Fugard's play [a cul-tural outlet which Nelson Mandela cites as inspirational during his long incarceration] whereby Africans, in a almost shaman like procedure, sum-mon up the spirit of past warriors and heroes to give them inspiration for the present, is particularly pertinent to Plato's endorsement of dialogue as the path to *alethiea*, for as Gadamer observes:

> [it is] Plato's observation that the only poetry which withstands his criticism is hymns to the gods and songs in praise of good individuals. To be sure, something "unreal" is poetically represented in these; gods and men themselves appear as speakers here in an imitation in the strictest sense. Nevertheless such poetry differs from the powerfully suggestive representation of the rest of poetry. It is representation in praise of someone. But in the song of praise and in the form thereof which transcends the human realm, i.e., the hymn to the gods, there is no danger of that self-estrangement induced by the potent magical play of poetry. In praising, neither the one who praises nor the one before whom the praise is made is forgotten. On the contrary at every moment both are present and ex-pressed as they are in themselves. For praising is not a representation of what is laudable. Of course, the song of praise will always contain an element of repre-sentation of the laudable, but in essence it is something distinct from this repre-sentation. He who praises addresses both himself and the one before whom he praises (and in a certain sense even the one who is being praised) for he speaks of that which binds them all to one another and gives them all a something, for in

praising the standard by which we evaluate and comprehend our existence is
made manifest.[85]

Indeed, by implicitly deriding the iconography of "Antigone" and the 'tradition of the oppressed', Fugard is indirectly foregrounding the African liberation shamanism of praise poetry whereby activists in the present don the attire of past African warriors and heroes to inspire those who struggle for the future.

Fugard's Rewrite contests incongruous and anachronistic interpretative stasis through dramaturgical dialogue driven not by easily digestible and consoling pleasure principles, but through what Plato identified as the sole route to experiencing real truth, philo [love of] sophia [wisdom], the sating of desire through a striving for wisdom, that is, through philosophical discussion in the present. Plato's endorsement of speech as the route to alethiea (the disclosure of truth) is elaborated upon by Gadamer's notion of Erlebnis, that is to be alive to the moment when interpreting tradition, and it is the immediacy of a dialogue with the past as presented by the Rewrite which echoes the project of the Platonic dialogue. It is such immediacy of interpretation which leads us back to the re-emergence of the pharmakon once more, for it is the spirit of Erlebnis which prevents us complying with interpretative stasis or received critical appreciations, such as the historical and ritualised acknowledgement of "Antigone" as a Christian icon of 'the tradition of the oppressed'.

The concept of the pharmakon, that is the expulsion of poison to elicit a cure, was closely linked to the practice of "ostracism" in fifth century Athens, whereby the very crimes which are ultimately held against the ostracised were at the same time born of the very superior qualities which raised him above the common herd. In this sense, the missionary quality with which imperialist educators introduced Christian interpretative stasis, such as their appropriation of Antigone, to South Africa, indirectly provided an interpretative justification for what was to evolve into Apartheid, and as such came to represent a socio-historical manifestation of the pharmakon, for as Sartre puts it "Humanism is the counterpart of racism: it is a practice of exclusion."[86] By extension, it is the pharmakon as represented by "Antigone" which subsequently provides the psychological poison to elicit the cure of a sense self-hood and identity in Winston, the pharmakon which facilitates his recognition that he is the "Antigone" that will not be silenced, that will not be immured by the frames of reference of an unjust interpretative stasis.

Notes

1   The source for the phrase "The Tradition of the Oppressed" is Section VIII from Walter Benjamin's *Thesis on the Philosophy of History* in *Illuminations* trans. by Harry Zohn, edited and introduced by Hannah Arendt (London: Jonathon Cape, 1970). Benjamin states:

> The tradition of the oppressed teaches us that the "state of emergency" in which we live is not the exception but the rule. We must attain to a conception of history that is in keeping with this insight. Then we shall realize that it is our task to bring about a real state of emergency, and this will improve our position in the struggle against fascism. One reason why fascism has a chance is that in the name of progress its opponents treat it as a historical norm.

Similarly, when our reading becomes ritualised, as is the case with many of the classics, including *Antigone*, the suffering depicted in such works becomes so aestheticised as to be distanced from the realities of our daily *praxis*. In this way the experience of, for example, Sophocles' art is supplanted by our ritualised reception of an iconographic representation of the interminable, and thus by extension, accepted struggle of the oppressed. Over the centuries "Antigone" has come to assume an iconographic status as the martyred champion of the oppressed, and by transplanting this image of Western liberal humanism to an Apartheid riven South Africa, Fugard questions the way our reading of the classics can often degenerate into a tacit cultural endorsement of suffering and injustice under the euphemistic guise of a textual "tradition" of the oppressed. In a sense the ritualised reception of "Antigone" as the champion of the oppressed may be considered as a tacit cultural acceptance of suffering in the name of sympathy and what Freire has identified as "false charity". In this respect Fugard rewrites *Antigone* in order to critique the way a supposedly liberal humanist culture not only endorses but actually helps to culturally contribute to an atrocity like Apartheid through the celebratory reiteration of such narratives. As Freire states in his seminal work *Pedagogy of the Oppressed*, trans. by Myra Bergman Ramos (London: Penguin, 1996) p. 27:

> True generosity consists precisely in fighting to destroy the causes which nourish false charity. False charity constrains the fearful and subdued, the "rejects of life" to extend their trembling hands.

2   The source for the term *pharmakon* is the ancient Greek ritual of banishing selected members of the city state (usually slaves or members of the lower orders) in a symbolic and celebratory act of community purgation. Concepts of the scapegoat and ostracism were to develop out of this practice. By symbolically purging and ridding the community of poison the Greeks believed they would elicit the remedy of community health and prosperity. This ritual would have been well known to the major dramatists of fifth century Athens and it is clearly alluded to

in their common treatment of tragic heroes as complex amalgams of vice and virtue who are subsequently destroyed or banished as a result of the gifts, qualities and attributes which set them above other men. Plato also refers to the *pharmakon*, most famously in the dialogue *Phaedrus* (c370 BC) in which he confronts the potential 'remedy' and 'poison' present in the practice of writing. Indeed, Derrida was to expand on Plato's treatment of the *pharmakon* in his seminal work *Dissemination*, as discussed during the course of this Chapter. For an illuminating insight into the social practices and rituals of ancient Greece, including the *pharmakon*, see George Thompson's *Aeschylus and Athens* (Lawrence and Wishart, 1980)

3   Walter Benjamin, *Gesammelte Schriften* (eds) R. Tiedemann, H. Schweppenhauser (Frankfurt am Main, 1974–1988) Vol I/3 p. 1231 cited by Irving Wohlforth in "The Measure of the Possible, The Weight of the Real and The Heat of the Moment: Benjamin's Actuality" in *New Formations* No. 20, Summer 1993, p. 2.

4   George Steiner, *Antigones: The Antigone myth in Western Literature, Art and Thought* (Oxford: Oxford University Press, 1989) p. 19.

5   Jacques Derrida, *Dissemination*, trans: by Barbara Johnson (London: Athlone Press, 1993) p. 70. Derrida explains the etymological roots of the *pharmakon* with:

> Pharmacia is also a common noun signifying the administration of the pharmakon, the drug: the medicine and/or poison . . . The pharmakon, this 'medicine' , this philter, which acts as both a remedy and poison, already introduces itself into the body of the discourse with all its ambivalence.

6   Jacques Derrida, p. xxv. In the Introduction Barbara Johnson states:

> Plato's 'original' text is thus itself already the battlefield of an impossible process of translation.

7   Garnier's original text provides a subtitle to this version of Antigone—*ou la pieté*—pertinent in the light of this discussion about the subsequent "christianising" of the source text.

8   G. W. F. Hegel as cited in Steiner pp. 22–27. Hegel's early writings and his later *Phenemonology* reveal much about the author's thoughts about Sophoclean tragedy for as Steiner observes:

> Hegel will name Antigone twice only. But beginning with section V, her presence is vivid. It is in this segment that Hegel spells out the axiom of existentialism.

9   J. W. Goethe presented a truncated version of *Antigone* in 1808. Like Hegel, consideration of Sophoclean tragedy holds a central position in his works.

10   Philip Cohen "It's racism what dunnit"- hidden narratives in theories of racism" in *Race, Culture and "difference"*(eds) James Donald, Ali Rattansi (London: Sage/ Open University, 1992) p. 71.

11   Cohen, p. 74.

12   Steiner, p. 139.

13   Steiner, p. 139.

14   Jean Pierre Vernant and Pierre Videl-Naquet, *Myth and Tragedy in Ancient Greece* trans: by Janet Lloyd (New York: Zone Books, 1990) p. 21

15   Vernant, p. 84.

16   C. W. Oudemans, A. P M. H. Lardinois, *Tragic Ambiguity: Anthropology, Philosophy and Sophocles' 'Antigone'* (Leiden, New York: E. J. Brill, 1987) p. 1

17   Shelley in a letter to John Gisborne in 1812

18   Thomas De Quincey in a review of 'The Antigone of Sophocles as Represented on the Edinburgh Stage' in *De Quincey's Works: The Art of Cnversation and Other Papers* Vol XIII (Edinburgh: Adam and Charles Black, MDCCCLXIII) pp.199–233. p.205.

19   Thomas De Quincey in an essay "Theory of Greek Tragedy" in *De Quincey's Works: Leaders in Literature with a Notice of Traditional Errors Affecting Them* Vol. VIII (Edinburgh: Adam and Charles Black, MDCCCLXIII) pp. 54–75. p. 65

20   Steiner, p. 7.

21   Steiner, p. 9.

22   Matthew Arnold from "Preface to First Edition of Poems" (1853) in *On the Classical Tradition* (ed) R. H. Super (Michigan, Ann Arbor: University of Michigan Press, 1960) p. 12.

23   Oudemans, p. 3.

24   Gayatri Chakravorty Spivak from "Criticism, Feminism and The Institution" in *The Postcolonial Critic: Interviews, Strategies, Dialogues* (ed) Sarah Harsym (New York and London: Routledge, 1990) p.9

25   Gadamer, *TM* p. 301–2.

26   Simone Weil's interpretation of *Antigone* is a good representation of the Judeo-Christian appropriation of the play and the subsequent interpretative demise of the *pharmakon*. See *Intimations of Christianity among the Ancient Greeks*, trans: by E. C. Geissbuhler (New York: Beacon Press, 1958):

> Among the Greek poets, Sophocles is the one whose quality of inspiration is the most visibly Christian and perhaps the most pure (he is to my knowledge

much more Christian than any tragic poet of the last twenty centuries). This Christian quality is generally recognized in the tragedy of Antigone which might be an illustration of the saying: We ought to obey God rather than men. (p. 9.)

and

Antigone is a perfectly pure being, perfectly innocent, perfectly heroic, who voluntarily gives herself up to death to preserve a guilty brother from an unhappy fate in the other world. At the moment when imminent death approaches her her nature betrays her, she feels betrayed by men and by the gods . . . What is called Fate in Greek tragedy has been very badly understood. There is no such agency apart from this conception of the curse, which once produced by a crime, is handed down by men from one to another and cannot be destroyed except by the suffering of a pure victim obedient to God" (p.10.)

27   Chinua Achebe, Chapter 3, "The African Writer and the Biafran Cause" in *Morning Yet on Creation Day: Essays* (New York: Doubleday, Anchor Press, 1975) p. 78.

Also Dhlomo has advocated the need to confront one's near past and present predicament in order to forge a cultural sense of history, because it is as much a part of that history as the native artforms and cultural activities of pre-colonial Africa. See Herbert Dhlomo's "Drama and the African" in *The South African Outlook 66* (1st October 1936) p.234:

The African dramatist cannot delve into the past unless he has grasped the present. African art cannot grow and thrive by going back digging up the bones of the past without dressing them with modern knowledge and craftmanship . . . We want African playwrights who will dramatise and expound a philosophy of history. We want dramatic representation of African Oppression, Emancipation and Evolution.

28   Catherine Zuckert, *Postmodern Platos* (Chicago and London: University of Chicago Press, 1996) p. 74.

29   Derrida, *Dissemination* p. 97.

30   Plato, *Gorgias,* trans: by W Hamilton (London: Penguin,1971) p. 32.

31   Plato, *Gorgias*, p. 46.

32   "Necklacing" did not really become apparent until the 1980's although, especially with respect to the interruptive character with which Gadamerian hermeneutics treats sequential time and chronology, it is fair to say that Fugard's reference to a necklace of thorns has assumed a retrospective pertinence. Martin Orkin (*Drama and the South African State*, p. 222) explains the rise of retribution crime and 'necklacing":

In the townships this included in the 1980's the continuing presence of the police with their hippos, caspirs and sten guns, the use of stone throwing as a means of defiance, and for a period in response to the problem of township informers and as a means of retribution, the use of necklacing.

33   Gadamer, *TM* p.112.

34   Gadamer, *TM* p. 102.

35   Linda Hutcheon, *A Theory of Parody* p. 4.

36   Gadamer, *TM* p. 102.

37   Gadamer, *TM* p. 117.

38   Gadamer, *TM* p. 112.

39   There have been numerous studies of crude stereotyping of racial groups in literature, including *The Merchant of Venice*, and its subsequent implication in historical events. It is worthwhile to note that throughout the play Shylock is referred to as "the Jew" no less than 58 times, emphasising the reduction of the character to a racial stereotype, although it is important to distinguish between Shakespeare's representation of Shylock and the overall effect of the play with historical hindsight. Annabel Patterson has carried out illuminating work on the esoteric "meaning" of texts. See A *Reading Between the Lines* (London: Routledge, 1993).

40   Gadamer, *TM* p. 117.

41   Orkin cites Brian Astbury, the Director of the The Space theatre to reveal the risks and dangers involved in producing and staging dramatic works during the Apartheid years (*Drama and the South African State*, p. 151.)

> Even Fugard, working with John Kani and Winston Ntshona was afraid of censorship, refusing to commit either 'Sizwe Bansi is Dead' or 'The Island' to script form until it had been performed abroad.

Astbury goes on to give a terrifying account, although not without a certain degree of humour, of a first night in 1972:

> . . . two plain-clothes policemen who after trying to buy seats without membership [The Space was run as a club to circumvent Apartheid legislation] identified themselves to me and tried to stop the show. I refused on the grounds of our legal opinion. They asked to see the director and cast. Athol, John, Winston and I gathered in the office and were warned that we would be charged if we went on with the performance. The other three decided that if I, as management, was prepared to go on, so were they. The policemen repeated their warning and asked to see the performance. They very obviously enjoyed the first half and then left. We were never charged.

42   Walter Benjamin, "Theses on the Philosophy of History" in *Illuminations* (ed) Hannah Arendt, trans. by Harry Zohn (New York: Cape,1970) p. 259.

43   Albert Camus, *The Plague* trans. by Stuart Gilbert (London: Penguin Books, 1960) p. 252.

44   Gadamer, *TM* p. 61.

45   Maurice Blanchot, *Vicious Circles: Two Fictions and 'after the fact'* trans. Paul Aster (New York: Station Hill, 1985) p.60.

46   Shoshona Felman, Dori Laub, *Testimony: Crisis of Witnessing in Literature, Psychoanalysis and History* (New York and London: Routledge, 1992) p. 122.

47   Plato, *Phaedrus* from "The Inferiority of the Written to the Spoken Word" lines 274–5, pp. 96–7 trans. by W. Hamilton (London: Penguin, 1973).

48   Benjamin, "Theses on the Philosophy of History" *Illuminations*, p. 257.

49   Derrida, *Dissemination* p.99.

50   Derrida, *Dissemination* p. 99.

51   Derrida, *Dissemination* p. 78.

52   Derrida, *Dissemination* p. 109.

53   Camus, "Neither Victims nor Executioners", trans. Dwight McDonald, *World Without War Publications*, (San Francisco: 1972) p. 44.
      ["Ni victimes ni borreaux" *Combat* 1948, reprinted in *Actuelles, Ecrits politiques*, Paris: Gallimard, 1950.]

54   Camus, "Neither Victims nor Executioners" p. 44

55   Camus, "Create Dangerously" lecture given at the University of Uppsala in December 1957; in *Resistance, Rebellion and Death* trans. Justin O'Brien, (New York: Knopf, 1961) pp. 250–2.

56   Indeed, it is noteworthy that Fugard did not receive a classical education and was initially and vicariously exposed to the classics via his reading of Camus. Also it is noteworthy that Fugard's first excursion into revisiting the classics for dramaturgical effect was the unscripted *Orestes* which marked his attempt to transpose the reality of the situation in South Africa onto the stage through unrehearsed "life" theatre, a process which he relates in the Introduction to "Statements" in *Two Workshop Productions Devised by Athol Fugard, John Kani and Winston Ntshona* (London, Cape Town: Oxford University Press, 1974):

      My work had been so conventional. It involved the writing of a play; it involved setting that play in terms of local specifics . . . I had an idea involving an incident in our recent South African history . . . a young man took a bomb into the Johannesburg station concourse as an act of protest. It killed an old woman. He was eventually caught and hanged. I superimposed almost in the sense of a palimpset this image on that of Clytemnestra and her two children, Orestes and Electra. There was no text. Not a single piece of paper passed between myself and the actors.

      Although *Orestes* (first shown on 24th March 1971) was unscripted, Fugard did make notes during the performance, which are reproduced in *Theatre One: New*

South African Drama (ed) Stephan Gray (Ad. Donker: Johannesburg, 1978) p. 82.

57   Shoshona Felman, Dori Laub, Testimony: Crisis of Witnessing in Literature, Psychoanalysis and History (New York and London: Routledge,1992) p. 114.

58   Felman, Laub, p. xv.

59   Gadamer, TM p. 294.

60   Felman, Laub, p. 108.

61   Felman, Laub, pp. 200–203.

62   Felman and Laub, p.102..

63   Felman, Laub, p. 103.

64   Elie Wiesel "The Holocaust as Literary Inspiration" Dimensions of the Holocaust, ed., Lacey Baldwin Smith (Evanston: Northwestern University, 1977) p. 14.

65   Felman, Laub, p. 85.

66   Walter Benjamin, "The Task of the Translator: An Introduction to the Translation of Baudelaire's "Tableaux Parisiens", Illuminations, ed. Hannah Arendt, trans Harry Zohn, (New York: Schocken Books, 1969) p.76

67   Paul de Man The Rhetoric of Romanticism (New York: Columbia University Press, 1984) pp. 121–122. (hereafter referred to as RR).

68   Paul de Man, RR p. 123

69   Felman, Laub, p. 160.

70   Benjamin, "The Task of the Translator" p. 76.

71   Gadamer, TM pp. 138–139.

72   De Man, RR p. 85.

73   Christopher Norris, The Truth about Postmodernism (Oxford: Blackwell, 1993) p. 191.

74   Gadamer, DD pp. 17–18.

75   Gadamer, DD pp. 61-2.

76   Julia Kristeva enunciates the psychoanalytic "abjection theory" in Powers of Horror: An Essay on Abjection (New York: Columbia University Press, 1982)

77   Kristeva, p. 5.

78   Gadamer, TM p. 138.

79   Gadamer, TM p. 100

80   Gadamer, *TM* p.97.

81   Cohen, p. 248.

82   Bhekizizwe Petersen "Apartheid and the Political Imagination in Black South African Theatre" in *Politics and Performance: Theatre, Poetry, Song in South Africa* (ed) Liz Gunner (Johannesburg: Witwatersrand University Press, 1994) pp. 35–54, p. 36.

83   Fugard, Introduction to "Statements" (1974)

84   Fugard in an article from Eastern Province Herald, 5th February 1974 reiterated Kani's statement: "I am not using the stage as a political platform." Nonetheless, on 2nd November, 1985 Kani and Ntshona announced in the Cape Town Weekend Argus:

> We John Kani and Winston Ntshona declare every single performance of the play, The Island, as an endorsement of the local and international call for the immediate release of Mr. Nelson Mandela and all political prisoners and detainees.

85   Gadamer, *DD* p. 65.

86   Jean Paul Sartre, *Critique of Dialectical Reason: I. Theory of Practical Ensembles*, trans: by Alan Sheridan-Smith (London: New Left Books, 1976) p. 762.

Chapter Five

Steven Berkoff and the Dramaturgy of Bile

The Hap of Intratextuality and the Oedipal Propriation

Berkoff's *Greek* (1980, revised 1988) exposes the psychoanalytic intratextuality which has appropriated our 'understanding' of Sophocles' *Oedipus Rex*, most notably the Freudian theory of the primal scene,[1] formulated in 1900 in *Die Traumdeutung* which, as commented upon by Goux, has effected a hermeneutic "enframing" or *Gestell*[2] of the source text:

> When Freud discovered—first in himself, through self-analysis, and then in the dreams of his male patients—persistent fantasies of patricide and maternal incest, he was promptly reminded of the fate of King Oedipus, on which Sophocles based the most perfect tragedy of Greek theatre. But Freud saw the myth and the tragedy as the literary expressions of a fantasmatic core; for him, the task of interpretation belonged to psychoanalysis alone. The persistence and universality of the psychological "complex" would account for the myth's existence and the power its theatrical deployment has for us. From Freud's standpoint, then, no increase in our understanding of the logic of the myth could be expected to shed any light at all on the formation of the complex. For Freud the complex explained the myth; he did not see the myth as a purveyor of knowledge that would be entitled as such to interrogate the psychoanalytic experience.[3]

Although Foucault's "repressive hypothesis"[4] tends to see Freudian psychoanalysis as heralding a limited amelioration of the repressive attitudes to sexuality of previous centuries, Freud's Oedipal Complex has proven to be a deterministic and rationalist imposition upon not only Sophocles' tragedy but ultimately our "understanding" of human sexuality, as modelled on a retroactive reading of the Sophoclean play, and it is this intratextuality which is addressed in *Greek*:

But have we not liberated ourselves from those two long centuries in which the history of sexuality must be seen first of all as the chronicle of an increasing repression? Only to a slight extent, we are told. Perhaps some progress was made by Freud, but with such circumspection, such medical prudence, a scientific guarantee of innocuousness, and so many precautions in order to contain everything, with no fear of "overflow".[5]

Berkoff's play posits that although the Freudian Oedipal Complex supposedly sets out to explain and thus free us from symptomatic neuroses, it has had the effect of generating another strain of neuroses, which in keeping with the Foucauldian idea of the backlash against the repressive hypothesis, derives from a society submerged in the discourse of sexuality as desire, as opposed to exalting in the natural and spontaneous pleasures of human life. Such neuroses, emphasized by the almost ranting rhythm and metre of the text, is portrayed by Berkoff in the form of mindless violence against casually selected scapegoats, the greed and excess of the 1980's at the expense of others deprivation, and the degeneration of the language to the level of the pornographic and obscene—all reflecting a society driven by the acquisitive and consumeristic quest for the immediate gratification of desire, with:

MUM: Transport sits idly at the docks where workers slink around and for a hefty bribe may let you have your avocado or Dutch cabbage . . . petrol's obsolete as thousands of rusting cars lay swelling up our streets to vital services like ambulances which take a month to get from place to place [p. 152]

and

. . . armed killers snipe from the shattered eyes of buildings and death stalks in the foul and pestilent breath of friends whose eyes are drunk with envy and greed at your success / people shake your hand with limp grips as if afraid to catch it . . . Masturbating shops line every High Street and the pneumatic drill of strong right wrists ensures a girl a fat living, the country's awash in spunk not threshing and sweetening the wombs of lovers but crushed in Kleenex and dead in cubicles with red lights. [p. 167]

In this respect Berkoff exhibits a Foucauldian approach to the Freudian Oedipal Complex, and he incorporates such a critique within his Rewrite of Sophocles' play not only to highlight the effects of such deterministic intratextuality upon our reception of the source text, but in order to reinvoke the source text to respond to its previous intratextuality in the present. *Greek* dramaturgically highlights the intratextuality of the source text to show how the discourse about sexuality pervades modern life under the guise of freedom, and in this way the Rewrite dramaturgically facilitates the source text to 'experience' through Eddy, the effects which its own intratext has promulgated as well as being able to respond to them— effects which are powerfully expanded on by Foucault:

> Let us consider the stratagems by which we were induced to apply all our skills to discovering its [sex] secrets, by which we were attached to the obligations to draw out its truth, and made guilty for having failed to recognize it for so long. These devices are what ought to make us wonder today. Moreover, we need to consider the possibility that one day, perhaps, in a different economy of bodies and plea- sures, people will no longer quite understand how the ruses of sexuality and the power that sustains its organisation, were able to subject us to that austere mon- archy of sex, so that we became dedicated to the endless task of forcing its secret, of exacting the truest confessions from a shadow. . . . The irony of this deploy- ment is in having to believe that our "liberation" is in the balance. [6]

Greek negotiates with the hap of Freudian psychoanalysis to critique the theoretical "containment" of the classic as well as its subsequent con- trolling influence on our understanding of human sexuality. In this sense, the Rewrite highlights how the "overflow" potentiality of our understand- ing of both the source text and aspects of human life is repressed by the containing and continuing influence of the general application of subse- quent 'Freudian' theories to the source text, such as that posited by Anzieu:

> The first act takes place on the road from Delphi to Thebes. Oedipus is returning to consult the oracle that revealed to him his destiny of parricide and incest. He has decided, in order to escape this destiny, not to go back to Corinth. (It is a remarkable mistake if he knows that those in Corinth are his adoptive parents. It is precisely by returning to them that he would have nothing to fear. And similarly, if Oedipus had decided to marry a young girl he would have guarded against committing incest with his mother.) In contrast, by setting out to seek his fortune (and giving himself over to free associations) Oedipus is going to fulfill his destiny (that is to say fantasy). [7]

However, through a hermeneutic imbued with a historically effected con- sciousness of the source text and its intratext for the present the Rewrite facilitates the "overflow" of the classic in a different yet intrinsically pro- ductive way. [8] The Rewrite dramaturgically enables the source text to be freed from the deterministic effects of its subsequent intratextuality, but more importantly the source text is further liberated to participate in a dialogue *about* the effects of that intratextuality with and for the present through the Rewrite. Thus, as opposed to Freudian psychoanalysis liber- ating Man from the power-administered discourse about sexuality, it has merely altered the discursive strategy whilst operating within the self-same parameters, and it is the effects of this intratextual hap which forms the central concern of Berkoff's Rewrite. Indeed, the constraints of Freud's interpretative determinism upon not only the source text but also human sexuality, as dramaturgically represented by Berkoff's *Greek,* are explained by Vernant:

> [Freud's theory] . . . elaborated on the basis of clinical cases and contemporary dreams is "confirmed" by a dramatic text from another age. But the text can only provide this confirmation provided that it is itself interpreted by reference to the framework of the modern spectator's dream—as conceived at least by the theory in question. For it not to be a vicious circle it would be necessary for the Freudian theory not to present itself from the outset as a self-evident interpretation but rather to emerge, on completion of a painstaking analysis, as a necessity imposed by the work itself, a condition for the understanding of its dramatic organisation, the tool for the whole decoding of the text.[9]

Unlike Marowitz' *Variations on The Merchant of Venice* and Fugard's *The Island* which both elicit a Gadamerian transformation-into-structure through negotiation with the historical hap of actual events, The Holocaust and Apartheid, *Greek* exemplifies a hermeneutic transformation of the source text wrought by intratextual hap as encountered in the present. *Greek* revisits Sophocles' tragedy in the full consideration of the socio-historical and hermeneutic repercussions and ramifications of Freudian psychoanalysis in which the "primal scene" based on the Oedipal myth as presented in *Oedipus Rex* holds a central position.[10]

In stark contrast to the idea that Being is eternal, unchanging, intelligible and self-subsistent as espoused by Parmenides and later Plato, Gadamer sees Being as essentially historical, and it is this historicity which is central to our understanding of the Rewrite. Thus, the Rewrite gives back to the source text the power to speak not only about the past, but to speak in a more radical sense about the present, a voice raised not in spite of the classic's historicity but because of it. Although Gadamer cites the classic text as that which proffers "greater freedom"[11] and scope for interpretation because of its historicity and an element of agreement through commonality, such textual plurality is by virtue of the interpretation itself, through historically effected dialogue, as opposed to deeply embedded secrets intrinsic to the text awaiting interpretative discovery. Historicity enriches the potential for such a hermeneutic dialogue, as indicated by the complex intratextuality of *Oedipus Rex*. Berkoff's *Greek* does not seek to offer an alternative or oppositional re-reading of Freud's reading of Sophocles' tragedy; rather, through intratextual hap and historically effected consciousness, the play encompasses the historicity of the source text, including Freud's appropriation and its repercussions for the "present" that is, Thatcher's Britain during the 1980's. The Rewrite's negotiation with the intratextual 'hap' thus dramaturgically exemplifies one of the basic tenets of hermeneutics; namely, to proceed from that which is clear, the distorted familiarity of the intratext, to that which is obscure, an "understanding" of the source text. Thus, instead of prefacing either implicitly or explicitly with standard interpretations or presenting binary interpretative strategies for the text, Berkoff negotiates with the "between space" and silence which relates the multiplicity of different translations, the previous ones and his own reading, for as Bernasconi observes:

> The reference to inadequate translations and blatantly metaphysical interpretations belongs to the ambiguity of the text, and is supported by the memory of what has gone before. The memory is kept alive in a history of textuality, a history of reading . . . If the translations and previous interpretations were forgotten or ignored, the so-called ambiguity would be lost, the ringing of stillness would fade into silence, the discontinuity of rupture would dissolve into continuity.[12]

Freud's 'primal scene' reading of the Oedipal myth and, by extension, Sophocles' tragedy, is not merely replaced or opposed in *Greek*; rather, the Rewrite confronts the legacy of the repressive hypothesis and the subsequent reaction against it in the present as made manifest by the representation of fragmentatory and divisive pressure groups and sects. In this way the implication is made that the "Theban plague" persists today, in the form of the self-destructive "symptoms" created by the deterministic rationalism of the Freudian psychoanalytic paradigm as based on the source text:

DAD: The nights in Hyde Park are lit by fires and the sound of tom toms from the Brixton black workers revolutionary gay lib joins forces with white is ugly forced abortions / wanking is not a town in China but an alternative to the filthy men female party group.

MUM: Meanwhile the rats head down Edgware Road up to Oxford Street preparing to turn right into Bond Street / get down Piccadilly and raid Fortnum's, pick up their mates at Forte's and join forces to make all resistance impossible seeing how all resistance is locked in internecine strife. [Act 1, Scene 3 p. 153]

In this respect *Greek* is the dramaturgical *Erlebnis* of an historically effected consciousness which engages in dialogue not only with the source text but also with its intratextual accretions, which in this particular case is the intratextual hap. As such the Rewrite does not seek to ignore or disregard the Freudian intratextuality in some vainglorious attempt to re-construct the source text, a pursuit which Gadamer condemns as little more than handing on a "dead" meaning. Even though the Rewrite drama-turgically explores and contests the subsequent intratextual rationalisation of the source text, this does not mean that the Rewrite is more akin to Romantic reconstructionism or that which Nietzsche would have consid-ered to be the 'antiquarian' use of history, for as Gadamer points out, *Erlebnis* cannot be elicited by an attempt at slavish faithfulness based on misguided notions about an 'original' text.[13] Thus the Rewrite can neither be assessed as replacing one rationalistic discourse with another or as being concerned with the reconstruction of a supposed sense of the 'origi-nal', rather it synthesises the historicity of the source text including the intratext for and through the present.

The Nietzschian emphasis upon the Platonic "necessary lie" to co-vertly impose a teleological and ordered framework upon society to deter-mine Man's function is an opinion which presumably would designate Freud's deterministic Oedipal Complex as a theoretical "will to power", analogous to that sense of megalomania experienced by Zarathustra (*Thus Spoke Zarathustra*, 1883–5)

> The lust to rule—but who would call it *lust* when what is high longs downward for power? . . . That the lonely heights should not remain lonely and self-sufficient eternally; that the mountain should descend to the valley . . . who were to find the right name for such longings? "Gift giving virtue"—thus Zarathustra once named the unnamable.[14]

Although Freud's intratextual "reading" of the source text has had the effect of a deterministic theoretical "will to power" upon our subsequent reception, we cannot necessarily uncover its motivation and so as op-posed to focusing upon such metaphysical hypotheses the Rewrite drama-turgically addresses and incorporates within its own dramaturgical frame-work the *effects* of intratextuality. In this respect, the Rewrite uncovers the deterministic effects of the intratext in a manner more akin to Heidegger's theory of "enframing", which considers such ordering as an intrinsic facilitator for our reaching a different and more pertinent under-standing at a later stage. Enframing, whereby Man attempts to impose an order on the chaos of human existence, although whether this can retro-actively be ascribed to a Nietzschian 'will to power' is debatable, facilitates in time a process called *propriation* or in Gadamerian terms, historically effected consciousness, to elicit a *different*, although not superior under-standing of the source text for the present. *Propriation* through enframing is founded on the premise that saying or the spoken does not constitute language but rather that all language comprises silence in the voice, the said in the unsaid:

> Silence corresponds to the noiseless ringing of stillness, the stillness of saying that propriates and shows. The saying that rests on propriation is, as showing, the most proper mode of propriation.[15]

Similar to a process akin to Heidegger's *propriation,* Berkoff's *Greek* is not concerned with replacing the said with another said, privileging an oppositional discourse in place of another, rather through negotiating with the hap of intratextuality the Rewrite elicits the said in unsaid, the voice in the silence, which has been drowned out by the condemnatory chorus of psychoanalytical disapproval for almost a century. *Propriation or Ereignis* encompasses the silence that enables us to listen, and is more significant than all the noises of signification, and as such has particular pertinence to our understanding of the Rewrite because it is Oedipus' great failing that he refuses to hear the said in the unsaid, the voice in the silence when he asks the Delphic Oracle "Are Polybus and Merope my parents?", to which Apollo simply offers the prediction that he will sleep with his mother and kill his father. Berkoff's *Greek* exemplifies a reading imbued with the unsaid of the source text as well as the said, for by incorporating the intratextual hap of *Oedipus Rex,* most notably the Freudian Oedipal Complex within its own dramatic structure, the intratextuality of our reception of the source text is polemicised to reveal *our* hermeneutic failure to hear the said in the unsaid—an uncanny echo of the perpetuation of the Oedipal destiny in our own hermeneutic experience.

In this respect, *Greek* and its dramaturgical reinvocation of not only the source text but also the source text's intratextuality, exemplifies the Heideggarian notion that all language is infused with silence, and that the only way to bring the essence of language to the sounded word is to bring the silence to the sounded word, the unspeakable to the spoken. As such, one can view Berkoff's Rewrite as a dramaturgical example of releasing, through *propriation,* the effects of what Heidegger identified as the peculiarly modern phenomenon of "enframing":

> The enframing, because it sets upon human beings—that is, challenges them—to order everything that comes to presence into a technical inventory, unfolds essentially after the manner of propriation; at the same time, it distorts propriation, inasmuch as all ordering sees itself committed to calculative thinking and so speaks the language of enframing. Speech is challenged to correspond to ubiquitous orderability of what is present.[16]

Berkoff's play, precipitated by the hap of intratextuality, shows how both hermeneutic freedom and understanding about human sexuality have been circumvented by the deterministic attempts of Man to "enframe" the Sophoclean tragedy, although in turn, it is the process of this self-same enframing that initiates the *propriation* elicited by the Rewrite that reveals the said in the unsaid and thus elucidates further hermeneutic potential in the source text. Indeed, the Heideggerian theory of *propriation* is similar to Gadamer's ideas about tradition and historically effected consciousness, for both are concerned with reaching "understanding" for the present through the *propriation* or historically effected consciousness of the past:

> All coming to presence, not only modern technology, keeps itself everywhere concealed to the last. Nevertheless, it remains, with respect to its holding sway, that which precedes all: the earliest. The Greek thinkers already knew of this when they said: The earlier with regard to its dominance becomes manifest to us men only later. That which is primally early shows itself only ultimately to men. Therefore, in the realm of thinking, a painstaking effort to think through still more primally what was primally, though is not the absurd wish to revive what is past, but rather the sober readiness to be astounded before the coming of the dawn.[17]

Through historically effected consciousness or *propriation* the intratextual hap of the Oedipal complex is questioned and reassessed in respect to our understanding of the source text, and by extension this leads us to consider how far such deterministic intratextuality as prompted by source text has contributed to the present society, where materialistic consumerism has infested politics to such a degree that people almost maniacally "buy into" their so-called freedom to "choose" from a plethora of pressure groups and causes:

> DAD: The country's in a state of plague / while parties of all shades battle for power to sort the shit from the shinola / the Marxists and the Workers' party call for violence to put an end to violence and likewise the wankers suggest hard solutions like thick chains and metal toecaps / Poisoned darts half-inched from local taverns / anyone who wants to kill maim and destroy / arson, murder and hack are being recruited for the new revolutionary party / the fag libs are holding violent demos to be able to give head in the public park when the garbage strike is over and not to be persecuted for screwing on the top deck of buses.

By presenting the modern day Oedipus, Eddy, as being unwillingly submerged into the yuppie culture of the 1980's, Berkoff prompts us to consider to what extent the intratextuality of the source text has not only contributed to hermeneutic nihilism, as alluded to throughout *Greek* by for example DAD's apathetic cliché-ridden speech, but also how it has materially contributed to a physical manifestation of the textual plague presented in *Oedipus Rex*, in the form of a backlash administered against the repressive hypothesis of previous times, as perpetuated by Freudian psychoanalysis. In this respect, *Greek* dramaturgically acknowledges that all "understanding" of knowledge is shaped by the historical, be it on a personal, cultural or social level, and as such the Sophoclean tenet taken from the source text, "Know thyself", meaning knowledge must not become distanced from our individual power to understand, acquires an even more powerful and resounding cadence for us today, for as Glover emphasises:

> Developed moral thought is not a static state of imprisonment within social norms imposed by childhood, but a process of interaction between general beliefs and particular responses.[18]

Spoken Silence, Changing Continuum

Foucault has commented upon the way in which the discourse of sexuality—the ostensibly liberal and open backlash against the repressive hypothesis—is in fact discursivity founded upon controlled and administered silence:

> What is peculiar to modern societies, in fact, is not that they consigned sex to a shadow existence, but that they dedicated themselves to speaking of it *ad infinitum*, while exploiting it as *the* secret.[19]

Similarly, the Rewrite considers the psychoanalytic intratext, Freud's Oedipal Complex, in order to reveal how such deterministic discursivity in the name of openness has in fact had the effect of silencing the said in source text, whilst simultaneously revealing, through historically effected consciousness, the paradox that such a rationalistic discursivity of silence is, in time, the outlet for another, different and present voice in the source text. Ironically, the silencing of the source text by the intratext engenders the Rewrite's representation of a cacophony of competing voices which are raised against the repressive hypothesis under the guise of "freedom of speech" in the present, and as an indirect result of the intratext. Thus, Berkoff gives voice to the stream of expletives and profanities of "hate speech"—the social manifestation of this backlash—as fragmented tirades and crusades competing to be heard amidst the divided and divisive reaction against the repressive hypothesis of which they form a part, and which is to some extent the result of the psychoanalytical intratext:

> . . . Macdougal and his paddies from Belfast are raring to blow up anything that moves. Thick-eared with hands like bunches of bananas / their voices from afar were like a pack of baying hounds . . .

and

> Hanging's no answer to the plague madam / you'd be hanging every day / I'm human like us all / we're all the same linked

and

> . . . the sturdy chiselled chins fresh shaved of our fine and brave John English ready to defend the queen and all her minions who represent all that is fine in this drab of grey / this septic isle . . . (Chorus of 'Rule Britannia, Britannia rules the waves . . .' etc)

The preponderance of violent, aggressive and divisive voices represented in the Rewrite, the dramaturgy of bile which serves to offend the audience into hermeneutic re-cognition, also suggests the extent to which the voice of the source text has been drowned out by the effects of the intratext, so much so, that Eddy's tragic dilemma is decentred and diminished amidst the thundering melee of hatred and violence, as emphasised by:

> Then I awoke / and rudely saw the world just as it is and started on my adventures thrust all young and sweet into the seething heaving heap of world in which I was just a little dot. [Act 2 Scene 4, p. 157]

In this respect the Rewrite presents, both through form and content, the passage of time between the source text and our reception as being hermeneutically productive as opposed to alienating, for it addresses the way in which the intratext has had the effect of giving voice in the present at the expense of the voice of the past, with the result that the tragedy of Oedipus is marginalised by the everyday tragedies which typify the culture of complaint; a culture which Berkoff's play emphasises as being the psycho-social effect of the intratext. Greek negotiates with the historicity of our reception to comment upon how the supposed unconscious Oedipal "guilt", as deterministically imposed upon the source text by the intratext, has resulted in a psychoanalytic pardon or expiation for any subsequent manifestation of neuroses in the present. Thus, the Rewrite exhibits an interpretative acknowledgment of the historicity of Being and as such exemplifies a reading where, in accordance with Gadamerian hermeneutics, time is no longer a chasm to be bridged because it separates, rather time provides the foundations and the support for the course of events in which the present is undoubtedly rooted.

Edward Bond has stated in the unpublished "Rough Notes on Olly's Prison" that mimesis is central to effective modern drama, and in keeping with this, mimetic transference is produced by the Rewrite, not just for the sake of the contemporanaeity of recontextualisation, but in order to dramaturgically put into relief the historical effects, including those of the intratext, which have undoubtedly contributed to our altered, although often unacknowledged, reception and "understanding" of the source text:

> Now it is first necessary to describe—so that the contents of chaos, of meaninglessness may be discerned; We must begin by showing the audience what they can recognise. The stage must mirror reality. Ibsen represented recognisable rooms because the rooms—in their bourgeois solidity—were recognisable maps of the audience's world; the rooms had meaning. We need only indicate a room [say] and put in it the things we shall use dramatically—not all the things the audience uses socially—we need only enough of those things to substantiate reality.[20]

By dramaturgically alluding, through mimetic transference, to the changing concerns and expectations with which we receive the source text today, the Rewrite further implies how our reception of classical tragedy can often, albeit imperceptibly, degenerate into the "cultivated" reverence and aesthetic distanciation that typifies vague notions of "taste" and the canonical, far removed from realities of the present. As Ricoeur has noted ". . . mimesis serves as an index of the discursive situation. It reminds us that discourse does not suspend our belonging to the world."[21] and in the same way it is the contemporisation of the source text that preempts our slipping into a reception typified by aesthetic distanciation.

Berkoff domesticates and urbanises the source text through setting, characterisation and language to invite us not only to reassess it through modern eyes but also to consider the effects of the intratext for the present and for our present reception of the source text. Thus the marginalisation of the Oedipal "hero", in part effected by the generalised application of the Oedipal Complex, suggests heroic marginalisation in our everyday experience, and is emphasised in *Greek* by reference to the lack of the modern "heroic" as conveyed by MUM's complaint that "Maggot is our only hope" and by the representation of the casual venting of any pent-up frustration and repressed anger upon any available scapegoat to be found on the streets of London:

EDDY: . . . 'Hitler got the trains running on time' . . . you got a lot of Nazi
lovers among the British down and out. Lazy bastards wondered why at
the end of skiving and strikes Moisha down the road copped a few bob or
why the Cypriots had a big store full of goodies . . . [p. 147]

The anti-heroic postures assumed by characters on the grounds of nationalism and racism as presented in *Greek* are horrifying manifestations
of a society with a distinct lack of or, at least, an extremely distorted
notion of standards and aspirations, and are presented by Berkoff as just
one more example of the backlash against the repressive hypothesis under the guise of freedom of expression. Indeed, Foucault has observed
that Modernity has to be envisaged less as an era than as an attitude, "a
mode of relating to comtemporary reality"[22] which can, in part, be
characterised by the "will to heroize"[23], and Berkoff dramaturgically articulates this need for the heroic through juxtaposition with the tragic
hero as presented in *Oedipus Rex* in order to comment on the dangerous
way in which it may manifest itself. Additionally, the victimization perpetrated in the spirit of distorted heroism is an uncanny inversion of the
ancient Greek ritual of banishing the once exalted city *Tuche* or good luck
in human form as the *pharmakon*, the embodiment of ejected, rejected
and purgated malevolence, as commented upon by Vernant:

> *Divine King* and *pharmakos*: These are the two sides to Oedipus that make a
> riddle of him by combining within him two figures, the one the reverse of the
> other, as in a formula with a double condition, Sophocles lends general signifi-
> cance to this inversion in Oedipus' nature by presenting the hero as a model of
> the human condition. But the polarity between king and scapegoat (a polarity
> that the tragedy situates at the very heart of the figure of Oedipus) is something
> that Sophocles did not need to invent. It was already part of the religious practice
> and social thought of the Greeks.[24]

Indeed, the doubling of Oedipus as hero and *pharmakon* in the source
text is emphasised by a series of other "double roles" throughout the play;
Jocasta as mother and wife; the Corinthian messenger who at once brings
news of Polybus' death but who, it transpires, also first gave the infant
Oedipus to Polybus and Merope; and the Theban herdsman who besides
being the witness to Laius' murder also emerges as the man who took
baby Oedipus from Jocasta and gave him to the messenger from Corinth.
Such doubling in the source text serves to emphasise the sense that the
Fates are conspiring against Oedipus, and that he is inextricably and inescapably bound by the uncontrollable forces of the curse, but Berkoff, as
opposed to transposing such incongruous and less theologically signifi-

cant effects to *Greek* specifically edits such minor characters. Through such editing not only are the weakened community links of modern life in contrast to the ancient city-state of the source text emphasised, but also it is suggested that the representation of the god-willed confusing pattern of interlinked coincidences and chances at the root of the Oedipal myth, is anachronistic for a modern day diasporic audience which has been shaped and formed by the dislocation and rupture wrought by two world wars, a reality which is summoned to account for the circumstances of the foundling Eddy's birthright:

> DAD: . . . Well all of a sudden in that hot August afternoon no bananas in the shops and coupons for four ounces of sweets each week, pictures of Auschwitz just come out / thousands of bodies like spaghetti all entwined / all done in the name of Adolf / all of a sudden in the hot blue day . . . they're all swimming look at them, look at all that blood and oil, bad mix, the sky turned black. What a terrific hell of a bang, and soot dropping all over us plus bits of people, all the fish dropped dead, from shock, hey let's help them out. Look let's get some help, they're all in the water. Some jerry ball of hate stacked full of painful promise and carrying the names of the future dead blew the Southend tripper to the moon and down they fell in deadly mash of Guinness and Gold Flake . . . We threw the bear back in the slick, and lifted the toddler out all dripping wet and covered in oil looking like a darkie so, no one about we took him home and washed him / he was a beaut / and mum was double chuffed to see a little round soft ball of warm goo goo / 'don't want to give him up' quoth Dinah, 'must we' she said. 'Nah', I said 'his mum will think he's dead anyway' / so let her go on thinking it . . . [p. 181]

Descriptions detailing the circumstances surrounding Eddy's parentage serve to make the audience aware of the post-war environment in which *Greek* takes place, and by extension the global fight against fascism is presented as an ominous and lurking backdrop to the racist victimization, nationalism and violence foregrounded in the present. In this way Berkoff introduces what might be considered the potentially unsaid intratextual psychoanalytical theories of the Oedipal myth, such as Reich's *Mass Psychology of Fascism*[25] into the Rewrite.

Berkoff's editing and emphasising of certain parts of the source text is not merely in order to convey the discontinuities and continuities with the source text for our present reception; rather, he is further suggesting that such continuities and discontinuities have been partly shaped and effected by the psychoanalytic influence of the intratext upon the source text and by extension the society which is mimetically represented in *Greek*. By emphasising how the intratext has contributed not only to

textual but also societal discontinuities and continuities Berkoff is dramaturgically putting into relief just how unstable are the foundations upon
which the intratext still operates, consigning us, as Hospers astutely observes, to the repetitive expiation offered by a reified psychoanalytic discourse based on a myth which ultimately has little realistic and practical
palliative application for the present not least because it is in part responsible for the present:

> The patients are not responsible for their neurotic manifestations, but then nei-
> ther are the parents responsible for theirs; and so, of course for their parents in
> turn, and theirs before them. It is the twentieth century version of the family
> curse, the curse on the House of Atreus.[26]

The psychoanalytical abrogation of responsibility, as enunciated by the
intratext, is thus presented by Berkoff as a root cause for so much of the
divisiveness, violence and antagonism present within modern society. In
this way, an implicit contrast is made with the ancients' confrontation
with the question of responsibility, particularly during the Attic Period,
when the debate about responsibility under man-made laws in contrast to
Man being destined to act in accordance with the will of the gods, was at
its height:

> The development of subjective responsibility, the distinction made between an
> action carried out of one's own volition and performed despite oneself, and the
> account taken of the agent's personal intentions are all innovations of which the
> tragedians were aware; and through the advances made in law, they had a pro-
> found effect upon the Greek concept of the agent and also altered the individual's
> relation to his own actions.[27]

Thus, *Greek* reintroduces the debate about the agent's responsibility which
to some extent the intratext has abrogated from our reception of the
source text and by extension from the present socio-political realities as
represented in *Greek*. Berkoff dramaturgically asserts, through silent allusion to the source text, that in today's godless society surely the concept
of responsibility needs to be addressed with even greater urgency if we
are not to repeat the destruction and barbarism of a society which is prey
to the often double-edged properties of the "hero" or the "will to heroize",
be that in the form of "Adolf" or "Maggot", a perjorative allusion to Mrs
Thatcher.

Thus, the Rewrite plays upon the said and unsaid, familiar and strange,
continuities and discontinuities with the source text through the intratext,
and as such echoes the Gadamerian opinion of the peculiar potential of

tragedy for continuity with the modern experience, whereby the spectator's encounter with the tragic theme and work becomes a self encounter. Even though Eddy "knows" the Oedipal story, and even alludes to the Oedipal tragedy within his own autobiographical account, the tragic dimensions of the source text are maintained by the eucatastrophe ending of the Rewrite which, freed from the Freudian imposition of predetermined unconscious "guilt", is still open-ended, leaving Eddy and by extension, us, not knowing his or, indeed, our own fate or path to self-knowledge and "understanding". In this way, Berkoff reaffirms the source text's emphasis upon the hermeneutic quest to self knowledge and understanding despite the intratextual information-based sedimentation of the source text's supposed "meaning" formed independently of interpretation, which as Weinsheimer observes is a hermeneutic impossibility:

> An old building suffers decay; but an old book is quite meaningless, dead, indeed not a book at all, until it is revitalised in interpretation. Yet that very alienation of voice into the meaningless of writing is the indispensable condition of the fact that the past returns more present to us in literature than in the architecture that survives uninterrupted from the same period. In great books the past does not live still, but rather again, and the more fully for being interrupted. Books are not a direct expression of mind then, but an indirect one. Indirection is the condition of our most direct access to history, as death is the price of resurrection.[28]

Although the Rewrite's eucatastrophe[29] ending does not ostensibly conform to Gadamer's analysis of tragedy whereby "the excess of tragic consequences is characteristic of the tragic" it does exhibit continuity with the source text thematically, but for the present and in recognition of the intratextual influence of the source text on our present reception. In fact, the Rewrite does capture *a sense of the 'excess of tragic consequences'* in the present by *not* specifying or particularising them and rather leaving such consequences as undisclosed potentialities in an imaginative space that, hopefully, cannot and will not be able to surmount the horrors which comprise the present reality of modern life. Even though the Rewrite does not appear to present Eddy as a tragic hero, it does structurally and thematically allude to the tragic fate of his predecessor, Oedipus, dramaturgically compelling the audience to address and confront the "tragic" for today, as opposed to perceiving the classic through a process of aesthetic distanciation as a venerated literary model which has physically as opposed to hermeneutically survived the "test of time".[30]

Thus, by virtue of the historically effected consciousness which informs its dramaturgy, the Rewrite addresses not only the source text's thematic concerns but also the changing attitudes to genre, and in this particular case, how our reception of tragedy may to a great degree become subject to the aesthetic distanciation which leads to hermeneutic alienation.[31] Of course it is essential to be aware of the crucial distinction between the dramaturgical *Erlebnis* of the Rewrite which is inextricably bound up with the historicity acknowledged in the experience of *Erfahrung*, and the aesthetic *Erlebnis* which motivates aesthetic distanciation.[32]

Greek further addresses the altered states which history imposes upon the source text through intratextual hap with respect to the riddle of the Sphinx, and the contrast between the answers given in response to the riddle by Oedipus and Eddy. Eddy's answer reflects the psycho-sexual and desire-driven focus of the intratext although he ironically reaches the same conclusion as his tragic precursor, Oedipus:

> EDDY: Man. In the morning of his life he is on all fours, in the afternoon when he is young he is on two legs, and in the evening when he is erect for his woman he sprouts the third leg.

Eddy's retort to the Sphinx's subsequent indignant accusation of trickery suggests that even reason such as that posited by the intratextual determinism, never mind hermeneutic analysis, is not stable or eternal, as well as suggesting the extent to which the intratextual psycho-sexual concerns have reached pervasive proportions in the present:

> SPHINX: You bastard, you've used trickery to find out the riddle.
> EDDY: No, just reason. All right, sorry to have to do this, I was growing quite fond of you. [Act 2, Scene 3 p. 171]

The altered states bestowed by historicity, and which an interpretation imbued with historically effected consciousness elucidates, are also emphasised by the Rewrite's emphasis on Eddy's self-conscious and self-reflexive rite of passage, from youth to manhood, a rite of passage which develops from the imperative of "to have to" repeat the cyclical determinism of the Oedipal formula, to his renunciation of the Oedipal fate at the end of the play:

> EDDY: . . . Why should I tear my eyes out Greek style, why should you hang yourself . . . Oedipus how could you have done it, never to see your wife's golden face again, never again to cast your eyes and hers on your eyes. [Act 2 Scene 4 p. 183]

Thus, just as Eddy's characterisation is not static, it is also implied that his reading of the source text, which he refers to in an ironically detached manner within the parameters of the Rewrite, does not remain unchanged but is imbued with the effects of his own historicity.

Eddy's personal development puts the hermeneutic nihilism and aspirationless demeanor of his parents into stark relief. MUM and DAD symbolise the apathetic, unimaginative and spiritless textual residue of the controlling theoretical determinism wrought by intratextuality, as illustrated by their cliché-ridden repetitive and predictable speech:

> DAD: Nah son but thanks and double ta. You're very kind to us . . . how thoughtful / bless you, you're welcome, have a nice day, but we're used to wot we got, can you teach an old dog new tricks, a bit long in the tooth you're as old as you feel, and I feel like a worn out old fart . . . we know the familiar faces / our rotten neighbours / . . . [p. 176]

Indeed the hermeneutic nihilism exemplified by Eddy's parents' uninspired and apathetic language contrasts with the veracity of Eddy's hate-speech during the murder scene, in which Eddy actually kills his father with words:

EDDY:	Hit hurt crunch pain stab jab
MANAGER:	Smash hate rip tear asunder render
EDDY:	Numb jagged glass gouge out
MANAGER:	Chair breakhead split fist splatter splosh crash
EDDY:	Explode scream fury strength overpower overcome
MANAGER:	Cunt shit filth remorse weakling blood soaked
EDDY:	Haemorrhage, rupture and swell. Split and cracklock jawsprung and neck break
MANAGER:	Cave in rib splinter oh the agony the shrewd icepick
EDDY:	Testicles torn out eyes gouged and pulled strings snapped socket nail scrapped
MANAGER:	Bit swallow suck pull
EDDY:	More smash and more power
MANAGER:	Weaker and weaker
EDDY:	Stronger and stronger
MANAGER:	Weak
EDDY:	Power
MANAGER:	Dying
EDDY:	Victor
MANAGER:	That's it
EDDY:	Tada.
WAITRESS:	You killed him / I never realised words can kill. [[159–160]

Just as the repetitive sterility and hermeneutic reification of the "parents" speech suggests a lack of imaginative space, so too, like the pornographic language which punctuates the play, Eddy's language in this scene exhibits the desire-driven and goal oriented acquisitiveness of modern society to such a degree that it leaves no imaginative space and is bereft of the said in the unsaid, the voice in the silence.[33] Indeed, the contrast between such pornographic and desire-driven vocabulary with the poetic and erotic reverie with which Eddy addresses his wife later in the play not only suggests his developing maturity, but also reveals his motivation as being one based on a pleasure principle befitting their "love story" as opposed to the goal-driven sating of desire which typifies the consumeristic culture of the 1980's. The comic-book register of the scenes of violence in *Greek* also allude to the developmental stage which Eddy's character has reached at this point in the play, and is another indication of the way *Greek* emphasises historicity by representing Eddy's rite of passage as analogous to attaining hermeneutic *Erlebnis* from childhood to adulthood, from containment to liberation and from hermeneutic nihilism to imaginative space. By employing such active and onomatopoeic language Berkoff implies a lack of imagination or descriptive ambiguity, and by extension he asserts that hermeneutic familiarity as effected by the intratextual Freudian imposition can only ultimately demean language to this level of comic-book determinism. Later, MUM and DAD's speech in Act 2, Scene 4 also serves to further emphasise Berkoff's critique of the wider psycho-social *effects* of ceding to such theoretical "containment", such as economic oppression facilitated in part by the instilled sense of repression and desubordination produced by intratextual enframing, like the Oedipal Complex, and as reflected in the parents' unconscious resignation to their lowly and unfulfilled existence both hermeneutically and socially:

> . . . it can't be now undone with words
> Fate makes us play the role we're cast. [p. 164]

The Rewrite emphasises the hermeneutic nihilism wrought by the deterministic intratextuality in order to expand upon the way in which such enframing under the guise of freedom can invariably result in the often silent and unheard effects of socio-economic and class oppression as echoed by DAD's pathos-filled but misplaced nostalgia:

> DAD: . . . he gave me fifty quid when I retired, handsome and watch with
> fifteen jewels / right proud I was / so what I got asbestos in my lung / so
> what I got coal dust in my blood / so what I got lead poisoning in my brain
> / so what I got shot nerves from the machines / so what I lost two fingers
> in the press / so what I'm going deaf from the steel mills / so what I lost a
> lung for our old king in Dunkirk / I'd do it again / yes I would I tell ya / so

what I got fuck all for it from our fair state / so what they're gliding past in
their Rolls-Royces / and their fat little kids come tumbling out on piggy
little legs / so what they thieve and murder and get away with it / so what
our royals pay no tax / they're figureheads mate / . . . [p. 177]

In this respect, Berkoff links his critique of the hermeneutic nihilism that
allows intratextual imposition or aesthetic distanciation to take place, with
the aspirationless sense of "security" to which the London working classes,
like Eddy's parents, cling, thriving on nostalgia and ritualistic notions of
tradition at the expense of the possible, but uncertain, social mobility and
betterment, which their "son" ultimately achieves. Indeed, the dangers of
generational reification are alluded to throughout *Greek* with, for example,
the repetitive tone of "DAD'S" limited and apathetic language and by
continual reference to "dads who have caught the British plague that ce-
ments their heads and puts vitriol inside their hearts" [Act 2, Scene 4 p.
178] a dystopic symptom identified by Eddy with:

EDDY: Still you can't help it / you're drowned in aggro since a kid and dad has
fed between your flappy lugs not love but hate / has fed the history of ye
old past to give you causes / something to do at night / has woven a
tapestry of woe inflicted on him from the distant foggy patch called past.
[Act 1, Scene 4 p. 156]

In this sense Berkoff alludes to the sins of the fathers with respect to the
"inertia" and apathetic reification of hermeneutic nihilism from ". . . a
distant foggy patch called the past.", in order to further reinforce how
psychoanalytic paradigms like the Oedipal complex all too often provide
an escape route or "get-out" clause from present responsibilities.

Indeed, it is worthwhile recalling Gadamer's view as to the way in
which we often subordinate hermeneutic "understanding" to the pursuit
of knowledge.[34] Such a subordination is a central theme of the source
text, which the Rewrite, through negotiation with historically effected
consciousness, reinvokes with reference to the effects of the 'blinding
knowledge' of the source text's subsequent intratextual history. *Greek*
thus "bridges the temporal distance" between ourselves and the source
text, not by replacing the source text's intratextual determinism, but by
incorporating it as part of the hermeneutic totality of *Oedipus Rex* for
our reception, and more importantly our "understanding" today, for as
Bernasconi has observed:

. . . once we have freed ourselves from the supposition that the meaning of a
text resides in reconstructing the sense it had for its authors or their contemporaries we are in a position to experience historical distance as something positive.

> It is when we no longer treat Plato and Aristotle as our contemporaries that we are in a position to be struck by what they have to say and have our horizons opened by them.[35]

The Rewrite dramaturgically emphasises in spite and because of the intratextual imposition of silence, what the source text has to say through a true hermeneutic experience imbued with historically effected consciousness and not canonised or ritualised reading practices which, in the case of *Oedipus Rex*, have also contributed to shaping the wider area of our "understanding" of human sexuality. Thus, just as the Rewrite initiates the release of the source text from the past silencing of the intratext, so too the source text is given a voice concerning the wider sociopolitical effects of the intratext in the present. Through such hermeneutic dialogue between past and present the transformation into structure of the Rewrite's eucatastrophe ending is elicited—a dramaturgical acknowledgment of the following "task":

> The hermeneutic task consists in not covering up this tension [between the text and the present] by attempting a naive assimilation of the two, but in consciously bringing it out. [36]

The autobiographical form of the Rewrite, puts the confessional mode of the psychoanalytic discourse of the intratext into stark relief, and it allows the Oedipus of the source text to reassume his status as a "character" which can in turn respond, as Eddy, to the intratextual casting of him as psychoanalytical paradigm. By breaking free of the psychoanalytic structure which has been imposed upon our reception of *Oedipus Rex* the generalised Freudian application and its inherently confessional and expiative interchange is replaced by the dialogue and questioning which shapes the autobiographical form. Thus, the intratextuality of the source text which is negotiated by Berkoff elicits the said of the unsaid, the unsaid of the said, for by including the subsequent hap of the Freudian intratextuality he illustrates the effect which Freud's contribution to the "repressive hypothesis" and the subsequent backlash against it has wrought upon our reception of *Oedipus Rex* in the present, as well as drawing attention to the wider socio-political ramifications of the effects of the psychoanalytic "industry". Indeed, Berkoff alludes to the psychoanalytic industry within *Greek*, and in so doing he pointedly makes reference to the suppliant posture of unequals, as opposed to the liberational space of parity, which such theories have imposed upon us in what Foucault has identified as the "confessing society"[37] of modernity:

EDDY: I'll send the chauffeur down to pick them up / that's if my dad has rid
himself of that old hoary myth that like a louse ate inside his nut, to tell
him of patricide and horrid incest / or subtitled could be called the story
of a mother fucker / a tale of kiddiwinks to send them mad to bed and
cringe in shadows in the night, and in their late years to bring good gelt to
shrinks in Harley Street. [Act 2, Scene 3 p. 172]

The autobiographical form of the Rewrite allows Oedipus a voice beyond
the deterministic appropriation of the source text, through his historical
successor Eddy, and is in keeping with Miething's observation that:

. . . autobiography observes just one question: who am I? . . . The autobiographical project obeys the order given by the Delphic oracle, the command-
ment, *gnothi se auton*.[38]

Meithing's opinion of autobiography affirms the basic emphasis upon dialogue and the perpetual questioning which serves as the impetus for the
autobiographical form. It is the *questioning* intrinsic to the autobiographical
form, culminating in an inescapably unanswered final question that evades
resolution or closure, that earmarks it as the quintessential literary recognition of the necessary *quest* to "know thyself", and this is a most fitting
form for the Rewrite of *Oedipus Rex* which seeks to expose the deterministic intratextual closure which has silenced the source text for so long.
The autobiographical form thus reinvests the source text with the imaginative space that has been circumscribed by the hermeneutic closure of
the intratext whilst addressing the effects of that intratext on the present
within the parameters of the Rewrite, dramaturgically emphasising what
Bernasconi sees as:

. . . the logic of supplementarity [whereby] the parasite is more original than the
original.[39]

In a sense Oedipus ventriloquises through Eddy his opinions about his
own intratextual fate, and the ventriloquist role which Eddy plays is further emphasised by the stage directions about movement, mask and the
almost impersonatory atmosphere of *Greek* in performance (by
impersonatory it is suggested that Berkoff's play almost appears to be
artifice responding to art):

The faces are painted white and are clearly defined. Movement should be sharp
and dynamic; exaggerated and sometimes bearing the quality of a seaside cartoon.

In an almost Pirandello-like way such impersonatory and self-consciously
theatrical devices (including the use of mime and strobe lighting which

evoke the filmic effect of the silent screen) has the effect that *Greek* in performance forestalls the illusory and deluding effects of the aesthetic distanciation with which the classics, in particular, are often approached. However, this does not entail that the interpretation becomes thematic, rather the intratextuality and its thematic and theatrical effects are incorporated into the dramatic *Erlebnis* of the Rewrite, and as such *Greek* perfectly conveys the Gadamerian premise that all interpretation should be undifferentiated from the work itself so that:

> The performance . . . does not become as such thematic but the work presents itself through it and in it . . . The fact that works stretch out of a past into the present as enduring monuments still does not mean that their being is an object of aesthetic or historical consciousness.[40]

The disrupted temporal sequence evoked in the Rewrite by the use of slow motion/fast forward strobe lighting effects suggest the way in which intratextuality has determined and administered our hermeneutic focus upon certain parts of the source text as opposed to others, in a fashion similar to film editing which selectively and deterministically consigns aspects of an artwork to the cutting room floor. Berkoff uses such theatrical devices within the theatrical event that is *Greek* as opposed to employing awkward and superimposed didacticism to arouse us from the inertia of accepting and apathetically consuming the imposed editing and emphases wrought by the intratext. The employment of such theatrical effects adds to the successful mimetic transference from ancient Greece to the technological age of the present, with the effect of conveying the extent to which technological expertise creates the almost imperceptible and silent effects of enframing which ultimately shape and administer our view of the world.

Gadamerian hermeneneutics does not posit the discovery of a privileged or superior reading of a text, rather it emphasises that *all* "understanding" is located in the different. Thus the privilege of the "familiar" interpretation of the text is disturbed, but not in favour of another oppositional model within the realm of metaphysics, for as Gadamer points out if we are to "understand" the historical text at all, it is through a different "understanding."

Besides facilitating a sense of history in our reception of *Oedipus Rex* via the depiction of an individual's rites of passage, the autobiographical form of *Greek* also preempts the repetition of a sense of the familiar at the expense of eliciting the strange. For example, *Greek* omits the reconstruction of the Sophoclean dramatic tension created by the source text's famous scenes of *stichomythia* and silence, prior to the revelation or *anagnorisis* of the "dreadful knowledge" which as commented upon by Rudynytsky contributes to:

> The tension between antithetical movements of haste and delay [which] is a direct expression of the self-analytic structure of *Oedipus the King*, wherein Oedipus' quest for himself is simultaneously a flight from himself.[41]

In this way Berkoff acknowledges that the Oedipal "story", albeit "known" through the deterministic framework of the Oedipal Complex has become all too familiar to us in the present, and that by extension, the "awful knowledge" has become as sanitized and rationalised to the level of theory, a sterility which Gadamer warns against:

> Art is not merely a tool of sociopolitical will; art documents a social reality only when it is really art, and not when it is used as an instrument.[42]

Of course, familiarity in the modern sense as 'methodological sureness' should not be confused with the familiarity of the previously known or that which is not novel to our understanding, for as Heath points out novelty was not a concern of the ancient tragedians either:

> . . . one of the basic aesthetic principles of tragedy (that of tragic dignity) has a moral content, so that—quite independently of any specifically didactic purpose—there are pressures within the aesthetics of the genre which would impel tragedians towards writing in accordance with accepted and acceptable values. Consequently, the tragedian will not have to try at all hard to write in an edifying way; this will follow naturally from his writing within the generic conventions . . . The idea that the tragedians wrote, in whole or in part, to explore or commend philosophical or religious opinions of any novelty or intellectual depth is not supported by this external evidence.[43]

In this respect, it is the intellectualisation of the source text, wrought by the determinism of intratextuality that has the effect of containing our spontaneous and emotive responses and replacing them with the certainty and repetition of familiarity.[44] The familiarity wrought by the "enframing" over-intellectualisation of *Oedipus Rex* is addressed in and by *Greek*, which through editing and form conveys the intratext as both a cause and product for the altered expectations we have of art, in particular tragedy, the genre which encompasses the source text. Thus familiarity, albeit through the distorting prism of intratextuality, has in part altered our concerns and expectations with respect to the reception of tragedy, from the originary ancient Greek expectation of *hedone* based on the physical manifestation of *eleos* and *phobos* elicited by dramaturgical expertise, as opposed to the modern expectation for novelty in the form of intellectual stimulation. The Rewrite draws attention to the way the institutionalisation of expectations or 'foreunderstandings' may compel us to cede to the sterile reception of familiarity, a sterility that can only be combatted by our reintroduction to the strangeness of the unsaid in the text, for as Gadamer states it is the tension between familiarity and strangeness which leads us to hermeneutic *Erlebnis*, and which the traditionary text or classic has the most potential for above most other texts.[45]

Indeed, there are numerous examples which reaffirm the view that *hedone* was central to the appreciation of tragedy in fifth century Athens, as exemplified by Herodotus' anecdote about a performance of Phrynichus' *Sack of Miletus* which led to the poet being fined and the play banned, not because the audience was moved to tears which was, in any case, a requirement of tragedy, but rather because the tears were shed over misfortunes that touched the audience too closely, reminding them of their own troubles and thus failing to adhere to the Hesiodic function of poetry, pleasure or *hedone*. Dramaturgical expertise and creativity was thus paramount for the competitive spirit of fifth century Athens, far removed from our twentieth century expectation of novelty, surprise or intellectualism. Over the centuries the *eleos and phobos* which elicits *hedone* have become intellectualised as terms of reference based on aesthetic distanciation, a transformation which Gadamer comments upon:

> Aristotle is not at all concerned with pity or with the changing valuations of pity over the centuries and similarly fear is not to be understood as an inner state of mind. Rather both are events that overwhelm man and sweep him away. Eleos is the misery which comes over us in the face of what we call miserable. Thus we commiserate with the fate of Oedipus (the example that Aristotle always returns to).[46]

As opposed to attempting to dramaturgically reaffirm the power of these emotions for a modern audience through the Rewrite, Berkoff incorporates our changing attitudes toward areas of human existence including our reception of tragedy into its own narrative parameters. In this way Berkoff clearly emphasises how our modern expectations of tragedy have altered in keeping with an "information-based" society which facilitates almost casual and voyeuristic access to the horrors of genocide and atrocity on a daily basis and in which the vicarious expectation founded upon the theoretical premise put forward by intratextual generalisations about *our* subjectivity and *our* identity are taken for granted as scientific and rationalistic "knowledge". Thus *Greek* suggests that today's society has forsaken the aleatory, serendipitous and deeply personal experience of pleasure for the power-driven instantaneity of desire, and in the case of our reception of *Oedipus Rex* the attainment of the pleasure of 'understanding' and self-knowledge which was at the root of ancient tragic dramaturgy has evolved into the deterministic and generalised information gathering desire to 'know' and store. Such a perception of tragedy is far removed from that of the ancients which emphasised the tragic genre as fulfilling the desire for pleasure or *hedone*, providing the subject matter and its handling was sufficiently detached from the immediate personal concerns of the audience. Indeed, in *Works and Days* Hesiod points out how the Muses induce the forgetfulness of ills (55); how a bard eases a man's grief and helps him to forget his troubles (98–103); and he does so precisely because of the sweetness and beauty of song (97, 104). Also Homer's *Odyssey* is replete with references to the pleasure-inducing function of poetry, the larger part of which was dedicated to the tragic, but it is emphasised that such an effect cannot arise from one's own tragedy since song is supposed to be forgetfulness of one's ills and a refuge from care, a point which is emphasised when Democdocus moves Odysseus to tears by a story that touches his own personal sorrows (1.325–71 and 8. 43–107) Thus, through the analepsis and prolepsis of the autobiographical form Berkoff's play reveals how far removed we have become from the emotive responses of *eleos* and *phobos enjoyed* by the audience of fifth century Athenian tragedy, and how the over-intellectualisation and theorising of such art has denied us the *hedone* or pleasure of the source text.

Thus, although tragedies like *Oedipus Rex* necessarily have an intellectual and moral content, and indeed may have acquired over the centuries the influence of instilling moral and intellectual effects on audiences, the function of tragic drama for the ancient audiences was indubitably *hedone* or pleasure. Moral didacticism was not the primary concern (much to Plato's chagrin) of the fifth century Athenian tragedian who in keeping with the principle of *hedone* was most interested to elicit an emotional response from the audience, but not emotion stemming from recognition of one's own sorrows. Instead the ancient tragedian:

> . . . was writing for the theatre, where his overriding task—the one on which competitive success would depend—was to satisfy an audience that looked for emotional stimulus and aesthetic satisfaction. In this sense Plato was right when he argued that the tragedian necessarily subordinated moral to hedonistic consideration: it is only that his somewhat eccentric moral outlook led him to infer from

the priority of emotive interests that tragedy could have no moral concern or intent at all. That on the present view, would be an exaggeration; but so would the view that assigned priority to didactic over hedonistic intentions. We might say therefore that it is not the presence of a didactic strand in the tradition that is misleading but the prominence it is accorded in some parts of the tradition. [47]

Indeed, Berkoff alludes to the loss of *hedone* in our reception of ancient Greek dramaturgy by presenting London, the focal point for the "septic isle" and "the decaying island", as a putrid, seething and sick body devoid of pleasure or *hedone*. By metaphorically presenting London as a cadaverous organism invaded like a "stinking woodpile" by "rats" and "maggots" Berkoff is simultaneously addressing the way that the detrimental and persisting symptoms of intratextuality continue to prevent the pleasures or *hedone* normally available to a healthy, productive and creative city, body or text. The psycho-corporeal language of the text in the form of pornography, invective and verbal bile emphasises the repressed and ailing body of a city that is replete with the multifarious pressure groups and sects which form the micropolitical backlash against the repressive hypothesis including a particularly vituperative strain of feminism in the shape of the Sphinx:

> SPHINX: . . . / when women were women, androgynous and whole and could reproduce themselves but somewhere and some time a reptile left our bodies, crawled away and became man, but it stole our little bag of seed and ever since the little reptile has been trying to crawl back, but we don't want it anymore, all we need is your foul little seed you gnat . . .
> [Act 2, Scene 2 p 169]

Indeed, the unhealthy and unproductive state of London in the 1980's, fragmented by the competing forces spawned as a result of the repressive hypothesis, as perpetuated by the intratextual influence, is emphasised by the Sphinx's antagonism toward men. The gender division is further conveyed by descriptions of repressed and unexpressed pleasure which manifests itself in sordid, asocial and destructive outlets like pornography, obscenity and violence:

> Masturbating shops line every High Street and the pneumatic drill of strong wrists ensures a girl a fat living, the country's awash in spunk not threshing and sweetening the wombs of lovers but crushed in Kleenex and dead in cubicles with red lights. Meanwhile men in white masks are penetrating the holy crucible where life may have slipped in, and armed with scalpels and suction pumps tear out the living fruit and sluice it down the river of sewage, the future Einsteins, Michelangelos and Eddys. The blood of creation is swept and flushed away with gasps of "don't" inside the tender packages not yet fulfilled. [Act 2, Scene 1 p. 167]

The combination of the intratextual hap with the violent, pornographic and profane description of London as a lonely, destructive, violent and divisive place devoid of pleasure not only alludes to the sexually repressed body, but by extension the loss of the *hedone* in our reception of tragedy is also recalled. In this respect, the Rewrite simultaneously presents the city-as-body-of-text, and in so doing emphasises not only the intratextual effect upon our reception of the source text, but also the wider intratextual ramifications upon sexuality, and by extension society.

The ancient Greek emphasis upon *hedone* or pleasure founded upon the emotive effect of tragedy is no longer the central concern of the modern interpretation of tragedy, and in a sense the determinism of contemporary morality and intellectualism often subsumes the imaginative space, or that which Heath identifies as the "poetics of tragedy". Just as mimesis is a prerequisite for the *Erlebnis* of the Rewrite, this must be balanced with imaginative space which Berkoff tries to re-illuminate by highlighting the way intratextual determinism has appropriated our understanding of *Oedipus Rex*, for as Gadamer explains in connection with the attainment of the "truth" of *Erlebnis*:

> A play in which everything is completely motivated creaks like a machine. It would be a false reality if the action could all be calculated out like an equation. Rather it becomes a play of reality when it does not tell the spectator everything, but only a little more than he customarily understands in his daily round. The more that remains open, the more freely does the process of understanding succeed . . .[48]

It is the altered states brought about by the historicity of our reception of the source text that is addressed in *Greek* not only by way of the autobiographical narrative but also with the implicit and explicit references to events in *Oedipus Rex* through the devices of analepsis and prolepsis, and the Rewrite's re-cognition of the over-intellectualisation of our reception of tragedy includes confronting the silencing effect of familiarity within its own textual parameters. Indeed, the silencing effects of familiarity are actually incorporated into Eddy's reassessment of his "fate" (as prescribed by the Oedipal Myth and its subsequent intratextuality):

> What a foul thing I have done, I am the rotten plague, tear them out Eddy, rip them out, scoop them out like ice-cream, just push the thumb behind the orb and push, pull them out and stretch them to the end of the strings and then snap. Darkness falls. Bollocks to all that.[Act 2, Scene 4 p. 183]

In this final scene Berkoff emphasises that our emotional response to tragedy has been supplanted by the critical intellectualisation of the intratext to such an extent that Eddy's "choice" has actually evolved into an intellectual and theoretical blue print known as the Oedipal Complex. However, by presenting Eddy's eucatastrophic 'decision', Berkoff is not merely positing an ending that is in opposition to the manifestation of the psychoanalytic "guilt" in the intratext; rather, in a similar process to that of the source text we are made aware of the aporia at the end of play. That is, the aporia whereby ". . . tragic man does not have to "choose" between two possibilities; rather he "recognizes" that there is only one way open before him." For Oedipus and the fifth century audience who observed his "fate" such an *ananke*[49] was imposed by the gods whereby the tragic subject recognised the religious necessity that makes him internally compelled, *biastheis*, even while he is making his "decision", and similarly, Berkoff reintroduces the concept of Eddy's responsibility to decide in accordance with the *ananke* imposed by his hermeneutic re-cognition of the source text for the present through historically effected consciousness. As the odyssey through his own intratextual history reveals, both to himself and to us, if Eddy does not choose his "twice known" mother as wife he is submitting once more to the proven reification of hermeneutic death as subsequently imposed by the psychoanalytic intratext, the Oedipal Complex. Instead, the eucatastrophe re-opens and reinvigorates not only the hermeneutic potential of the source text for the present, but also by reclaiming the imaginative space of the source text for the present and by extension the hap for the future, the socio-political effects wrought by the intratext may be diminished if not overcome, for as Ricouer has convincingly argued:

> It is in the realm of the imaginary that I try out my capacity to do something; that I take the measure of 'I can'.[50]

Of course, the "I can" of the imaginative space precipitated by the transformation-into- structure of the eucatastrophe should be carefully distinguished from the goal-driven objective of the ideological—be it the "will to power" of the pressure groups, the capitalists, the racists, the warmongers or the theoretical appropriations which all form part of Berkoff's dramaturgy of bile. Rather, like the originary dramaturgical project of ancient Greek theatre, the imaginative space reopened in and by *Greek* is defined by the pleasure or *hedone* of the aleatory, serendipitous "nowhere" of utopia not the predeterministic desire which characterised the dystopia of the 1980's. In this respect Berkoff's Rewrite is a celebration of acceptance that to know thyself is to "understand" the unknowable, as conveyed by the semantic ambiguity about Eddy's Utopian "nowhere" destination at the end of the play to "exit from paradise / entrance to heaven."

Notes

1 Freud developed the theory of the "primal scene" which states that the content of Sophocles' play corresponds to the latent content of our dreams:

> It is the fate of all of us, perhaps, to direct our first sexual impulse towards our mother and our first hatred and our first murderous wish against our father. Our dreams convince us that is so . . . While the poet, as he unravels the past, brings to light the guilt of Oedipus, he is at the same time compelling us to recognize our own inner minds, in which those same impulses, though suppressed are still to be found. [Sigmund Freud, The Standard Edition of the Complete Psychological Works of Sigmund Freud, 24 vols, ed. and trans. James Strachey with Anna Freud, Alix Strachey and Alan Tyson (London: The Hogarth Press 1953–1974) Vol 4 pp. 262–63.]

2 "Enframing" or Gestell is most comprehensively used by Heidegger in "The Question concerning Technology" in *Basic Writings* (ed: David Farrell Krell, Routledge, London 1996) p. 324. Heidegger does not merely posit that enframing is hermeneutic determinism, rather it is a "setting upon" that challenges us forth to revealing, a process that is even more in evidence in the age of technology:

> The word stellen [to set] in the name Ge-stell [enframing] does not only mean challenging. At the same time it should preserve the suggestion of another Stellen from which it stems namely that producing and presenting [Her-und Dar-stellen] which in the sense of poesis, lets what presences come forth into unconcealment. This producing that brings forth, eg., erecting a statue in the temple precinct, and the ordering that challenges now under consideration are indeed fundamentally different, and yet they remain related in their essence. Both are ways of revealing, of aletheia. [p. 326]

3 Goux, Jean-Joseph *Oedipus, Philosopher*, trans: Catherine Porter (Stanford: Stanford University Press,1993) p. 1

4 Michel Foucault, *The History of Sexuality Part One* p. 10

5 Foucault, *The History of Sexuality Part One* p. 5

6 Foucault, *The History of Sexuality Part One* p. 159

7 Vernant, "Oedipus Without the Complex" in *Myth and Tragedy in Ancient Greece* p. 103

8 See *TM* p.140 from . . . *Essential to an emanation* . . .

9 Vernant, *Myth and Tragedy in Ancient Greece* p. 87

10 Claude Levi-Strauss in "The Structural Study of Myth" (1955) has stated:

> . . . not only Sophocles but Freud himself should be included among the recorded versions of the Oedipus Myth on a par with earlier or seemingly more authentic versions. [p. 217]

11   Gadamer, *TM* p. 577

12   Bernasconi, "The Transformation of Language at Another Beginning" in *Heidegger in Question* p. 209

13   See Gadamer, *TM* p. 273, from . . . *paradoxical tendency toward restoration* . . .

14   F. Nietzsche *Thus Spoke Zarathustra: A Book for Everyone and No One* trans. R. J. Hollingdale (London: Penguin, 1969 p. 208

15   Heidegger, "The Way to Language" in *Basic Writings* (ed) David Farrell Krell (London: Routledge, 1996) p. 421

16   Heidegger, "The Way to Language" p. 421

17   Heidegger, "The Way to Language" p. 327

18   D. Glover, "Freud, Morality and Responsibility" in *Philosophy and Psychoanalysis* (ed) Brian A. Farrell (New York: Macmillan Publishing Company, 1994) p. 152

19   Foucault, *The History of Sexuality Part One* p. 135

20   Personal unpublished notes obtained from Edward Bond as a consequence of a period of correspondence and interviews during Christmas 1994.

21   See Paul Ricoeur's article "Imagination in Discourse and in Action" in *Rethinking Imagination: Culture and Creativity* eds., G. Robinson, J. Rundell (London: Routledge, 1994) pp. 126–135. Also refer to Editor's Preface.

22   Foucault "What is Enlightenment" in *The Foucault Reader* (ed) Paul Rabinow, p. 39

23   Foucault "What is Enlightenment" p. 40

24   Vernant, pp. 131–2

25   Wilhelm Reich, *The Mass Psychology of Facism* trans. by Vincent R. Carfagno (London: Souvenir Press, 1991).

26   John Hospers in 'What means this Freedom?' in *Philosophy and Psychoanalysis* (ed) B. Farrell (New York: Macmillan College Publishing Company, 1994) p. 142

27   Vernant, p. 69

28   Weinsheimer, (a) p. 129

29   *Eucatastrophe* is used here to describe a tragedy which does not end in catastrophe or disaster. Many critics consider that the final part of the Theban plays prevents them from being representative of the more familiar catastrophic ending of the ancient tragedies. However, with respect to Berkoff's Rewrite the term is used to suggest an alternative (although not a simplistically happy one) to the relatively catastrophic demise of Oedipus in Sophocles' *Oedipus Rex*. For a more

detailed discussion of *eucatastrophic* tragedy see Malcolm Heath's *The Poetics of Greek Tragedy* (London: Duckworth, 1987)

30 See Gadamer, *TM* p. 159 from . . . *Tragic pensiveness flows from the self-knowledge* . . .

31 See Gadamer, *TM* p. 85 for a further explanation of the effects of aesthetic consiousness, from . . . *Through reflection* . . .

32 Gadamer provides a fuller explanation of the distinction between the conjoined experience of *Erlebnis* and *Erfahrung*, and the *Erlebnis* which motivates aesthetic distanciation in *TM* p. 97 from . . . *The pantheon of art* . . .

33 See Eugene Ionescu's play *The Lesson* which explores semantic 'power' and 'hate speech'.

34 See Gadamer, *TM* p. 311 from . . . *the miracle of understanding* . . .

35 Bernasconi, p. 175

36 Gadamer, *TM* p. 306

37 Foucault, *History of Sexuality Part One* p. 59

38 Christophe Meithing, "Le grammaire de l'ego . . ." cited by Robert Smith in *Derrida and Autobiography: Literature, Culture, Theory 16* (Cambridge, Cambridge University Press, 1995) p. 55

39 Bernasconi, *The Art of Existing*, p. 210

40 Gadamer, *TM* p. 120

41 P. L. Rudnytsky,. *Freud and Oedipus* (New York: Columbia University Press, 1987) p. 268

42 Gadamer, *TM* p. 579

43 Malcolm Heath, *The Poetics of Greek Tragedy* (London: Duckworth, 1987) p. 47

44 Gadamer's analysis of the strangeness of familiarity is worthy of note here, *TM* pp. 361–2 from . . . *The axiom of familiarity* . . .

45 Gadamer explains why the strangeness of familiarity is best tested with respect to the classics or the eminent text. See *TM* p. 295 from . . . *Hermeneutics must start from the postion* . . .

46 Gadamer, *TM* p. 130

47 Heath, *The Poetics of Greek Tragedy* p. 47

48 Gadamer, *TM* p. 498

49 *Ananke* is usually translated into necessity, and suggests a necessity that is inescapable in its operations but which controls only specified events and not the whole range of necessitated occurrences. Plato considered necessity to be anti-

thetical to reason, as "errant cause" and the irrational element in the Universe; According to the ancient Greeks such necessity can be rationalised by persuasion but not wholly eliminated; it is a blind, aimless force akin to *tyche*.

50   Ricoeur, "Imagination in Discourse and in Action" in *Rethinking Imagination: Culture and Creativity* eds., G. Robinson, J. Rundell (London: Routledge, 1994) p. 126

Chapter Six

The Trackers of Oxyrynchus and the Hermeneutics of the Aesthetic

Invention as Destruction—The Genre of Self-Immolation

Satyr drama is the earliest known dramaturgical example of a concerted institutional evaluation of art, even though for a short period it transcended such categorisation at the competitive Dionysian festivals which Harrison pinpoints as rare occasions when a "great amalgam" of spectators, from "the shoemaker" to "the philosopher" voted, according to their particular response on the "effect" of art.[1] In this respect, Harrison's Rewrite of the Sophoclean Satyr drama, *Ichneutae*[2], as prompted by archaeological hap, is an ideal resource for his dramaturgical consideration of the aestheticisation of art, not only because of the demise of the genre but with respect to the overriding thematic concern of the source text, the Apollonian rationalisation of art. Because Satyr drama was a short-lived aesthetic category its subsequent "reception" has been negative and it has been casually disregarded as a frivolous unstructured aberration with which the Greek tragedians completed their tetralogies. However, Harrison's Rewrite,(*The Trackers of Oxyrynchus*, 1988) in keeping with the hermeneutic emphasis on questioning rather than answering, interrogates our complacent acceptance that the demise of the Satyr was of necessity due to its intrinsic worthlessness and, in an almost Foucauldian interrogation of the very discursive practices that shape us, Harrison assumes a critical scepticism towards the naturalised state of "aesthetic consciousness" because as Hernnstein Smith states:

> [The] . . . classics have been so thoroughly evaluated and interpreted *for* us by the very culture and cultural institutions through which they have been presented and by which we ourselves have been formed.[3]

The earliest recorded attribution of a Satyr play is to Pratinas of Phleious, who later competed with Aeschylus for the tragic prize between 499 and 496 BC. Archaeological evidence has revealed that Pratinas wrote fifty plays, of which thirty two were satyric, implying that he must have been competing at Athens before the rule of tetralogy came into force in 502–1 BC, for "otherwise the ratio between these two figures cannot be explained."[4] Such empirical facts suggest that the genre of Satyr drama was probably far more popular than the textual evidence would suggest, but that further investigation is circumscribed to a large degree because the Satyr drama flourished before its retrospective categorisation as the first dramaturgical "creation", and its subsequent demise, soon after, as the first "victim" of the aestheticisation of art.

There is considerable debate as to whether the Satyr provided the kernel of the tragic form, or whether it was a later accretion, and a large part of the confusion has been exacerbated by Aristotle's ambiguous description of the part played by Satyr drama in the evolution of the tragic dramatic form:

> Beginning with small plots and humorous diction, on account of its satyr-like origin (ek satyrikou), tragedy eventually became serious, and the iambic trimeter was substituted for the trochaic tetrameter, the latter having been employed at first on account of the satyr-like (satyriken) and dance-like character of the poetry.[5]

It has been popularly assumed that Aristotle is stating that tragedy was originally boisterous, wanton and obscene, leading to the deduction that the form originated from the Satyr drama, but Thompson refutes such a conclusion as one which conveniently conflates the dithyrambic origins of tragedy with Satyr, and which relies upon translating "satyr-like" as necessarily related to Satyr drama. Undoubtedly, the dithyramb was a wild and impassioned choral hymn sung in honour of Dionysus and was a form which preceded Attic Tragedy, but there is little evidence to suggest that this intrinsic part of the cult of Dionysus was in any specific way connected with the Satyr drama. Indeed, Herodotus attributes the first dithyramb to Arion in the latter part of the seventh century BC without making any mention of Satyr drama, and there is clear evidence to suggest that the primitive dithyramb provided the foundation for the first stages of ritual drama when the musicality of the earlier form came to be superseded by words, which, in turn, led to the emergent tragic form:

> . . . [Words] became so dominant as to shake themselves free of their musical integument, while the leader became an actor, then two actors and finally three. Yet long after it had grown wings, there still clung to the art of tragedy fragments of the chrysalis that had once secreted it."[6]

Indeed, the confusion created by Hermes when he leads the cattle in a number of directions to literally put the satyr off his track is an uncanny preamble to our difficulty in discerning the origins of Satyr drama, namely whether it evolved out of the Tragic form or whether it preceded it and, as a result, the "trackers" of Harrison's play not only allude to the satyrs in the service of Apollo, but also to the audience/reader who searches for the source of the Satyr drama:

(*The* SATYRS' *maze/tracking dance continues and becomes faster as though they are getting closer to their prey, then, following their different tracks they end in collision. They fall down, then they begin to look at the tracks closely.*)

1

If these are bull's tracks, their back legs go first
These bulls have had their bums reversed.

2

These tracks of god's herd, if that's what we've found
Look they're all of 'em the wrong way round.

3

Hey, look here at this! It's stupid, daft.
Their backlegs are forrad, their front legs are aft.
[Delphi version p. 32.]

Thompson convincingly suggests that Tragedy arose from the less organised parameters of cultic worship, procession and hymn which gradually came to be assimilated into the new form only to become subject to the organised sanitisation befitting the city-state festivals of Dionysia. It was only the gradual "refinement" of the tragic form, born of and imbued with the Dionysian frenzy of cultic worship, that led to the almost organic evolution of the satyr drama, as explained by Thompson:

This [the absorption of the Dionysian cultic rituals into the official state festivals] created a new tension, which had an important effect on its development. While the middle class strove to refine its intellectual content and to remove it from direct contact with reality, the peasantry and plebeians continued to seek in it the fulfilment of its earlier function. The result was that, as Aristotle says it took a long time to become serious. Indeed, the comic element was never entirely eliminated. While it was being extruded from the tragedies, it reappeared in the satyr play and on this basis at the end of the sixth century the art-form attained a final equilibrium, which owed its stability to the fact that in the meantime the comic element was finding a new and independent outlet. Thus, the evolution of tragedy and the emergence of comedy were both directly related to the interplay of internal tensions which is the dynamic of society.[7]

Thus, in a way, the fading Satyr genre retrospectively defined what was to become the genre of Tragedy, besides also paving the way for the emergence of the genre of Comedy, leaving a less well delineated bucolic and Arcadian space for itself that in effect did not really conform to or reflect the urban and civic concerns of the increasingly sophisticated and irreligious society of fifth century Athens. Of course, this is not to suggest the Satyr drama disappeared suddenly; in fact there is evidence to suggest that it was still relatively popular up until the third century, and Seaford argues this clearly proves that the ancient rituals, soil and nature which unite the mythological satyrs were nostalgically lauded by the Athenians during a period of rapid urbanisation:

> . . . satyric drama was created out of the urbanisation of Athens and then recre-
> ated in Alexandria. In an urban culture the pre-urban *thiasos* acquires a sharper
> significance.[8]

Of course, the precise details of how the Athenians responded to the Satyr drama are unclear, and as the divergence of opinion between Thompson and Seaford illustrate, open to debate, but undoubtedly the Satyr Drama has been erroneously categorised as a short-lived frivolity which provided a concluding element of humour to the tetralogies. Indeed, as Todorov points out all genres, however obscure, are intrinsic to other genres and even more so with respect to the formation of the two genres which were to provide the bedrock of our cultural heritage, Tragedy and Comedy:

> A new genre is always the transformation of an earlier one or of several: by
> inversion, by displacement, by combination . . . There has never been a litera-
> ture without genres; it is a system in constant transformation and historically
> speaking the question of origins cannot be separated from the terrain of genres
> themselves.[9]

Thus, the Satyr Drama was the generic sacrifice that assured the creation of both Tragedy and Comedy[10], as echoed in *The Trackers of Oxyrynchus* by the reference to the myth of Marsyas who was flayed alive by Apollo for deigning to play the flute, a myth which not only represents the first 'tragedy' but which also tells of how the remaining fearful satyrs hencefor-ward assumed the "role" of the frivolous, mischievous but innocuous clowns of Comedy who would not incur the wrath of Apollo. In this respect, Foucault's observation about the way we often misguidedly and idealisti-cally "theogenise" origins is correct, because as I have just shown any real investigation of "origins" invariably heightens our understanding of their "disparity":

. . . historical beginnings are lowly; not in the sense of modest or discreet like the steps of a dove, but derisive and ironic, capable of undoing every infatuation.[11]

The genre of Comedy coming after the Satyr drama also consolidated the supposed 'refinement' of theatre, most notably with respect to the gradual erosion of the free interaction accommodated between audience, chorus and stage by action and parabasis. Indeed, there is evidence that by the end of the fifth century, *proedria,* that is, a front row of seats of honour designated for civic dignitaries, had been instituted, marking a permanent division within and between the audience and the performers which was to result gradually, by the time of Menander, in the chorus degenerating into an almost subsidiary convention within the main drama. In the introduction to his Rewrite of Aristophanes' *Lysistrata, The Common Chorus* (1992) Harrison comments on the way the institution of such divisions has had the result of depriving us of the temporally transcendent sense of event which imbued the early ancient performances, leaving us conditioned by modern theatre into entering into a psychically and thus hermeneutically time-bound spectacle in which "We know in proscenium terms that once the curtain has risen it has to fall."[12] In his essay "The Festive Character of Theatre", (*Die Aktualitat des Schonen/ The Relevance of the Beautiful,* 1977) Gadamer also discusses the sense of event so intrinsic to early Greek theatre, a festive feature which he cites as essential to our escaping ". . .our thoroughly specialised existence"[13] and which all modern dramatists should aspire to by reinvoking the festive potential of our theatrical tradition, including the classics:

. . . the festive occasion possesses its own sort of temporality. It is an essentially recurrent phenomenon, and even a unique festival celebration bears the possibility of repetition within itself . . . Now for the first time in the history of the theatre, we see the repetition of performances and the revival of previously performed stageworks as standard practice. Now for the first time we are faced with the task of mediating between the contemporaneity of the present and the presence of our historical cultural heritage . . . However, this does not mean that the purpose of a classical theatrical programme is to give authentic performances whose historically accurate style has been established by scholars. On the contrary, the characteristic value of this chapter in the history of theatre is precisely the power of fusion that the present possesses as such when it succeeds in elevating past life into presence.[14]

Indeed, by playfully overturning our generic expectations Harrison alludes to the dramaturgical development that divided the audience and stage subsequent to the demise of the Satyr drama (that could well be considered an embryonic precursor to the proscenium arch) by incorporating a level of audience participation normally associated with the circus

as opposed to a work which has evolved into "high" art staged at illustri-
ous venues like The Royal National Theatre, as illustrated by the following
stage directions:

> (*Silenus* takes a papyrus scroll and unrolls it to reveal some fragments of the
> Greek papyrus, in fact, the first words of the Chorus of Satyrs in their fragmen-
> tary, incomplete state. They should be legible to all. With this he begins to teach
> the audience to chant the fragments until there is a strong chant which is echoed
> by the ancient voices of 8000 ghosts at the ancient Pythian games.) [p. 28.
> Delphi Version]

Additionally, Harrison refers to the divisive and often "obscene" effects of
urbanisation and "civilisation" and their continuing effect upon our production and reception of art in the present throughout his play, whether
it be the social insulation of the bourgeois theatre from the excluded but
very real tragedy "outside", or whether it is made manifest by the cultural
imperialism of Grenfell and Hunt who dismissively ridicule what they consider to be the primitive "fellaheen" as the latter attempt to transform the
papyri into natural fuel for their crop-growing, heat and general sustenance.

The irony of the aestheticisation of art which evolved into the use of
formal generic categorisations was that it proved to be the very process
that almost simultaneously created and precipitated the demise of the
newly defined Satyr drama, even though it would appear that similar
dramatic forms which had yet to be 'classified' were in existence prior to
this process, and that after its demise the 'effect' of Satyr was to imbue
perhaps the most cited generic categories, Comedy and Tragedy. Harrison
alludes to the paradoxical productivity of sacrifice with "Summat's been
flayed/for this sweet serenade." [p. 45] and Ferguson[15] has drawn attention to the centrality of the strange symbiosis between destruction and
creativity in the source text, thematic concerns which have retrospectively
acquired the dramatic irony of the finest examples of tragedy when one
considers not only the material demise of the Satyr drama, but also the
rather disconcertingly prophetic myth concerning the flaying of the Satyr
Marsyas for deigning to "make" music:

> SILENUS: No dead animal could produce a strain like that.
> CYLLENE: It's true
> SILENUS: How do you expect me to believe that booming voice comes from
>   beyond the grave!

It is unclear whether Sophocles intended to polemicise Apollo's implication in the manifest rationalisation of art which occurred during his own
lifetime, but nonetheless the irony that Apollo's quest resulted in the first

'tragedy' being born of the satyrs—the flaying of Marsyas—is further expanded by Harrison when at the end of the Royal National Theatre version he presents Apollo's wrath as ultimately redundant in a society which is already populated with downtrodden and "tragic" human satyrs. Thus Harrison presents the brutal possibility of a second flaying of the satyrs not for "aesthetic effect" but in order to highlight the hypocrisy of "aesthetic effect" in a society which is prepared to calmly and unfeelingly countenance the very real and human tragedies which daily confront them when they leave the theatre.

Indeed, Satyr drama's intergeneric residual and formative influence on both Tragedy and Comedy is suggested and reflected in the way *Trackers* is presented as a combination and conflation of a whole host of generic classifications including the tragic, the comic, the musical, the detective story and the farce. The dramaturgical form of the Rewrite absorbs and thereby demolishes, albeit in a transitory way, generic categorisation, the aestheticisation of art and evaluative opinions about "high" and "low" art, by evoking a multitude of genres, styles and forms within its own dramaturgical parameters. Some examples of this are monumental architecture and Victorian idealisation of the classical simultaneously represented by Kyllene, the Caryatid; the "musical" atmosphere of the synchronised Satyric "hoofers"; the detective genre represented by the "Holmes and Watson" of archaeology; Fauvist-like vandalism and defacement of institutional art; music, be it melodious, atonal, divine, classical, popular and folk; and a pastiche of generic classifications including comedy, tragedy, satyr and farce.

The evolutionary vicissitudes of what we call the Satyr play are thus extremely complex and shrouded in silence, and such an investigation highlights the way in which we too often comply with such a generic term, or to put it another way, "frame of acceptance"[16] without question, with the result that art is not only evaluated according to such artificial categories but even produced within their pre-set parameters, a process which is alluded to when the satyrs are patronisingly "rewarded" with what are presumably considered culturally "appropriate" and aptly named "ghetto-blasters". Indeed, Weinsheimer has made some acute observations about the effect of the frame on pictorial art and his comments are equally pertinent to this discussion of the way we simplify art with generic frames and categorisations:

> The frame, a symbol of aesthetic differentiation and of aesthetics itself, announces first the dividing line between art and non-art. The frame makes the painting a picture, and this involves distinguishing between the picture and its world, so that the picture is freely transportable into any world, as accords with the simultaneity

of aesthetic consciousness to all worlds. Second, the frame marks the difference of the picture itself from copies of it, or more generally from the particular conditions of our approach to it. In both respects the integrity, autonomy and immediate presence of the framed picture apparently obviate the work of historical mediation. It is already present, and thus neither historical investigation nor reproduction is necessary to represent it to us.[17]

Perhaps even more than other art, our reception of the Satyr drama, is framed by generic evaluation and thus expectations which normally supersede even a cursory knowledge of, for example, the only extant complete example of the Satyr drama, Euripides' *Cyclops*[18], or indeed familiarity with the papyri and fragments of other Satyr plays. In a sense the most we know about the Satyr drama is its generic label, save perhaps, certain vague and simplistic notions about Dionysian revelry and lewdness, with the effect that "Satyr drama" resembles an empty or barely marked canvass surrounded by an ornate and highly embellished frame, an image which is powerfully echoed by Harrison's use of a blank projection screen to the rear of the stage from which vague "shadow puppets" of satyrs begin to slowly emerge:

(SILENUS *gazes towards the papyrus where we can see the waiting shadows of the* CHORUS OF SATYRS. SILENUS *takes out a whistle.*)

SILENUS
I'll clog to life them loyal lads of mine.
(SILENUS *blows the whistle. The* SATYRS *do not enter.*)

APOLLO
You've lost your herd like me. I see no sign.

SILENUS
Well, 2000 years spent under the ground
might have take the edge off my clogs' old sharp sound.
But you wait, your Godship, once I strut my stuff
my satyrs'll come like a shot, sure enough
(*The* SATYRS *do not come.*)

In a sense, Harrison dramaturgically unframes the "Satyr drama" with the effect that it almost takes on a life of its own, and in a free-play of indulgent experimentation which the interpretative bind of intratextuality cannot subdue or control, his "satyr play" absorbs a host of "genres" which have evolved since its own demise over two thousand years ago. Indeed, Harrison further questions the generic "framing" of the Satyr drama by drawing attention to the practice either in terms of the institutional 'framing' of art by projecting a number of images of "various opera houses and theatres" onto the screen at the back of the stage, or with respect to his reference to a variety of architectural and decorative 'frames' such as Kyllene, the Caryatid and the mock 'Theatre of Dionysus' made from crates, and framed by pillars of "living" satyrs. Indeed, with respect to the frame of "living" satyrs, Harrison makes the analogy with the very real suffering and human sacrifice which has provided the edifice which supports what is commonly assumed to be a sensitive and humanist "culture", but which in reality has often been aestheticised art in the service of a state or nation's "will to power". Additionally, the archaeological hap which informs Harrison's Rewrite of Sophocles' *Ichneutae* provides a historical "frame" between source and destination, the "then" and the "now" of Sophocles' play, surrounding a blank canvas of intratextual void which as Harrison's play testifies is an invitation to inventively create and recreate art freed from the cultural swathes of aestheticisation.

Harrison's Rewrite does not hermeneutically negotiate with any specific intratextual appropriation or representational iconography subsequent to the source text, but rather it is concerned to reinvoke the Satyr to polemicise not only our generic responses but also to shed further light on the foundations which have contributed to the consolidation of our "aestheticised" responses to art and that which Nietzsche laments as the subsequent loss of "effect":

> The work never produces an effect but only another 'critique'; and the critique itself produces no effect either, but again only a further critique. There thus arises a general agreement to regard the acquisition of many critiques as a sign of success, of few or none as a sign of failure. At bottom, however, even given this kind of 'effect' everything remains as it was; people have some new thing to chatter about for a while, and then something newer still, and in the meantime go on doing what they have always done. The historical culture of our critics will no longer permit any effect at all in the proper sense, that is an effect on life and action: their blotting-paper at once goes down even on the blackest writing, and across the most graceful design they smear their thick black-strokes which are supposed to be regarded as corrections: and once again that is the end of that. But their critical pens never cease to flow, for they have lost control of them and instead of directing them are directed by them. It is precisely in this immoderation of its critical outpourings, in its lack of self-control, in that which the Romans call *impotentia* that the modern personality betrays its weakness.[19]

Nietzsche highlights how the aestheticisation of art, which he dates to the heyday of Euripidean drama when Socratic rationalism superseded the Dionysian spirit of the Satyr play, has engendered in us a distanced appreciation of art devoid of "effect", often obscured by the opaque web woven by criticism as well as, I would argue, the obfuscatory result of generic "framing" and classification.

Thus, by rewriting an example of a fragmented Satyr drama and, in a more particular sense Sophocles' *Ichneutae*, Harrison addresses an issue which is pertinent to all of the classics considered in this study—the aestheticisation of art—and he confronts this issue, not only with respect to the thematic presentation of the suppression of the satyrs' musicality in the source text, but also by consideration of the reasons and the consequences of the demise of the Satyr drama. In addition, the play's antiquity coupled with our rather vague knowledge about the Satyr drama's origins makes an ideal source for a dramaturgical exploration of the aestheticisation of art, because not only is the Satyr drama' s relationship with Tragedy and Comedy unclear, but by extension the generic basis of our literary heritage and thus any subsequent discourse based on such generic classification is put into question.

Through his Rewrite Harrison dramaturgically poses questions about the foundations of our cultural heritage because the Satyr drama in terms of both its invention and demise represents the embryonic stages of aesthetics; that is, the very processes through which we receive, evaluate and even produce "art", a point eloquently made by Silenus in *The Trackers of Oxyrynchus*:

> SILENUS
> Satyrs in the theatre are on hand to reassess
> doom and destiny and dire distress
> Six hours of tragedy and half an hour of fun
> But they were an entity conceived as one.
> But when the teachers and critics made their selections
> they elbowed the satyrs with embarrassing erections.
> Those teachers of tragedy sought to exclude
> the rampant half-animals as offensive and rude.
> *But* whose eyes first beheld the Promethean blaze?

Harrison further stresses how the aestheticisation of art and the subsequent 'refined' and evaluative terms of reference employed when discussing art have become so institutionalised that such evaluative language has actually progressed from being descriptive to being the impetus for the production of "art", rather like the retailer's orders which set the factory conveyor belt into action, a prescriptive and aestheticised notion of art which is clearly exhibited by Grenfell, as he manically scours the Oxyrynchus site for what he and the scholastic academy have already evaluated as "high art" and masterpieces. Indeed, C.M. Hinsley has described European archaeology during the second half of the nineteenth century as being very much motivated by constructively idealised and sanitised agendas which, in keeping with the Victorian morality personified by Grenfell and Hunt, reflected ". . . notions of colonial power and appropriation, technological prowess, and male presentation of treasures to metropolitan females."[20] Such idealisation is addressed by Harrison, not only with respect to the chauvinistic and high flown nationalistic aims expressed by Grenfell and Hunt throughout the play, but also by way of Kyllene who represents the Victorian's vicarious idealisation of womanhood through classical artefacts, haughty, poised and unapproachable. Thus, late nineteenth century British archaeology was very much directed towards and shaped by an agenda infused with Victorian morality and ideals, and was a far cry from being a serendipitous, impartial and objective approach to the past, a point elaborated by the archaeologist Shelby Brown:

> Classical archaeology has been tied ever since to the collecting and displaying of "good art" and the value judgements that accompany the identification of "art" as well as the definition of "good" (hence the traditional focus, for example, on fine wares rather than household ceramics, and patrician or imperial rather than plebeian imagery.[21]

Indeed, the image of a "goal oriented"[22] aesthetic production line racing against time for survival as being the basic indices of "value", as well as being the process which abets personal histories to 'victory' over the vicissitudes of historical time, is symbolised in the *The Trackers of Oxyrynchus* by not only the farcical "relay race" but also by the almost drill-like militarism exhibited by Grenfell and Hunt to reach their destination, the finishing line; that is, the material physical object of the text, any text, by Sophocles. In this sense, it is the relative obscurity and intratextual "loss" of art which motivates Grenfell and Hunt to value such art, and they characterise the extent to which art has become aestheticised and prejudged according to extratextual criteria even before it has even come to light.

Of course, *The Trackers of Oxyrynchus* is not concerned to offer an extratextual interpretation of genre and other areas of aesthetics at the expense of engaging with the source text, as to do so would be to forfeit the "hermeneutic" experience of the classic through a process of aesthetic differentiation, for as Gadamer asserts:

> . . . the being of art cannot be defined as an object of an aesthetic consciousness because, on the contrary, the aesthetic attitude is more than it knows of itself. It is a part of the *event of being that occurs in presentation*, and belongs essentially to play as play.[23]

Thus although Harrison's play may appear to be focused on extratextual and formalist concerns, namely the demise of a genre and the aestheticisation of art, these issues are not only interchangeable with the main themes of the source text or what is available of it, Apollo's desire to dominate and rationalise art, but also *pace* Plato they resonate with broader issues about the social effects of aestheticisation. In this respect, *The Trackers of Oxyrynchus* is not a dramaturgical consideration of cultural intratextuality in order to highlight the aesthetic distanciation that can often obfuscate our hermeneutic experience of a *specific* text; rather, by virtue of the source text's antiquity and long hermeneutic "absence", its re-emergence in the form of the Rewrite, elucidates the extent to which our cultural heritage is based on an "aesthetics of hermeneutics", of which the ideological coherence and containment of genre forms a part. Indeed, it was the encroaching "aesthetics of hermeneutics" that compelled Plato[24] to argue that the poets be banished from the Republic, on the premise that if our very culture is based on and sustained by such an aesthetic myth every aspect of our life is likely to be distorted, for as Gadamer has observed:

> [Plato's] critique of mimetic poetry cuts much deeper than it had first appeared. It not only criticises the false and dangerous contents of mimetic art or the choice of an unseemly mode of representation. *It is at the same time a critique of the moral consequences of "aesthetic consciousness"*[25]

However, Harrison is not oppositionally positing that because culture is necessarily based on aesthetic mystification it should be unceremoniously dismantled; rather' he rewrites Sophocles' *Ichneutae* to raise our consciousness about aestheticisation and thus our understanding of art, and there is no better resource for raising such consciousness than "the classic" which inhabits the ill defined ground between constituting "culture" and being constituted by "culture", rather like the disturbed and trammelled earth scoured by the satyrs as they participate in a search leading to Apollo's herd and the first strains of what we now know to be Music, and which, it transpires, are simultaneously present in the one and the same source. Indeed, Gadamer has pointed out that too often Plato's dialogues in *The Republic* are taken at face value, as opposed to being viewed as a hermeneutically inspired dialectical negotiation with what he perceived to be the encroaching dangers of Sophistry in his own society:

> One misses the full seriousness and importance of that requirement, however, if one takes the projected educational program and the ordering of the state literally.[with respect to Plato's Republic]. This state is a state in thought, not any

state on earth. That is to say, its purpose is to bring something to light and not to provide an actual design for an improved order in real political life. Plato's state is a "paradigm in heaven" for someone who wants to order *himself* and his own inner constitution. Its sole raison d'être is to make it possible for a person to recognise himself in the paradigm..[26]

In a similar vein to Plato's forewarning about the mentally binding and often mystifyingly dangerous properties of the aestheticisation of art, Harrison reinvokes Sophocles' *Ichneutae* to draw attention to the continuing aestheticisation of art that defines what we call "culture". However, Harrison is not suggesting we join with the urban outcasts in their Fauvist-like destruction of culture at the end of his play or that we revert to something approximating the Platonic unacculturated state of the "city of pigs"[27] invoked by the culturally imperialistic Grenfell and Hunt when discussing the fellaheen, but rather that with the Rewrite we re-cognise and thus imaginatively overcome the institutional attempts to further aestheticise our consciousness of art.

Indeed, Harrison ingeniously manages to involve his audience in the imaginative leap out of aesthetic consciousness by actually involving them in the 'play' of his play, be it through audience participation, chanting, dissolving the dramaturgical boundaries between audience and actors, or by rescripting each version of his play for a specific and particular setting. This means, for example, that the audience at the Royal National Theatre who are literally members of the cast in that specific version of the play are prevented from dissociating themselves from the reality of the 'satyr' strewn walkways of the South Bank outside the theatre through either a process of aesthetic distanciation or by the even more dangerous propensity to aestheticise life. In this respect Harrison's dramaturgy appears to echo Gadamerian hermeneutics[28] which emphasises play as possessing the potential to transcend the subject/object dichotomy of subjectivist aesthetics, which in turn so easily falls prey to the process of the aestheticisation of art, because it is through play that the artwork is ". . . no longer an object for a subject, but rather when the two are reunited. The work of art is the playing of it."[29]

Thus, *The Trackers of Oxyrynchus* is a complex amalgam of issues pertaining to the thematic, generic and social which dramaturgically interconnect the Sophoclean presentation of the suppression of the satyrs by Apollo with the generic and physical demise of the Satyr drama, which occurred not only as a result of an encroaching consciousness of rank wrought by the ascendancy of democracy and civic spirit, but was also effected by the waning of religiosity, whereby plays which focused on

mythological characters placed at the mercy of the whims and peccadil-
loes of the gods became less popular. In a sense, Harrison's play conveys
the way the thematic tracks which the satyrs follow to the source of Hermes'
musical invention in Sophocles' play have become indiscernible from the
generic tracks we follow to the source of Satyr Drama in the present, as
well as subtly implying that today we are similar to the tracking satyrs in
that we too have been deprived of the experience of art, if not as a result
of Apollo's dictum, as a consequence of the aestheticisation of art wrought
by the mythological and dramaturgical demise of the "satyr". Harrison
not only conveys how our tracks have become irretrievably muddied with
the satyrs' tracks but also he ironically suggests that our tracks have assumed a similarity to the original tracks of Apollo's lost cattle whereby as
a result of our production and appreciation of art according to predetermined aesthetic evaluations we trail into the next 'sell-out' production or
exhibition like naive and unsuspecting "herds".

Harrison's dialogue with Sophocles' *Ichneutae* highlights that as opposed to developing a liberating hermeneutic of aesthetics we have become imbricated in an incremental aesthetic of hermeneutics that defines
art in accordance with an abundance of extratextual concerns such as
antiquity, authorial oeuvre, survival and morality, but as opposed to attempting a futile suprahistorical critique to overturn a process which has
evolved over two millennia Harrison reinvokes the aesthetic category and
cultural cachet of the 'classic' to raise consciousness in his audience about
the aestheticisation process. By extension, Harrison suggests that like
the satyrs silenced by Apollo's dictum, we have been denied the
spontanaeity and freedom of hermeneutic *inventio*, as a result of the
almost imperceptible bind of aestheticisation which denies the liberating
hermeneutic of the aesthetic as advocated by Gadamer:

> Every work of art, not only literature, must be understood like any other text that
> requires understanding, and this kind of understanding has to be acquired. This
> gives hermeneutical consciousness a comprehensiveness that surpasses even that
> of aesthetic consciousness. *Aesthetics has to be absorbed into hermeneutics.*[30]

In this sense Harrison does not just arouse the audience's consciousness of the part played by aestheticisation in the formation of what we
know to be "culture" but he compels us to confront the wider social impli-
cations of continuing to adhere to an aesthetic myth which in effect serves
as an inhumane and impervious shield against not only the real tragedies
which abound in modern society but also the imaginative and productive
exertion of our hermeneutic faculties to question. Indeed, the relative

ignorance which surrounds the Satyr drama is alluded to in *The Trackers of Oxyrynchus* when the audience are invited to blindly "read" and recite the projected ancient Greek text, with the result of dramaturgically emphasising how aesthetic distanciation leads most of us to complacently accept and rely on scholastic evaluations, given by "experts" like Grenfell, for information about our cultural heritage, a far cry from the celebratory and festive "great amalgam" cited by Harrison, and further evidence of that which Nietzsche identified as art's loss of "effect":

> The reason is that he [reader/spectator] has lost and destroyed his instincts and, having lost his trust in the 'divine animal', he can no longer let go of the reins when his reason falters and his path leads him through deserts. Thus the individual grows fainthearted and unsure and dares no longer to believe in himself; he sinks into his own subjective depths, which here means into the accumulated lumber of what he has learned but which has no outward effect, of instruction which does not become life. If one watches him from the outside, one sees how the expulsion of the instincts of history has transformed man almost into mere *abstraction* and shadows; no one dares appear as he is, but masks himself as cultivated man, as a scholar, as a poet, as a politician.[31]

Thus, a generic "knowledge" of the Satyr play has overwhelmed textual 'understanding', and as such the Satyr play is invariably but erroneously categorised as being the final "light relief" of the tetralogies, indicative of the often sedimented, predetermined and elitist approach with which we receive art as characterised by Kyllene, when she states:

(*Enter* KYLLENE *through papyrus curtain.*)

(*Looking down from stage*)

> I have a feeling I'm in the wrong show!

[Delphi Version p. 37]

Of course, it is unlikely that *Ichneutae* will become a popular or even well 'understood' work, but nonetheless Harrison's Rewrite dramaturgically raises consciousness about the dynamics of cultural formation, beneath what is often perceived to be the monolithic, incremental and linear manifestation of what we unquestioningly refer to as "culture". Generic categorisation can, rather like intratextual appropriation, have a distorting effect upon our reception and "understanding" of a play, reducing the reader's reactions from that which Benedetto Croce identifies as the "intuitive" to the "logical" response or from the discursive to the codified.[32] Harrison rewrites Sophocles' Satyr drama, not only to highlight our unsatisfactory classification of a specific genre, but also to critique generic classification in a wider sense. This process is perpetuated by a naively historicist approach to art which on the one hand consigns an intrinsic part of our 'culture' to the level of an archaeological exhibit ascribed to careerist adventurers like Grenfell and Hunt, and on the other hand persists in promoting aesthetic distanciation through prescriptive generic classifications whereby, for example, we "see" as opposed to "feel" the tragic in Tragedy because we are "told" to do so, and because we fail to hermeneutically comprehend that, as Todorow perspicaciously observes:

> . . . Genre is not so much subject matter but the state of mind it induces.[33]

Archaeological Hap and the Aesthetics of Cultural Imperialism

> If we determine an event on the basis of a concept, we fall into Knowing; if we measure the phantasm against its supposed origin in reality, we are judging. These two conditions, the concept and the philosophy of representation, make up 'Philosophy'; whereas *thinking* as an event is a repetition without a model, a dice throw. This nomadic, rather than sedentary thinking produces difference within its very repetitions.[34]

Central to our appreciation of *The Trackers of Oxyrynchus* is the archaeological hap which uncovered the source text, not only because it was the event that revealed the text which we subsequently engage with hermeneutically, but because the hap or event that brought the text to light is in itself intrinsically informative about our culture, and indeed is an historical event that potentially alters the meaning of the source text in the present. In this respect, the archaeological hap which brings Sophocles' play to our attention, elicits a maieutic effect on our understanding about more recent events which are subsequent to the source text, most notably cultural imperialism. Of course in this respect the archaeological hap of the Rewrite, which to refer back to Gadamer is always ". . . beyond willing and doing", is not the same thing as the programmatic hap which drives Grenfell and Hunt onwards, but rather the archaeological hap retrospectively subsumes, by virtue of historical hindsight, the explorers' futile attempts to "make" history, by emphasising the inescapable certainty that it is *we* who are continuously made and shaped by history. Indeed, the failure of the rationalism of Grenfell's quest is clearly illustrated by the way in which he concertedly overlooks the "petitions" as being merely administrative "non-art", which subsequently, through historically effected consciousness, have not only become intrinsic to our understanding about the "selectivity" of cultural imperialism, but also shed further light on what was perceived by the Athenian hegemony to be the overly democratising effect of Satyr drama, with the result that it was consigned to obscurity alongside other manifestation of potential civic unrest and truculence, such as the petitions.

Just as the event or hap which eludes the hegemony of method is the defining aspect of history, because it shows that history is *not* determined or rigid, total or finalised, so too, the archaeological hap which prompts Harrison's play, hermeneutically precipitates the liberation from the chronologically binding process of the aestheticisation of art to which the source text and Satyr drama has been tied, for as Foucault points out with respect to archaeology:

> . . . it seeks rather to untie all those knots that historians have patiently tied; it increases differences, blurs the lines of communication; and tries to make it more difficult to pass from one thing to another. [35]

Harrison's Rewrite as prompted by archaeological hap, not only precipitates a revision of our reception of art, drawing attention to the often unnoticed aestheticisation of art of which the Satyr drama was apparently the first institutionalised victim, but also, by virtue of the very site-specific nature of archaeology, it precipitates a consideration of the spatiality of history, and thus the effects of cultural diaspora and imperialism upon our reception of art. Harrison, thus, acknowledges archaeological hap as being rooted not only in chronological time but also spatial time. The potential cultural dislocation suggested by the archaeological is frequently and victoriously alluded to by the colonial plunderers, Grenfell and Hunt, and in this way the archaeological hap summons up not only the "then" and "now" of chronological time, but also the "there" and "here" of cultural appropriation:

> GRENFELL
> Here are treasures crated, waiting to be shipped
> From Egypt to Oxford where we work out each script.
> [Delphi version p9]

In this way Harrison's rescripted Rewrite refuses the audience the luxury of consigning the less comfortable and ignoble aspects of our culture to the "past" because the very materiality and physical presence summoned up by archaeological hap, which tangibly brings the "then" to the "now", and the "there" to the "here", emphasises the continuing effects in the present of a dark and murky, but frequently and constructively "forgotten"[36] past, in keeping with Said's observation:

> To a very great degree the era of high nineteenth century imperialism is over:
> France and Britain gave up their most splendid possessions after World War Two,
> and lesser powers divested themselves of their far-flung dominions. Yet, once
> again, recalling the words of T. S. Eliot, although that era clearly had an identity
> all its own, the meaning of the imperial past is not totally contained within it, but
> has entered the reality of hundreds of millions of people, where its existence as
> shared memory and as a highly conflictual texture of culture, ideology, and policy
> still exercises tremendous force . . . we must try to grasp the hegemony of the
> imperial ideology, which by the end of nineteenth century had become com-
> pletely embedded in the affairs of cultures whose less regrettable features we still
> celebrate.[37]

In this respect, Harrison's Rewrite expands upon the geopolitical and spatial dimension one encounters with Fugard's *The Island* which, although a play which addresses the radical hermeneutic potential of the classic within a different geo-political space, does not address the simultaneous polysemicity of a hermeneutic which encompasses space-time. Thus, although the two re-scripts of Harrison's Rewrite can be "understood" individually, they can, and arguably, should be approached as a composite whole of juxtaposing versions of the simultaneous effects of the aestheticisation of art on either the culture of the 'empire builders' or the appropriated culture of the plundered. Harrison dramaturgically implements that which Edward Said identified as a "contrapuntal"[38] approach to culture and history, which resists the impetus to follow the dominant and thus most frequently disseminated narrativisation of culture whereby, in a process akin to that which Bhabha identifies as "narrating the nation"[39], the imperial powers appropriate other cultures to such an extent that they actually naturalise their plunder as *their* "national" heritage. Thus, Harrison, prompted by the cultural dislocation of archaeological hap, dramaturgically explores not only excavated art from the perspective of the empire builders, but also from the perspective of the plundered in keeping with Said's explanation:

> What an Algerian intellectual today remembers of his country's colonial past
> focuses severely on such events as France's military attacks on villages and the
> torture of prisoners during the war of liberation, on the exultation over indepen-
> dence in 1962; for his French counterpart, who may have taken part in Algerian
> affairs or whose family lived in Algeria, there is a chagrin at having 'lost' Algeria,
> a more positive attitude toward the French colonising mission—with its schools,
> nicely planned cities, pleasant life—and perhaps even a sense that 'troublemak-
> ers' and communists disturbed the idyllic relationship between 'us' and 'them'.[40]

In the Delphi version Harrison dramaturgically alludes to the continuing effects of the earliest stages of the aestheticisation of art into the present day, by presenting the modern day satyrs, that is the poor and dispossessed, who, no longer acquiescing to play the role of comic clown, retaliate against their cultural alienation by making a futile and self-immolatory gesture which repeats the demise of their ancient precursors:

CHORUS OF SATYRS
If I can't be a man I'll be wholly goat
and stuff the papyrus down Sophocles throat

4
Fellaheen, phallus bearers only for farce.
Well, show us a tragedy we'll show you our arse

3
Aeschylus, Sophocles gerroff our backs
We're hijacking Culture and leaving no tracks
(*The* SATYR *begin to burn down the papyrus of the* Ichneutae.)

SILENUS
Don't burn the papyrus. That's where we come from!
(*They watch the papyrus burn and drink beer and scatter the cans on the mounds where the papyri were extracted from. These are the new rubbish mounds of Oxyrynchus*)

To them old Silenus is an Uncle Tom
(*Shouting to* SATYRS)
Don't burn the papyrus. We're all inside.
Don't burn the papyrus. It's satyricide!
[Delphi Version p68]

Conversely, in the Royal National Theatre version, Harrison depicts the satyrs as driven by necessity to destroy the Satyr drama which provides the basis of the "culture" from which they are alienated, to provide material insulation against the biting cold and fearsome elements outside the theatre where simultaneously the "cultivated" audience attempt to psychologically insulate themselves from any external suffering which might impinge upon what they perceive to be their inviolable sense of "culture". In both plays Harrison critiques the effects of the aestheticisation of art on the culture specific to both settings, whether it be the plundered and degraded Greek culture of Delphi, which in a retaliatory reaction against an appropriated culture, lead the satyrs to abandon any claim to it, or whether the degree of aestheticisation of art is such that it has been used to prop up nationalistic and imperialistic barbarity under the guise of heroism and achievement, and has developed into an aesthetic consciousness which not only insulates against acknowledging the less beautiful areas of life, but actually promotes the aestheticisation of life.

In this respect, the archaeological hap which prompts Harrison's consideration of Sophocles' Satyr play is different to the historical and intratextual hap of *endurance,* which precipitates the retrospective dramaturgical consideration of the other classics considered in this study, because it summons up the intratextual void of *survival* between the textual source and its destination, simultaneously representing the latest and earliest stages of culture as we have come to know it, but without the source text having been perceptibly present or participating in its formation. In addition, the archaeological hap raises issues about the evaluation of art into "high" or "low", because the first artistic victim of negative aesthetic evaluation, the Satyr Drama, is transformed in the present, purely by virtue of its antiquity, authorial oeuvre and survival, into not only the "literature" and "high art" so much craved by Grenfell and Hunt, but also the sell-out runs at the Royal National Theatre, a phenomenon which Foucault observes in his consideration of the aesthetic bestowal of classic status: ". . . their ancientness, whether real or imagined, was regarded as a sufficient guarantee of their status."[41] Thus, by virtue of archaeological hap the Rewrite is provided with a focus which summons up debate about the 'value' of loss, and the way authorial oeuvre, antiquity and survival can bestow 'value' on texts which have not and most probably will not be read or performed, except, ironically in the form of a Rewrite presented by a highly modish and presently acclaimed dramatist.

The archaeological hap which conjures up our awareness of site-specific context and the spatiality of time is intrinsic to Harrison's consideration of the role played by imperialism and cultural appropriation in our further aestheticisation of art. Because *The Trackers of Oxyrynchus* is based on an essentially "unhistorical" source text without specific intratextual accretions it is an ideal resource for Harrison's polemical investigation of the variety of historiographical methods which help to shape, distort and perpetuate certain modes of art reception and evaluation. In this respect Harrison rewrites *Ichneutae,* in celebration of its potential as an archaeologically hermeneutic resource from which to explore and thus deepen our understanding of the historical, social and political ramifications of cultural formation and, more importantly, to raise our consciousness of the often simplistically homogenised perception of cultural formation we possess.

In keeping with Foucault's genealogical approach, *The Trackers of Oxyrynchus* revisits the past discursive strategies which inform our present discourse to highlight the disjunctures, anomalies and discrepancies upon which received knowledge is so often based:

> . . . genealogy retrieves an indispensable restraint; it must record the singularity of events outside of any monotonous finality; it must seek them in the most unpromising places, in what we tend to feel is without history—in sentiments, love, conscience, instincts; it must be sensitive to their recurrence, not in order to trace the gradual curve of their evolution but to isolate the different scenes where they engaged in different roles. Finally genealogy must define even those instances when they are absent, the moment when they remained unrealised (Plato at Syracuse did not become Mohammed).[42]

A historiography founded on effective history, as posited by Gadamer and as exhibited by Foucault's genealogy, is far removed from that displayed by Grenfell and Hunt, who, as discussed earlier, display an overwhelming historicism similar to that which Nietzsche identified as "monumental" and "antiquarian" uses of history.(*On the Usefulness and Disadvantages of History for Life*, 1874). In keeping with the arrogance of their cultural imperialism and colonial spirit, these scholastic empire builders do not question their motives, or indeed reflect on the havoc and destruction they wreak throughout the lands they pillage, for what is, in effect, cultural booty. In this sense, the Royal National Theatre version and the Delphi script complement each other as being the antithetical results of cultural appropriation, with the cultural imperialists being represented by the apogee of aestheticisation at the bourgeois theatre at one end of the spectrum and the pillaged and appropriated represented by self-conscious cultural abandonment in favour of the immediacy and competitiveness of sporting entertainment at the other. In this way Harrison's dramaturgy is imbued with a genealogical approach to the classic which, as opposed to presenting a totalised and continuous interpretative development of a particular text, emphasises the contradictory and overlapping arbitrariness of interpretation and evaluation whereby the " . . . universals of our humanism are revealed as the result of the contingent emergence of imposed interpretation."[43] By highlighting the interpretative and evaluative discontinuities, contradictions and fluctuations of art, Harrison's Rewrite also draws attention to his own interpretative contingency, ephemerality and finitude, ". . . and that he himself is produced by what he is studying: consequently he can never stand outside it"[44]. This interpretative finitude is further emphasised by Harrison's self-referential observation that in an age of accelerated gratification, the aestheticisation of art is transforming into the commodification of the aesthetic and that, as a consequence, his own plays, including *The Trackers of Oxyrynchus* will soon join the "rubbish heaps" outside the theatre.[45] Thus, Harrison's play negotiates with history from its own, acknowledged, limited and finite position and as the classic, more than any other literary form, represents our shared cultural practices, whether endorsed or critiqued, and since these practices have in part made us what we are, we are provided with a traditional and literary common ground from which to proceed, to "understand" and to act, for as Grondin astutely observes:

> The principle of effective history clearly implies becoming conscious of the continuing efficacy of tradition beyond our conscious awareness of these effects and therefore the impossibility of a complete self-awareness of consciousness about itself.[46]

Just as recognition of hermeneutic finitude does not entail abdication from the hermeneutic quest to interrogate received knowledge, as prompted by a self-consciousness of one's inescapable prejudices, equally one's interpretative stance should avoid straying into the historicist's pitfall of replacing one homogenised suprahistorical interpretation with another. Indeed, Harrison dramaturgically suggests the impossibility of escaping one's contingent and thus irreconcilably limited 'understanding' and interpretative stance with respect to the anachronistic presentation of Grenfell and Hunt's exploration which at once appears to have taken place in 1888, but which is transposed to 1988 by way of the confused dates cited during Grenfell's eulogy for his archaeological mentor, Flinders Petrie:

> GRENFELL
> Flinders Petrie's finds were the inspiration
> that puts us on the track of this present excavation.
> (A hundred years ago exactly.
> The date was July 1988)
> Petrie dug Hawara, and discovered there
> a papyrus of Homer with a lock of lady's hair.
> A hundred years ago almost to the day
> I gazed on that Homer in a Bodleian display.
> I swore, while still a teenager at Queen's,
> to rescue Greek papyri from enriching Egypt's greens.
> [Delphi Version p. 10]

By way of such anachronistic details, in addition to the use of a pastiche of styles, artistic, linguistic and otherwise, Harrison suggests just how enmeshed and implicated we are in our history and the deeds of our forefathers, including the inescapable legacy bequeathed by cultural imperialism to our reception and production of art in the present, and to emphasise the pervasiveness of these effects Harrison not only implicitly parodies the Royal National Theatre audience's "interest" in the classics, but even his own inextricable connection in the process of the aestheticisation of art:

> (. . . *The* SATYRS *move forward, shuffling towards the rubbish heaps, saying the petition in Greek and picking over the newspapers, the torn text of* The Trackers of Oxyrynchus, *National Theatre posters for* Trackers *etc* . . .)

However, this is not to suggest that *The Trackers of Oxyrynchus* is a vehicle solely for dramaturgical parody, for this would be to operate, albeit oppositionally, within the same discursive parameters of the aesthetics of hermeneutics which he critiques. Rather Harrison more productively illustrates through his extremely self-conscious use of parody just how self-perpetuating the aestheticisation of art is, particularly if we allow ourselves to become distanced from perceiving the classics as texts in the present and as hermeneutic resources *for* "understanding" today, as opposed to epistemological objects *of* knowledge. Harrison's simultaneously uses *and* critiques parody as being intrinsically bound up in and thus instrumental in the perpetuation of the aestheticisation of art, as illustrated by his parodic presentation of "Victoriana" which in the form of Kyllene, the Caryatid, is a corrupt, but somewhat naive and unsubtle, idealisation of antiquity that on one level arouses laughter but which, on another, raises an uncomfortable awareness of our own, although different, self-conscious aestheticisation of art. In a sense, Harrison suggests that just as the Victorians aestheticised and thus elevated what was in effect culturally appropriated plunder, we are complicit in a similar process of aestheticising the degradation and poverty which impinges upon us daily with, for example a similarly incongruous register like "pale boy" when referring to the down and outs on the streets of London. In this respect Harrison comments upon the way in which art has been corrupted into an aesthetic tool in the service of the 'will to power', whether that be motivated by imperialism, elitism or class division.

The Trackers of Oxyrynchus is far from being an exercise in melancholic recuperation of a lost Dionysiac spirit of the kind which informs, for example the Nietzschean selective "critical" historiography that the Nazis were to embrace so enthusiastically, although Harrison's confrontation with such historiography is in evidence along with his critique of the psychologically motivated reasons, such as nationalism and imperialism, which often lie behind the retrospective and highly selective re-construction of "culture". Harrison's presentation of Hunt and Grenfell suggests the deep-seated and traumatic repercussions of the loss of the Empire for the imperialists. Just as Hunt, who as his name suggests, symbolises the fearless and unsentimental acquisitiveness of the empire builders of the past, the tormented Grenfell, who as implied by Harrison's use of confusing dates and periodisation, personifies not only the past but also the present, symbolises the recurring psychological 'myth' of a fallen but benevolent, fertile and civilising mission that was England's "Old Empire". Indeed, the two explorers continually stress their mission to bring culture to England's 'green and pleasant land' at the expense of what they consider to be "compost" and "fertilizer" for a geographical, and with the supreme irony befitting their arrogance, cultural wasteland, and although these references may be literally juxtaposed to highlight the hypocrisy of Grenfell and Hunt's "civilising" mission in the face of poverty, they also symbolically convey the cost of depriving and withdrawing an "organic" sense of tradition and cultural "sustenance" from a nation. In a sense, when the "present" aspect of "Gren-fell" is foregrounded, he symbolises the melancholic disavowal of the loss of Empire, not least by the very nature of his frenzied determination to find and thus repeat Apollonian domination, a mythic metaphor not only for the aestheticisation of art but, by extension, the aestheticisation of plunder for the purposes of the imperial mission. As Wheeler explains, it is the melancholic's disposition to distractedly and unproductively repeat traumatic events in an attempt to disavow them, and one can consider the depiction of Grenfell's physical "possession" by the Apollonian spirit of dominion as being not only indicative of the self-generative power of aestheticisation but also expressive of the extent to which he has been overtaken by such a disavowal by repetition:

> . . . the melancholic remains caught in the compulsion to repeat the trauma of loss in order to master it (a thing that he has never properly done.) [47]

Grenfell, like the melancholic who remains caught in the compulsion to repeat the trauma of loss, exhibits what Santner identifies as the elegiac loop of disavowal, as emphasised by his elegiac reminiscences about Flinders Petrie and his early career which anachronistically appear to have reached the date of the performance of Harrison's play, 1988. In this respect, Grenfell's melancholia symbolises the oft-repeated and constructed histories of imperialism, or that which Santner calls fetish narratives. According to Santner such a retroactively constructed fetish narrative:

. . . is the way an inability or refusal to mourn emplots traumatic events; it is a strategy of undoing, in fantasy, the need for mourning by stimulating a condition of intactness, typically by situating the site and origin of loss elsewhere. Narrative fetishism releases one from the burden of having to reconstitute one's self-identity under 'posttraumatic' conditions; in narrative fetishism, the 'post' is indefinitely postponed.[48]

Similarly, in the Delphi version of the play one can consider the satyr's football match as a sporting repetition or "playing out" of the cultural loss suffered as a result of what Harrison calls "the struggle for art" with Apollonian/Imperial might, whereby the transitory excitement of the game provides some kind of melancholic recuperative compensation for their demise whilst materially bearing witness to it:

(*Enter the new generation of* SATYRS. *They are like football hooligans with scarves, flags, etc. , and chanting and clapping. The* SATYRS *spray the name 'Marsyas. . . first with red, then with white aerosol paints, the colour of the Greek team Olympiakos. They add Marsyas in blue for England. (Marsyas! Marsyas! Marsyas!) They slash papyrus. They spray Marsyas in inflammable fuel and set light to it so that the name of Marsyas blazes on the screen papyrus. They kick the smashed ghetto-blasters into life. They blare out the 'Marsyas Theme'*) [Delphi version, p67]

Thus, at the end of the Delphi version of the play Harrison presents the satyrs as participants in the spontaneous and immediate gratification of competitive sport, devoid of any conscious sense of tradition save for the ironic references made to Marsyas during the course of their repetitive and mindless supporters' chant. The irreverent context in which the satyrs make reference to Marsyas is indicative perhaps of how far removed and desensitised they have become from their cultural roots, although subconsciously they melancholically reinvoke the initial scene of their demise. In this way Harrison suggests that as a consequence of the imperialistic plundering and appropriation as perpetrated by colonial adventurers like Grenfell and Hunt, the Delphi satyrs, unlike Silenus and the older generation who accede to playing the demeaning role of "Uncle Tom" [p68], have reacted against and "hi-jacked" "culture" that is no longer theirs to participate in. Indeed, Harrison punctuates his play with vernacular and colloquial terms such as "hi-jacked" not only to contemporise the demise of the satyrs, but also to linguistically project the effects of, for example, imperialism, by reminding us of the multifarious terrorist groups which were to emerge as a direct result of the plundering and confiscatory project implemented by men like Grenfell and Hunt a century before.

Conversely, the accusatory and violent ending of the Royal National Theatre version of Harrison's play is directed at an audience which has been shaped and is thus implicated in an imperialistic heritage which has not only continued to aestheticise art but which has aestheticised art for imperialistic and nationalistic reasons. The incrementally binding effect of aetheticisation as highlighted by Harrison's re-script for the Royal National Theatre, not only emphasises the fact that 'civilisation' has been founded on a myth that obfuscates any real understanding of art, but it also stresses the way in which an aestheticisation process has evolved whereby "civilisation" inoculates itself from the omnipresent barbarity lurking beneath the institutional honours, medals and accolades of empire building, the laurels of victory which are ironically dismissed by the Satyrs when they barter for *their* reward with Apollo:

> . . . They'd have no quarrel
> with gold or food, or liquid from a barrel,
> but don't reckon too much to a wreath of laurel.
> Summat solid, Lord Apollo, please
> not leaf equivalents of OBE's
>
> . . .
>
> The prospect of promotion to Sir Satyr
> doesn't make my heart go pitter-patter.
> You know us, all prancing, getting pissed
> so forget your Olympian Honour List.
> [Delphi version p. 26]

As opposed to the abandonment of "culture" wrought in part by the effects of imperialism in the Delphi version of his play, Harrison presents the apogee of the aestheticisation process in the aptly named "Royal National" Theatre as a self-protective and insulatory mechanism which not only facilitates aesthetic distanciation from reality but which produces the increasing potential for a select minority to aestheticise and thus comfortingly sanitise the bleaker side of life. However, although it would appear that "culture" has in accordance with the "civilising" mission of Grenfell and Hunt flourished back in "Great Britain" Harrison has syllogistically presented a similar cultural demise to that in the Delphi version, whereby in the Royal National Theatre version the aestheticisation of art has reached such proportions that it has supplanted the "culture" of art and hermeneutics, transforming the classics into little more than a fashion accessory for the more affluent theatre-goers of the metropolis who, Harrison suggests, regard the name "Sophocles" as possessing about the same significance as the next "in vogue" designer label. *The Trackers of Oxyrynchus* not only reinvokes the Satyr drama and its subsequent demise to polemicise our inextricable implication in the aestheticisation of art, but it also implies that such aestheticisation has gradually assumed societal proportions whereby we not only endorse cultural division, but actually assume an innoculatory cynicism which allows us to aestheticise the injustice, horror and ugliness that stalks our divided society. Such aestheticisation of life is clearly problematised during the course of *The Trackers of Oxyrynchus*. One of the most moving examples occurs when Harrison evokes in his audience a disconcerting confusion that puts their value-system into question when they are implicitly asked if they embrace the retaliatory gesture of the 'fellaheen' and 'down and outs' against the symbolic power which suppresses them, namely using the fragments and papyri for sorely needed fuel *or* are their "aesthetic" sensibilities so affronted that their concerns rest with the deprivation their "civilisation" will incur as a result of this act of cultural hooliganism and philistinism?

Although both versions of the play ostensibly and syllogistically suggest that Grenfell/Apollo is victorious in his quest to suppress the Satyr play, the material and textual reality of the Rewrite of Sophocles' *Ichneutae* can be viewed as Harrison dramaturgically throwing down the gauntlet, and thus challenging the audience to contest the hermeneutic oblivion and distortion of the Satyr play, whether that takes the form of aestheticising plunder behind a showcase in the Bodleian, or whether it entails a second satyr being mercilessly flayed by the returning and revenging Apollo, both in the name of the rationalisation and further aestheticisation of our reception of art.

The polysemic re-scripts of the Rewrite thus represent what Gadamer would refer to as "thoughtful mediation with contemporary life" because they dramaturgically reflect the different and distinctive historical "effect" of the play at the Royal National Theatre to the "effect" at Delphi, in recognition of the plundering legacy of archaeological hap with its impetus to requisition and transport cultural booty from one part of the world to another. In this way Harrison dramaturgically counters any criticism that he is committing the very crime of aesthetic homogenisation that he critiques, as well as displaying the historically effected consciousness that typically motivates the Rewrite. Thus, Harrison's rewrites of the Rewrite display a sensitivity to the locus of the staging of the plays which facilitates a further emphasis and refinement of his historiographical critique of the aestheticisation of art, particularly relating to the effects of imperialism. In this respect Harrison takes full account of imperialism and its inevitable impact on the process of the aestheticisation of art which during the nineteenth century became even more complex in view of its association with cultural appropriation for nationalistic purposes.

Harrison prompts us to consider the psychological dimensions, including the "will to power", behind culture and its continuing construction, not least by virtue of the very fact that we are imaginatively transported into a world of satyrs and gods, through the psyches of two men, Grenfell and Hunt, and Harrison dramaturgically emphasises the humanity of myth by simultaneously casting the actors who play Grenfell and Hunt as the mythical Apollo and Silenus respectively. Harrison's dramaturgical humanisation of what is, in accordance with "aesthetic" practice designated a myth, prevents us, the cultural heirs to Grenfell and Hunt's legacy, from securing ourselves a fictional or mythical bolt-hole to which we might escape from our hermeneutic responsibilities, and in this way the Apollonian cruelty toward Marsyas and the subsequent demise of the Satyr drama wrought by the aestheticisation of art is very clearly portrayed as being pertinent to and connected with our present realities. By humanising the Apollonian spirit of dominion Harrison convincingly forges connections between such brutality and the self-same process which was to become intrinsic to the cultural imperialism of the nineteenth century and upon which 'culture' as we know it is founded and sustained today, and in so doing he reinvokes and reanimates the Sophoclean satyr play, which thematically and by its very form represents the effects of such domination, as being a far cry indeed from the popular, but evidently erroneous conception of Satyr drama—namely, fanciful creations which provided "light" entertainment and frivolity for the Ancients, and which for the most part are lost, and thus must be worthless and unimportant.

The Commodity Aesthetic and The Fragmented Vessel

The re-scripted Rewrite, *The Trackers of Oxyrynchus*, leaves us bereft of any certainty as to *which* play is the Rewrite of Sophocles' *Ichneutae*, and in this way Harrison asserts, by disrupting our sense of literary continuity and linearity, that the notion of the "original" or textual priority is and has to be defunct if we are to pursue literary art with a hermeneutic sensibility, a sentiment found in the work of Gadamer:

> . . . a hermeneutics that regarded understanding as reconstructing the original would be no more than handing on a dead meaning.[49]

Indeed, it is particularly fitting that Harrison re-scripts his Rewrite in this way because it disrupts the linearity so often artificially and misleadingly created and imposed by cultural imperialism and, in this respect, Harrison displays a great hermeneutic sensitivity to the archaeological hap surrounding the re-emergence of the source text, including all the usual connotations of cultural dislocation and displacement suggested by archaeological excavation, by referring not only to Grenfell and Hunt's cultural imperialism, but, in addition, by alluding to the Egyptian, as well as the Greek, and thus European, influences on such art. Indeed, Bernal has highlighted how many excavated classical artefacts have been historiographically and culturally "reconstructed" in the service of nationalistic interests or what he refers to as "continental chauvinism"[50], whereby, for example, the Egyptian and Semitic influences upon classical art are conveniently glossed over or ignored, a process which Said has commented on:

> Studies such as Martin Bernal's *Black Athena* and Eric Hobsbawm and Terence Ranger's *The Invention of Tradition* have accentuated the extraordinary influence of today's anxieties and agendas on the pure (even purged) images we construct of a privileged, genealogically useful past, a past in which we exclude unwanted elements, vestiges, narratives. Thus according to Bernal, whereas Greek civilisation was known originally to have roots in Egyptian, Semitic and various other southern and eastern cultures, it was redesigned as 'Aryan' during the course of the nineteenth century, its Semitic and African roots either actively purged or hidden from view. Since Greek writers themselves openly acknowledged their culture's hybrid past, European philologists acquired the ideological habit of passing over these embarrassing passages without comment, in the interests of Attic purity.[51]

Of course, the disruption of textual linearity and priority exhibited by *The Trackers of Oxyrynchus* may appear to be a contradiction in terms, especially in view of Harrison's "rewrite" of a *classic* which is, by its very status an emblem of textual linearity and priority, but this is a process which highlights how the Rewrite not only performs a textual hermeneutic, but also a hermeneutic with the very status which the term "the classic" summons up. Thus, Harrison does not only negotiate with the classic's historicity and intratextuality, present or absent, he also hermeneutically negotiates with the very classic status which has propelled and by a process of retroactive consolidation affirmed the source text's historicity and intratextuality. Harrison does not, therefore, rewrite the classic in order to further consolidate and perpetuate the aestheticisation which has created its status, firstly because he rereads and rewrites the text differently for and in the present, taking into account the culturally imperialistic but silent intratext which has appropriated the text. In addition, as befits his consideration of the archaeological hap and the cultural dislocation of our reception of the text, he hermeneutically confronts the classic as an aesthetic construct within history. This approach does not suggest either opposition to or reverence for our literary tradition *per se*; rather, it is a hermeneutic questioning which deepens our understanding of our cultural heritage, as opposed to the futile veneration or disparagement of tradition in accordance with conflicting extratextual political agendas which revere or oppose the classic as a "construct" for either nationalistic or elitist interests.

In this respect, Harrison displays a genealogical approach to rewriting the classic which refuses the piety which certainly motivates either the intrinsically "moral" opposition or "moral" veneration of tradition or that which Foucault has identified as *Herkunft* (stock or descent) in recognition that ". . . every origin of morality from the moment it stops being pious—and *Herkunft* can never be—has value as critique."[52] Undoubtedly, as Foucault points out *Herkunft* or tradition cannot escape some degree of prejudicial morality, but Harrison harnesses this ineluctable sense of tradition, and its inescapable demand for hermeneutic responsibility by rewriting a classic in order to elicit the hermeneutic "experience" or *Erlebnis* that alters or challenges our moralistic expectations or horizons with respect to the classic, whether they be oppositionally or venerationally motivated, for as Gadamer explains:

> . . . when we call something classical, there is a consciousness of something enduring, of significance that cannot be lost and that is independent of all the circumstances of time—a kind of timeless present that is contemporaneous with every other present.[53]

Thus in keeping with Gadamerian hermeneutics, Harrison's Rewrite displays the play on *Erfahrung,* that is, the gathered and received knowledge of tradition, and *Erlebnis,* the immediacy of experience, whereby a dramaturgical transformation into structure based on hermeneutic difference, is presented.

The disruption of textual linearity created by Harrison's re-scripting of the Rewrite, far from dissipating our hermeneutic reception of the source text, actually nourishes and enlarges our understanding whereby not only the fragmentary source text, of which only about one half has survived, becomes two plays; it is also shown to possess the potential to be hermeneutically self-generating according to hap. In this respect, Harrison's Rewrite exhibits a similar hermeneutic potential to that described by Benjamin with respect to the shattered vessel, which by virtue of its fragmentation does not suffer loss or damage, but rather gains the hermeneutic value and interest of each separate fragment within its greater, although transitory, whole. In this respect, Sophocles' *Ichneutae* can be likened to the shattered vessel, the fragments of which tell their own separate story, and Harrison in a similar way to Benjamin's ideal translator has painstakingly retrieved the fragments and shards of the source text that have been scattered from Delphi to Oxyrynchus to London, and hermeneutically encompassed not only their physical presence but also the diaspora from their source, both textually and culturally, into his own rewriting. Harrison examines the nature of the fragments of the whole, just as the chinks and gaps between a source and target language should be addressed by a good translator, not in order to cover up or to efface them but to enlarge our understanding, ". . . to make them *both* recognisable as the broken fragments of the greater language, just as fragments are the broken parts of the vessel."[54] In this respect, *The Trackers of Oxyrynchus* does not exhibit the rather fruitless reconstructional hermeneutics espoused by Schleiermacher which emphasises our sense of recapturing and thus repeating the "origin" of the source text; rather, it embraces dialogue between the present and the past in order to reach a different albeit transitory understanding. Conversely, the Rewrite's approach to the fragmentary source text does not mean the wholesale random and ahistorical use of pastiche and montage, but rather imbued with historically effected consciousness and prompted by archaeological hap, the Rewrite, like Benjamin's ideal translation, ". . . lovingly and in detail incorporate[s] the original's mode of signification . . ."[55]

Indeed, the Benjaminian allusion to the self-generative and fragmentary nature of translation, and for the purposes of this critique, by extension the Rewrite, is sharply contrasted with the ossifying and atrophying approach to art exhibited by Victorian imperialists like Grenfell and Hunt, and represented by Kyllene, the Caryatid, who despite "falling" off the stage rearranges herself with ease and without, quite literally, any 'real' damage. Kyllene's stoic indestructibility not only alludes to the hypocrisy-laden idealisation of womanhood promulgated by Victorian moralists; it also suggests the 'will to power' and resolve to sustain the artificial appropriation of classical art on the part of Victorian imperialist plunderers, a static inviolability referred to by the satyrs:

CHORUS OF SATYRS

1

So calm of body, so serene of face,
drapery discreet, and every hair in place

2
Them girls are straight but we're not straight
but bent and straining underneath the weight.

3
Though its tons of marble that she holds
A caryatid still looks like a centrefold,
[Delphi version p38]

Besides ironically critiquing the monumentalisation of art wrought by Victorian imperialists, Harrison is also suggesting the latent effects of the aestheticisation of art, including the insidious encroachment of the aestheticisation of life, whereby not only is the powerful hegemony provided with the comforting ability to delusionally insulate itself from acknowledging the harsh and unjust realities of life, but by extension and in keeping with a consumerist and technological age, art becomes corrupted into an aesthetic commodity, which by virtue of its ability to imperceptibly anaesthetise us from reality, is specifically designed "to please". In this way Harrison reinvokes the Gramscian[56] model of hegemony whereby even though art is demeaned to the level of a consumer item we are manipulated into feeling as though our evaluation and endorsement of such an aesthetic commodity in the guise of art is spontaneous and unfettered when in reality even our reception of supposedly radical "art" which ostensibly contests the status quo is tacitly sanctioned and thus shaped by the bastions of the status quo themselves, for as Said astutely observes:

> Well before Foucault, Gramsci had grasped the idea that culture serves authority, and ultimately the national State, not because it represses and coerces but because it is affirmative, positive and persuasive.[57]

Indeed, the satyrs actually prophesy the eventual aestheticisation of life, alluding not only to the aesthetic idealisation and sanitisation of world domination perpetrated by cultural imperialists in the name of the state, but also with respect to the encroaching trend to "buy into" the modish and pre-determined aesthetic of the day in order to attain the pleasurable gratification and self-satisfaction of what is frequently referred to as the "feel good" factor, regardless of either the torments and sufferings which exist in reality, or indeed the truly "free" bountiful beauty offered by nature:

CHORUS OF SATYRS
6
Every cave, every grot, every bosky retreat
'll soon be throbbing with Apollo's lyre beat.

7

Plucking piped out from morn till eve.
Here'll be unliveable. We'll all have to leave.

8

There'll be no stretch of sky, no bit of ground
that won't in the end be full of its sound.

9

When Hermes took cow-gut and tortoise shell
did he know that he'd turn our peace into hell?

10

You watch what'll happen. It'll force the poor birds
out of business. You mark my words.

. . .

6

Ay, birdsong's *passe*. This lyre'll usurp
the song of the skylark, the cricket's chirp.

7

Eventually everything's going to get drowned
in such all-surrounding and man-made sound.

. . .

9

This lyre contraption's the thin end of the wedge.
We'll soon have this Muzak behind every hedge.

. . .

(*By this time the* CHORUS OF SATYRS *have opened all their 'presents'. The
ghetto blasters lie on the ground in front of them forming a curve. Suddenly,
very loudly, the ghetto-blasters begin to play the same melody as* APOLLO
played during his lyre recital, but deafening rock-style . . .)
[Delphi Version pp. 57–9]

Also, Kyllene could be considered as representative of the way in which
classical antiquity was corrupted into an aesthetic commodity for and by
the Victorians, as suggested by her indestructibility and idealisation, factors designed to please and sycophantically reinforce the self-perception
possessed by her late nineteenth-century audience. Such an aesthetic
commodity, in accordance with the accelerated pace of fashion, not only
suggests the mechanistic power of novelty but also, paradoxically, the

mass-produced reification of the original, both of which are practices which emphasise form at the expense of any motivating sense of meaning except those of the market forces which shape them, whether this takes the form of box-office breaking and modish performances which can transform even the classics into self-aggrandising fashion accessories, or whether it is a glamourisation of the ill-nourished and weak, as suggested by Harrison's ironic use of aesthetic register with "the pale boy" and insulting euphemisms like "cardboard city". Indeed, the way in which the satyrs' "presents" in the form of ghetto-blasters (an implicit reference to the artificial and shallow 'freedom' offered by consumerism) emit the Apollonian victory song in another form, prompts one to consider the way the spirit of *inventio* with which art was once infused, has become little more than a repetitive treadmill of merely "modernised" aesthetic forms.

Thus, although Nietzsche somewhat hastily condemned Euripides as the arch villain of Socratic rationalism at the expense of Dionysiac *inventio*, his criticism of the dramatist's contribution to the loss of "effect" in art by primarily and concertedly aiming "to please" the judges and the audience is extremely perceptive, and indeed is a critique central to an understanding of *The Trackers of Oxyrynchus*. Harrison polemicises the way in which art, stripped, or perhaps more appropriately, flayed, of Dionysiac serendipity and *inventio* has become, in accordance with Apollonian dominion a mere shell of mechanistic and superficial aestheticism, which in the technological age has further evolved into the aesthetic commodity designed and specifically produced for a categorised and targeted audience. This development is powerfully conveyed when Apollo, like a marketing executive projecting future sales, decides that the best "product" name for his new-found instrument would be one that avoids sentimental, or even subsequently damming allusions to its makers:

> APOLLO
> Let's go back to 'lyre' and forget the whole zoo.
> [Delphi version p. 34]

Harrison thus illustrates how far removed we have become from the early Greek audience, who did not associate the pleasure of art with Apollonian victory, control or gratification—such as that depicted by the divisive and literally "goal" oriented 'football culture' at the end of the Delphi version of the play—but who embraced "a common wholeness", which incorporated both sufferer and celebrant with the relative sorrows and joys that are haphazardly thrown up by the unpredictable vicissitudes of life.

In this respect, Harrison's re-scripts of the Rewrite, *The Trackers of Oxyrynchus*, materially exemplify through their very textual polysemicity that the Apollonian dominion of art has not been total, and that the fragments of Sophocles' *Ichneutae* still possess and bear witness to the self-generative Dionysiac spirit of *inventio* to participate in what Harrison calls "the basic struggle of art." In a sense the polysemic Rewrite symbolises the further proliferation of the source text's nomadic "tracks", textual, historical and hermeneutic, which by and through its very return to the source text constructively defies the aestheticist's curfew to remain within its designated abode, origin or generic categorisation, a productive paradox of rewriting which Blanchot has elaborated on:

> The "re" of the return inscribes like the "ex", opening of every exteriority: as if the return, far from putting an end to it, marked the exile, the beginning in its rebeginning of the exodus. To come again would be to come to ex-centre oneself anew, to wander. Only the *nomadic* affirmation *remains.*[58]

Thus, Harrison's rescripted Rewrite represents a kind of dramaturgical nomadism, which in keeping with Nelson's[59] observation that "tracks" can only be constituted from behind, and after the event of their being made, emphasises that the Apolline "tracking" of aestheticisation must always be one or two steps behind art, if the "feel good" requirements of reception are not to further dictate what has in effect become the production of the aesthetic commodity devoid of *inventio*, but duplicitously in the name of art. Harrison's rescripted Rewrites disruptively disturb, muddy, and, to go back to the Benjaminian allusion, "fragment" the cleared pathway of textual linearity created by over two millennia of the aestheticisation of art. Moreover, by its very form and overlay of present "tracks" on the fading and effaced traces of the source text, *The Trackers of Oxyrynchus* dramaturgically initiates a further "struggle for art", which in the spirit of *inventio*, tests and challenges our dulled hermeneutic sensibilities to negotiate and explore the uncharted and unmapped territory *that is art*.

Notes

1   In *The Birth of Tragedy* Nietzsche polemicises the suppression of what he calls the "Dionysiac" spirit by encroaching rationalism and the Socratic aesthetic, which he pinpoints to the work of Euripides. The true spirit of tragedy, for Nietzsche was captured in the healthy antagonism between the Dionysiac and Apollonian aspects of life, but with the demise of the Dionysiac spirit as personified by the satyrs, tragedy degenerated into a theoretical representation of rational optimism and poetic justice.:

> But when a new artistic genre did spring into life, honouring tragedy as its predecessor and its master, it was frighteningly apparent that although it bore its mother's features they were the features she had borne during her long death-struggle. It was Euripides who fought tragedy's death-struggle; the later genre is known as New Attic Comedy. It was in comedy that the degenerate figure of tragedy lived on, a monument to its miserable and violent death. [BT p. 55]

Nietzsche's work provides an imaginative and thought-provoking introduction to considerations about the way Greek tragedy and comedy, as we know it, has been subject to aestheticisation, besides challenging us to consider the demise of the satyric impulse in art.

2   Sophocles' *Ichnethue* is based on a Homeric hymn to Hermes, and concerns the pilfering of Apollo's cattle whereby Hermes, the offspring of Maia, Atlas's daughter, and Zeus, led the herd in such a way so as to reverse and confuse their tracks and thus conceal his own footprints, in an attempt to elude apprehension by the angry Apollo. Only fragments of *Ichnethue* survive, about half the original text. See The Loeb Classical Library, Sophocles III (ed) G. P. Goold *Sophocles' Fragments: The Searchers/Ichnethue* trans. by Hugh Lloyd-Jones, LCL 483(Cambridge, Mass: Harvard University Press, 1996) pp.140–177.

Hugh Lloyd-Jones comments upon the fragmentary state of the play:

> In forming a judgement as to the play's quality we should remember that the discovery of the thief and the confrontation between the two gods which are missing must have formed the climax to which the whole action was designed to lead up. [p. 143.]

3   Herrnnstein Smith, *Contingencies of Value* p. 51.

4   George Thompson, *Aeschylus and Athens*, London, Lawrence and Wishart, 1980, p. 220. Thompson provides a detailed and lucid examination of Greek drama and its origins, as well as a useful consideration about Satyr drama, the demise of which he contextualises in relation to the social upheavals and developments of the sixth century BC.

5   Aristotle, *The Poetics* cited by Thompson, p. 220.

6   Thompson, p. 162.

7   Thompson, pp. 222–223.

8   R. Seaford in the Introduction to Euripides' *Cyclops* (Oxford: Clarendon Press, 1984) p. 31.

9   Todorov *The Fantastic: A Structural Approach to a Literary Genre* trans. by Richard Howard (Ithaca: Cornell University Press, 1980) p. 15.

10 Euripides' work provides us with the best indication of the gradual evolution toward what we refer to as 'comedy' especially with respect to his obvious experimentation with different types of drama, in an attempt, presumably to replace the Satyr drama, most notably *Alcestis*, a play which escapes firm generic categorisation or definition.

11 Michel Foucault, "Nietzsche, Genealogy, History" in *The Foucault Reader: An Introduction to Foucault's Thought* (ed) Paul Rabinow, p. 79. Here Foucault critiques the way in which we solemnly elevate 'origins' as being the source of purity and uncontaminated or undefiled innocence, when in fact if we look closely, in genealogical mode, we will find what he terms 'disparity'—that is, discontinuity, disruption and difference which uncover power struggles, leading Foucault to announce that "The genealogist needs history to dispel the chimeras of the origin . . ." [p. 80]

12 Tony Harrison, *The Common Chorus: A Version of Aristophanes' Lysistrata* (London and Boston: Faber and Faber, 1992) Introduction, p. v

13 Gadamer, "The Festive Character of Theatre" in *The Relevance of the Beautiful and Other Essays* (ed) Robert Bernasconi, trans; Nicholas Walker, (Cambridge: Cambridge University Press, 1995) p. 65. [hereafter referred to as *RB*]

14 Gadamer, *RB* pp. 58–63.

15 J. Ferguson, *A Companion to Greek Tragedy* (Austin and London: University of Texas Press, 1972). Ferguson provides an informative, although somewhat terse precis about the Satyr Drama and its demise, besides additional insights into the 'Satyr' work of other dramatists, like Aeschylus who, it is understood, completed his version of the Oedipus Tragedy with a Satyr drama called *The Sphinx*. Only thirteen plays of Sophocles are stated by ancient authorities to have been satyric, but Radt believes that Sophocles wrote some thirty satyric dramas. (Introduction to Loeb volume p. 4.)

16 Refer to H. Dubrow's analysis in *Genre: The Critical Idiom: 42* (London and New York: Methuen, 1982.)

17 Weinsheimer, (a) p. 120.

18 Euripides' *Cyclops*. This is the only complete extant Satyr drama; Seaford (1984) has translated and provided an informative inroduction to the play, which encompasses reflections about the Satyr drama, its purpose and its demise.

19   F. Nietzsche, 'On the Uses and Disadvantages of History for Life' in *Untimely Meditations* trans: by R. J. Hollingdale (Cambridge: Cambridge University Press, 1994) p. 87.

20   C. M. Hinsley, "Revising and Revisioning the History of Archaeology: Reflections on Region and Context" in Andrew Christenson (ed) *Tracing Archaeology's Past: The Historiography of Archaeology* (Carbondale and Edwardsville, Southern Illinois University Press, 1989) p. 88.

21   Shelby Brown, "Feminist Research in Archaeology" in *Feminist Theory and the Classics* (eds) Nancy Sorkin Rabinowitz and Amy Richlin, (New York and London: Routledge, 1993) p. 246.

22   Brown, p. 246.
     Brown refers to a useful distinction made by Sabloff with respect to the uses and implementation of archaeology—namely between the "dynamic" and the "static" past, the former of which, unlike Grenfell and Hunt's practices, takes a processual and postprocessual approach to archaeology. See Sabloff, Jeremy "When the Rhetoric Fades: A Brief Appraisal of Intellectual Trends in American Archaeology During the Past Two Decades" in *Bulletin of the American Schools of Oriental Research* 242: 1–6, 1981/ 3
     In a similar vein Walter Benjamin states in his autobiographical work *One Way Street* that:

     The true archaeologist is no treasure hunter though. For him or her, a shard of pottery, a broken comb, a worn out shoe, may have greater worth than the gold and silver treasures of the past . . . it is the archaeologist who recognises that beneath our feet are the countless bones and remains of those who have no monument, no landmark. [p314]

23   Gadamer, *TM* p. 116.

24   Plato's *The Republic* trans: Desmond Lee, Penguin, London 1987. Plato posited that "unsuitable" poets and their work, which form the greater part, should be banished from the Republic. [Book II, Part III] This argument is augmented by Part X.

25   Gadamer, *DD* pp. 64–65.
     In *Truth and Method* Gadamer critiques "aesthetic consciousness" and its correlate. the subjectification of the artwork, and here Gadamer argues that Plato foresaw the moral consequences of "aesthetic" education which advocated a ruinous and false dissociation from the practical world, and that in his ideal and imaginary 'republic' the Socratic self-knowledge which combatted the indifference and disinterestedness of aesthetic consciousness would reign supreme.

26   Gadamer, *DD* pp. 48–49.

27   Plato, p. 122. Having protested at the primitive society based on subsistence and the basic necessities of life, as outlined by Socrates, (a passage which has been cited as a parody of "the good life"), Glaucon further retorts "Really Socrates, . . . that's just the fodder you would provide if you were founding a community [often translated as city] of pigs!"

28 Gadamer, *TM* see Chapter II, Part I "Play as the Clue to Ontological Explanation", pp. 101–134. Here, Gadamer affirms play as the way of being of the work
of art. This does not however suggest that Gadamer slips into the very subjectiv-
ism toward art that he critiques, whereby we treat the artwork as an object, or
game to play for as Gadamer states "The mode of being of the game does not
permit the player [in this case the audience] to behave toward the game as to an
object". Rather, the play with respect to our reception of the artwork is serious
and assumes primacy over the consciousness of the players [the audience] to the
extent that "the players are merely the way the play comes into preentation."
Weinsheimer's analogy with Yeats's poem is particularly useful, [Weinsheimer, (a)
p 103]:

> As we cannot know the dancers from the dance,as Gadamer might say with
> Yeats, so also dance comes to be only through the dancers. Dance is the
> dancing of it, the game itself is the playing of it, and the artwork itself exists
> only in its working, only in its being experienced.

29 Wiensheimer, (a) p 103.

30 Gadamer, *TM* p. 164.

31 Nietzsche, "On the Uses and Disadvantages of History for Life" p. 84.

32 Tzvetan Todorow, *Genres in Discourse* (Cambridge: Cambridge University Press,
1991) p. 18.

33 Todorow, *The Fantastic: A Structural Approach to a Literary Genre* (Ithaca,
New York: Cornell University Press, 1975) p. 15.

34 Sean Hand, "Translating Theory, or the Difference between Deleuze and Foucault", Translator's Introduction to Gilles Deleuze *Foucault* (Athlone Press, London 1988) p. ix–x

35 Foucault, *The Archaeology of Knowledge* trans; A M Sheridan Smith, (London:
Routledge, 1995) p. 170.

36 Nietzsche, F "On the Uses and Disadvantages of History for Life" pp. 62–3. Here
Nietzsche puts forward his ideas about 'critical' historiography whereby he advocates the selective forgetting of history: ". . . one's being just as able to forget at
the right time as to remember at the right time; on the possession of a powerful
instinct for sensing when it is necessary to feel historically and when unhistorically.
This, precisely, is the proposition the reader is invited to meditate upon: *the
unhistorical and the historical are necessary in equal measure for the health
of an individual, of a people and of a culture.*" [p. 63.]

37 Edward Said, *Culture and Imperialism* (London: Chatto and Windus, 1993) pp.
11–12.

38 Said, p. 11. Said popularised the term 'contrapuntal' which in musical parlance
quite literally means "the art of combining melodies" [Chambers]. Here, Said
attempts to combat the monodimensional and often overwhelmingly eurocentric
approach, or what Bernal has labelled "contintental chauvinism", to cultural studies that have prevailed by advocating a simultaneous and multiperspectival focus
to the study of cultures.

39 Bhabha, H "Introduction: narrating the nation" in *Nation and Narration* (ed) Homi K. Bhabha, (London: Routledge, 1990) p. 1.

40 Said p. 11.

41 Foucault, "What is an Author" in *The Foucault Reader* p. 109.

42 Foucault, "Nietzsche, Genealogy, History" in *The Foucault Reader* p. 76.

43 Foucault, "Nietzsche, Genealogy, History" p. 76.

44 Foucault, "Nietzsche, Genealogy, History" p. 76.

45 In the Introduction to *The Common Chorus*, Harrison refers to the ephemerality of art in some detail, and he reflects on the temporality of fame, including his own:

> Theatre can only celebrate its presented moments by embracing its own ephemerality. In that is the glory of performance . . . The Egyptian fellaheen employed by Grenfell and Hunt in the excavations in "Trackers" used the papyri of Plato and Euripides as compost for their greens, and in the final version for the NT in 1991 the rubbish tips of the South Bank contained the poster, programme and text of the play being performed. The play contained the rubbish version of itself . . . This contemplation of the ruins of time is a common theme in all literature and thought. As the philosopher George Santayana wrote: 'The spectacle of change, the triumph of time, or whatever we may call it, has always been a favourite theme for lyric and tragic poetry, and for religious meditation. It is the condition of any beautiful, measured or tender philosophy.' It is to find the meaning of suffering in such a context that Greek tragedy exists. And out of the same source comes the laughter of comedy and celebration of the satyr play.[pvii–ix]

46 Jean Grondin, *Sources of Hermeneutics* (Albany, New York: State University of New York, 1995) p. 84.

47 Wendy Wheeler, "After Grief? What Kinds of Inhuman Selves?" in *New Formations: A Journal of Culture/Theory/Politics Number 25 Summer 1995 "Michel Foucault: J'accuse"* p. 81.

48 E. L. Santner, "History Beyond the Pleasure Principle: Some Thoughts on the Representation of Trauma" in S Friedlander (ed) *Probing the Limits of Representation: Nazism and the 'Final Solution'* (Cambridge, Mass: Harvard University Press, 1992) p. 144.

49 Gadamer, *TM* p.167.

50 Martin Bernal, *Black Athena: The Afroasiatic Roots of Classical Civilisation I: The Fabrication of Ancient Greece 1785–1985* (New Brunswick: Rutgers University Press, 1987) p. 2.

51 Said, *Culture and Imperialism* p. 16.

52 Foucault, "Nietzsche, Genealogy, History" p. 81.

53 Gadamer, *TM* p. 288.

54 Benjamin, "The Task of the Translator" *Illuminations* (1970) p. 78.

55 Benjamin,"The Task of the Translator" *Illuminations* (1970) p. 78

56 Gramsci, A *Selections from The Prison Notebooks* (ed) Quintin Hoare (New York: International Publishers) p. 57.

57 Edward Said, *The World, The Text and The Critic* (Cambridge, Mass: Harvard University Press, 1983) p. 171.

58 Maurice Blanchot, *The Step Not Beyond*, trans. by Lysette Nelson (Albany, New York: State University of New York, 1992) p. 33.

59 Lysette Nelson, Introduction to Blanchot's *The Step Not Beyond* pp. xiv–xv.

Conclusion

The Rewrite does not replace the classic in accordance with imposed or extratextual socio-political agendas in the present, rather it holds a self-consciously temporal bound conversation with a *text* that has become and has remained a "classic" as a result of the extratextual, and the often socio-politically motivated, conferral of status and value. By going back to the text that is a classic the Rewrite enables its textual precursor to speak through and not in spite of its and, by extension, *our* continuing and changing "cultural" formation. By virtue of its cultural cachet, subsequent appropriation and "intratextuality", the classic is engaged by the Rewrite as a literary vortex of cultural consciousness in order to elicit not only a reassessment of the classic but also, and more importantly, in order to prompt an interrogation of the presently held preconceptions and values which have been formed and perpetuated by artificial notions of "culture", and of which the classic forms a part. The Rewrite not only invites us to engage our historically effected consciousness of altered textual meanings and thus the instability of evaluative judgements, but also it initiates a reconsideration of the absolutes with which we attempt to rationalise and control the world and which are so often shaped by, reflected in and perpetuated through "culture".

At this juncture, and in view of the chapter in this study which attempts to grapple with our cultural implication in the Holocaust, it is apposite to recall Primo Levi's observation about the inescapable difficulties that we confront in our attempt to continually "understand" and, in keeping with the spirit of the Rewrite, "re-understand" the human situation:

> Have we—we who have returned—been able to understand and make others understand our experience? What we commonly mean by 'understand' coincides with 'simplify'. Without profound simplification the world around us would be an

infinite, undefined tangle that would defy our ability to orient ourselves and decide upon our actions. In short, we are compelled to reduce the knowable to a
schema . . .[1]

The Rewrite's self-conscious interpretative contingency and transience
is perhaps an attempt to escape epistemologically reductive schema without abdicating the responsibility to "understand", and indeed it is for this
reason that any sort of "conclusion" about the infinite conversation with
ourselves, as initiated in *Variations, The Island, Greek or The Trackers
of Oxyrynchus*, is and must be inappropriate. As Gadamer states:

> The ongoing dialogue permits no final conclusion. It would be a poor hermeneuticist
> who thought he [or she] could have, or had to have, the last word.[2]

Notes

1   Primo Levi, *The Drowned and the Saved* (London: Abacus, 1992) p. 22

2   Gadamer, *TM* p.579

Bibliography

1. Principal Dramatic and Philosophical Works Cited

a) Plays

Chapter III—The Merchant of Venice After The Holocaust

Shakespeare, William, *The Merchant of Venice: The Arden Shakespeare*, ed. by John Russell Brown (London and New York: Methuen, 1984)

Marowitz, Charles, *The Marowitz Shakespeare* (New York: Marion Boyars, 1990)

Wesker, Arnold, *Volume Four: Shylock and Other Plays* (London: Penguin Books, 1990)

Chapter IV—Antigone, Fugard and 'The Tradition of the Oppressed'

Sophocles, *The Theban Plays*, trans. by E. F. Watling (Harmondsworth, Middx: Penguin Books, 1977)

Fugard, Athol, *The Township Plays*, ed. by Dennis Walder (Oxford, Cape Town: Oxford University Press, 1993)

Chapter V—Steven Berkoff and the Dramaturgy of Bile

Sophocles, *The Theban Plays*, trans. by E. F. Watling (Harmondsworth, Middx: Penguin Books, 1977)

Berkoff, Steven, *Decadence and Other Plays* (London, Boston: Faber and Faber, 1990)

**Chapter VI—The Trackers of Oxyrynchus and the
Hermeneutic of The Aesthetic**

Sophocles, *Sophocles' Fragments: The Searchers/Ichnetheu*, trans. by
    Hugh Lloyd-Jones, Sophocles III of The Loeb Classical Library (ed)
    G. P. Goold (Cambridge, Mass: Harvard University Press, 1996)

Harrison, Tony, *The Trackers of Oxyrhynchus* (London, Boston: Faber
    and Faber, 1991)

b) Texts by Gadamer

Gadamer, Hans-Georg, *Truth and Method*, trans. by Joel Weinsheimer
    and Donald G. Marshall (London: Sheed and Ward, 1989)

————— *The Relevance of the Beautiful and Other Essays*, trans. by
    Nicholas Walker (Cambridge: Cambridge University Press, 1995)

————— *Philosophical Hermeneutics*, trans. by David E. Linge (Berke-
    ley: University of California Press, 1977)

————— *The Idea of the Good in Platonic-Aristotelian Philosophy* (New
    Haven: Yale University Press, 1986)

————— *Dialogue and Dialectic: Eight Hermeneutical Studies on Plato*
    trans. by P. Christopher Smith (New Haven: Yale University Press,
    1980)

————— "The Eminent Text and Its Truth" in *Bulletin of the Midwest
    Modern Languages Association* Vol. 13, 1980, pp. 3–10.

————— "The Western View of Inner Experience of Time and the Limits
    of Thought" in *Time and Philosophers* (Paris: UNESCO) 1974

2. Interviews

Material obtained from notes, taped interviews and a period of correspondence with Edward Bond (including extraneous notes for "Olly's
Prison" and "Lear") during the Christmas period of 1994.

Material and general information obtained as a consequence of a taped
interview with Arnold Wesker at the Hay-on-Wye Festival of Music and
Literature (May 1995).

Bibliography of Other Works

Abbott, Paul, "Authority" *Screen (incorporating Screen Education)* 20:2 (Summer 1979), 11–64

Ades, Dawn et al (eds) *Art and Power: Europe under the Dictators 1930–45* (London: The Hayward Gallery, 1995)

Adorno, T. W., *Negative Dialectics,* trans. by E. B. Ashton (London: Routledge, 1996)

Adorno, Theodor W., "Commitment" in Walder, D. ed., *Literature in the Modern World* (Oxford: Oxford University Press, 1990) 89–99

Adorno, Theodor, *The Jargon of Authenticity* trans. by Knut Tarnowski and Frederic Will (London and Henley: Routledge and Kegan Paul, 1973)

Alisdair MacIntyre, "Contexts of Interpretation: Reflections on Hans Georg Gadamer's *Truth and Method*" *Boston University Journal* 27:1, (1976) 41–46

Allport, G. W., *The Nature of Prejudice* (New York: Anchor Books, 1958)

Almog, S., ed., *Anti-Semitism through the Ages*, trans. by N. Reisner (Hebrew University of Jerusalem: Pergamon,1988)

Altieri, C., *Canons and Consequences: Reflection on the Ethical Force of Imaginative Ideals* (Evanston, Illinois: Northwestern University Press, 1990)

Anderson, B., *Imagined Communities* (London: Verso, 1983)

Arendt, H., *The Origins of Totalitarianism* (London: George Allen and Unwin, 1958)

Arendt, H., *The Human Condition* (Chicago and London: University of Chicago Press, 1970)

Aresty, N., *The Jew in the Victorian Novel* (New York: Routledge, 1980)

Arnold, M., *Culture and Anarchy* (Cambridge: Cambridge University Press, 1990)

Arnold, M., *Selected Prose* (London: Penguin, 1987)

Arnold, M., *Collected Works* ed., R. H. Super (Ann Arbor: University of Michigan Press, 1960)

Aronowitz, S., *Dead Artists, Live Theories and Other Cultural Problems* (New York: Routledge, 1994)

Artaud, A., *The Theatre and its Double*, trans. by V. Corti (Montreuil, London: Calder,1993)

Auerbach, E., *Figura: Scenes from The Drama of European Literature* (Manchester: Manchester University Press, 1984)

Bacon, F., *Essays* (London and Melbourne: Everymans Library, 1985)

Bakhtin, M., *Art and Answerability*, trans. by V. Liapunov (Austin Texas: University of Texas, 1990)

Barker, H., *Arguments for a Theatre* (London: John Calder, 1989)

Barthes, R., *Mythologies*, trans. by A. Lavers (London: Vintage, 1993)

Barthes, R., *Camera Lucida: Reflections on Photography* (London: Vintage, 1993)

Barthes, R., *S/Z*, trans.by Richard Miller (New York: Hill and Wang, 1974)

Barthes, R., *The Rustle of Language*, trans. by Richard Howard (New York: Hill and Wang, 1986)

Barthes, R., *The Semiotic Challenge*, trans. by Richard Howard (New York: Hill and Wang, 1988)

Bate, J., *Shakespearean Constitutions: Poltics, Theatre, Criticism* (Berkeley: University of California Press, 1989)

Bate, Walter Jackson, *From Classic to Romantic: Premises of Taste in Eighteenth Century England* (New York: Harper and Row, 1946)

Baudrillard, J., "The Hyper-realism of Simulation" (1976) in *Art in Theory, 1900–1990: An Anthology of Changing Ideas* (eds) Charles Harrsion and Paul Wood (Oxford: Blackwells, 1992) 1049–1051

Bauman, Z., *Modernity and Ambivalence* (Oxford: Polity, 1991)

Bauman, Z., *Modernity and the Holocaust* (Cambridge: Polity Press, 1989)

Bauman, Z., *Postmodern Ethics* (Oxford: Blackwell, 1993)

Bauman, Zygmunt, "Walter Benjamin, The Intellectual" in *The Actuality of Walter Benjamin: New Formations* No. 20 (Summer 1993) 47–59

Beinart, W., and Dubow, S., eds, *Segregation and Apartheid in Twentieth Century South Africa* (London: Routledge, 1994)

Belsey, C., *Critical Practice* (London: Routledge, 1980)

Benamou, M., Carmello, C., eds., *Performance in Postmodern Culture* (Milwaukee, Wisconsin: Centre for Twentieth Century Studies, 1977)

Benjamin, Andrew, "Shoah, Remembrance and The Abeyance of Fate: Walter Benjamin's 'Fate and Character'" in *The Actuality of Walter Benjamin: New Formations* No. 20 (Summer 1993) 93–111

Benjamin W., *The Origin of German Tragic Drama*, trans. by John Osborne (London: Verso, 1977)

Benjamin, W., "The Author as Producer" (1934) in *Art in Theory, 1900–1990: An Anthology of Changing Ideas* (eds) Charles Harrison and Paul Wood (Oxford: Blackwells, 1992) 483–489

Benjamin, W., "The Work of Art in the Age of Mechanical Reproduction" (1936) in *Art in Theory, 1900–1990: An Anthology of Changing Ideas* (eds) Charles Harrison and Paul Wood (Oxford: Blackwells, 1992) 512–520

Benjamin, W., *One Way Street and Other Writings*, trans. by E. Jephcott and K. Shorter (Norfolk: Verso, 1985)

Benjamin, W., *Illuminations* trans. by Harry Zohn (London: Cape, 1970)

Bennett, T., *Formalism and Marxism* (London: Routledge, 1979)

Bennington, G., *Legislations: The Politics of Deconstruction* (London: Verso, 1994)

Bentley, E., ed., *The Theory of The Modern Stage: An Introduction to Modern Theatre and Drama* (Harmondsworth, Pelican, 1979)

Bergonzi, B., *Exploding English: Criticism, Theory, Culture* (Oxford: Clarendon, 1990)

Bergson, H., *Matter and Memory*, trans. by Nancy Margaret Paul and W. Scott Palmer (London: George Allen and Unwin, 1962)

Berkoff, S., *I am Hamlet* (London, Boston: Faber and Faber, 1989)

Bernal, Martin, *Black Athena: The Afroasiatic Roots of Classical Civilisation. I: The Fabrication of Ancient Greece 1785–1985* (New Brunswick: Rutgers University Press, 1987)

Bernasconi, R., *Heidegger in Question: The Art of Existing* (New Jersey: Humanities Press, 1996)

Bernstein, M. A., *Foregone Conclusions: Against Apocalyptic History* (Berkeley and Los Angeles: University of California Press, 1994)

Betti, Emilio, "Hermeneutics as the General Methodology of the *Geisteswissenschaften*" trans. and ed. by Josef Bleicher, *Contemporary Hermeneutics: Hermeneutics as Method, Philosophy, and Critique* (London: Routledge and Kegan Paul, 1980) 51–94

Bhabha, H. K., "The Other Question" in *Screen (incorporating Screen Education)* Vol. 24, No.6 (Nov-Dec 1983) 18–36

Bhabha, H. K., *Nation and Narration* (London: Routledge, 1993)

Bhabha, H. K., *The Location of Culture* (London: Routledge, 1993)

Bharacha, R., *Theatre and the World: Performance and The Politics of Culture* (London and New York: Routledge, 1991)

Bigsby, C. W., *Contemporary English Drama Studies: Stratford Upon Avon* 19 (1981)

Billington, M., "A Short Sighted View of the World" in *The Guardian* Wednesday, April 13th 1994

Blanchot, M., *The Gaze of Orpheus and Other Literary Essays* (London: Station Hill, 1981)

Blanchot, M., *The Infinite Conversation* trans. by Susan Hanson, (Minneapolis and London: University of Minnesota Press, 1993)

Blanchot, M., *The Space of Literature* trans. by Ann Smock (London, Lincoln: University of Nebraska, 1989)

Blanchot, M., *The Writing of Disaster*, trans. by Ann Smock (Lincoln and London: University of Nebraska Press, 1995)

Blanchot, M., *Vicious Circles* trans. by Paul Aster (New York: Station Hill, 1985)

Blanchot, M., *The Step Not Beyond*, trans. by Lysette Nelson (New York: State University of New York, 1992)

Bleicher, Josef, *Contemporary Hermeneutics: Hermeneutics as Method, Philosophy and Critique* (London: Routledge and Kegan Paul, 1980)

Bloch, E., *The Principle of Hope*, 3 Vols (London: Blackwell, 1986)

Bloom, H., *A Map of Misreading* (Oxford: Oxford University Press, 1980)

Bloom, H., *The Western Canon: The Books and School of the Ages* (London: Papermac, 1995)

Bloom, Harold, *The Anxiety of Influence: A Theory of Poetry* (New York: Oxford University Press, 1973)

Boal, A., *Theatre of the Oppressed* (London: Pluto Press, 1992)

Bogdanov, M., "Shakespeare Lives!" in *The Guardian* 30th December, 1982

Bossy, J., *English Catholic Community 1570–1850* (London: Darton, Longman and Todd, 1975)

Bourdieu, P., *Distinction: A Social Critique of the Judgement of Art*, trans. by R. Nice (London: Routledge, 1979)

Boyarin, J., ed., *Remapping Memory: The Politics of Timespace* (Minneapolis, London: University of Minnesota Press, 1994

Bradford, R., ed., *The State of Theory* (London and New York: Routledge, 1993)

Brann, E. T. H. "The Canon Defended", *Philosophy and Literature*, Vol. 17, No. 2 (October 1993) 193–218

Brecht, B., *The Messingkauf Dialogues*, trans. by J. Willett (London: Methuen, 1965)

Brecht, B., *Parables for the Theatre*, trans. by Eric Bentley (London: Penguin, 1966)

Buck-Morss, S., *The Dialectics of Seeing: Walter Benjamin and the Arcades Project* (Cambridge, Massachesetts: The MIT Press, 1995)

Buck-Morss, Susan, "Aesthetics and Anaesthetics: Walter Benjamin's Artwork Essay Reconsidered" in *The Actuality of Walter Benjamin: New Formations* No. 20 (Summer 1993) 123–145

Bulman, J. C., *Shakespeare in Performance: The Merchant of Venice* (Manchester: Manchester University Press, 1991)

Burger, P., *A Theory of the Avant-Garde*, trans. by M. Shaw (Minneapolis, Universtiy of Minnesota Press, 1994)

Burgin, V., *The End of Theory* (London: Macmillan, 1993)

Burgin, Victor, "The City in Pieces" in *The Actuality of Walter Benjamin: New Formations* No. 20 (Summer 1993) 33–47

Calinescu, M., *Rereading* (London: Yale University Press, 1993)

Calinescu, M., and Fokkema, D., eds., *Exploring Postmodernism*: Selected Papers Presented at a Workshp on Postmodernism at XIth International Comparative Literature Congress, 20-24th August 1985 (Amsterdam: Utrecht Publications, 1990)

Calvino, Italo., *The Uses of Literature*, trans. by Patrick Creagh (San Diego: Harcourt Brace Jovanovich, 1986)

Calvino, Italo *The Literature Machine: Essays* trans. by Patrick Creagh (London: Secker and Warburg, 1987)

Camus, A., "Creation and Revolution"(1951) in *Art in Theory, 1900–1990: An Anthology of Changing Ideas* (eds) Charles Harrison and Paul Wood (Oxford: Blackwells, 1992) 615–618

Camus, A., *Resistance, Rebellion and Death*, trans. by Justin O'Brien (New York: Knopf, 1961)

Camus, A., *The Outsider*, trans. by Joseph Laredo (London: Penguin, 1982)

Camus, A., *The Plague*, trans. by Stuart Gilbert (London: Penguin, 1960)

Camus, A., *The Rebel*, trans. by Anthony Bower (London: Penguin, 1971)

Camus, A., *World Without War Publications*, trans. by Dwight McDonald (San Francisco, 1972)

Canary, R. H., Kozicki, H., eds., *The Writing of History: Literary Form and Historical Understanding* (London, Wisconsin: University of Wisconsin, 1978)

Caruth, C., *Trauma, Narrative and History* (Baltimore and London: The Johns Hopkins University Press, 1996)

Caute, David, *The Illusion* (New York: Harper and Row, 1972)

Cesarani, David, ed., *The Final Solution: Origins and Implementation* (London: Routledge, 1996)

Cheyette, B., *Construction of 'the jew' in English Literature: Racial Representation 1875–1945* (Cambridge: Cambridge University Press, 1995)

Chladenius, Johann Martin, "On the Concept of Interpretation", *The Hermeneutic Reader* ed., Kurt Mueller-Vollmer (New York: Continuum, 1985) 55–71

Coady, C. A. J., *Testimony: A Philosophical Study* (Oxford: Clarendon, 1992)

Cohen, M., "Shylock Through the Looking Glass" in *The Guardian*, 4th August, 1989

Cohen, P., " Monstrous Images, Perverse Reasons", Working Paper No.11, Centre for Multicultural Education, Institute for Education, University of London

Coleman, Edward Davidson., *The Jew in English Drama* (New York: New York Publishing, 1970 reprint of 1943 imprint with annotated bibliography)

Collier, P., and Geyer Ryan, H., eds, *Literary Theory Today* (Oxford: Polity Press, 1992)

Condren, C., "Towards an Explanation of Classic Status" in *The Status and Appraisal of Classic Texts: An Essay on Political Theory, its Inheritance and the History of Ideas* (Princeton, New Jersey: Princeton University Press, 1985) 253–285

Connor, S., *Theory and Cultural Value* (Oxford: Blackwell, 1992)

Connor, Steven, "On and Of Literary Value: A Reply to Antony Easthope" *Textual Practice* Vol. 5, No. 3 (Winter 1991) 326–333

Cook, Deborah, "Reflections on Gadamer's Notion of *Sprachlichkeit*" *Philosophy and Literature* Vol. 10, No. 1 (April 1986) 84–92

Cooke, L., and Wollen, P., eds, *Visual Display: Culture Beyond Appearances* (Seattle: Bay Press Seattle, 1995)

Coplan, D., *In Township Tonight: South Africa's Black City Music and Theatre* (London: Longman, 1985)

Cornis-Pope, M., *Hermeneutic Desire and Critical Rewriting: Narrative Interpretation in the Wake of Post-Structuralism* (London: Macmillan, 1992)

Cottom, D., *Ravishing Tradition: Cultural Forces and Literary History* (Ithaca and London: Cornell University Press, 1996)

Croce, B., "What is Art?"(1913) in *Art in Theory, 1900–1990: An Anthology of Changing Ideas* (eds) Charles Harrsion and Paul Wood (Oxford: Blackwells, 1992) 108–112

Crow, B. and Banfield, C., *An Introduction to Post-Colonial Theatre* (Cambridge: Cambridge University Press, 1996)

Cumberland, R., *The Jew* (1794)

Cunningham, V., *In the Reading Gaol: Postmodernity, Texts and History* (Oxford and Cambridge: Blackwell, 1994)

D'haen, T, and Barfoot, C. C ., eds, *Tropes of Revolution: Writers Reactions to Real and Imagined Revolutions, 1789–1989* (Amsterdam: Rodopi, 1991)

D'haen, T., and others, eds, *Convention and Innovation in Literature* (Amsterdam: J Benjamins Publishing Company, 1989)

Danto, A. C., *The Transfiguration of the Commonplace: A Philosophy of Art* (Cambridge, Massachusetts: Harvard University Press, 1981)

Danto, A. C., *Analytical Philosophy of History* (Cambridge: Cambridge University Press, 1965)

Davenport, Edward "Why Theorize About Literature?" in Hernadi, Paul ed., *What is Literature?* (Bloomington, Indiana University Press, 1978) 33–46

Davidowicz, L., *The Holocaust and the Historians* (Cambridge, Mass and London: Harvard University Press, 1981)

Davidson, Basil, *Modern Africa: A Social and Political History* (London and New York: Longman, 1994)

Davies, R., *A Voice from the Attic: Essays on the Art of Reading* (Middlesex: Penguin, 1990)

De Man, P., *The Rhetoric of Romanticism* (New York: Columbia University Press, 1984)

De Quincey, T., *De Quincey's Works* (Edinburgh: Adam and Charles Black, MDCCCLXIII)

Deleuze, G., *Foucault,* trans. by Sean Hand (London: Athlone Press, 1988)

Deleuze, G., and Guattari, F., *Anti-Oedipus: Capitalism and Schizophrenia* (London: The Athlone Press, 1984)

Deleuze, G., *Difference and Repetition* trans. P. Patton (London: Athlone Press, 1994)

Derrida, J., *Acts of Literature* (New York: Routledge, 1992)

Derrida, J., *Dissemination,* trans. by Barbara Johnson (London: The Athlone Press, 1981)

Derrida, J., *Glas,* trans. John Leavey and Richard Rand (Lincoln: University of Nebraska Press, 1986)

Derrida, J., *Spurs: Nietzsche's Styles,* trans. Barbara Harlow (Chicago: University of Chicago Press, 1979)

Derrida, J., *The Ear of the Other,* trans. by Peggy Kamuf (New York: Schocken Books, 1985)

Derrida, Jacques, *Of Spirit: Heidegger and The Question,* trans. by Geoffrey Bennington and Rachel Bowlby (Chicago and London: The University of Chicago Press, 1991)

Derrida, Jacques, *Writing and Difference* trans. by Alan Bass (Chicago: Chicago University Press, 1978)

Devereaux, Mary, "Can Art Save Us? A Meditation of Gadamer" *Philosophy and Literature* Vol. 15, No. 1 (April 1991) 59–73

Docherty, T., ed., *Postmodernism: A Reader* (London, Harvester Wheatsheaf, 1993)

Dollimore, J., *Radical Tragedy: Religion, Ideology and Power in the Drama of Shakespeare and his Contemporaries* (Hertfordshire: Harvester Wheatsheaf, 1989)

Donald, J., and Rattansi, A., *'Race', Culture and Difference* (London: Sage and Open University, 1992)

Drain, R., *Twentieth Century Theatre: A Sourcebook* (London and New York: Routledge, 1995)

Dreyfuss, H. L., and Hall, H., eds., *Heidegger: A Critical Reader* (Oxford: Blackwell, 1995)

Dreyfuss, H. L., and Rabinow, P., *Michel Foucault: Beyond Structuralism and Hermeneutics* (New York: Harvester Wheatsheaf, 1982)

Dreyfuss, Hubert. L., *Being-in-the-World: A Commentary on Heidegger's Being and Time, Division One* (Cambridge, Massachusetts: The MIT Press, 1995)

Dubrow, H., *Genre: The Critical Idiom, 42* (New York: Methuen, 1982)

Eagleton, T., *Walter Benjamin or Towards a Revolutionary Criticism* (London: Verso, 1981)

Eagleton, T., ed., *Ideology* (London: Longman, 1994)

Eagleton, T., *Ideology: An Introduction* (London: Verso, 1991)

Easthope, A., McGowan, Kate, eds., *A Critical and Cultural Reader* (Buckingham: The Open University Press, 1992)

Easthope, Antony, "The Question of Literary Value" in *Textual Practice* Vol. 4, No. 3, (Winter 1990) 376–389

Edgar, D., *The Second Time as Farce: Reflection on the Drama of Mean Times* (London: Lawrence and Wishart, 1988)

Edgeworth, M., *Harrington* in *Tales and Novels*, 18 vols (London: 1833)

Eliade, M., *Myths, Dreams and Mysteries*, trans. by P. Mairet (New York: Collins, 1960)

Eliot, T. S., *The Use of Poetry and the Use of Criticism: Studies in the Relation of Criticism to Poetry in England* (London: Faber and Faber, 1963)

Elsom, J., *Cold War Theatre* (London: Routledge, 1992)

Elsom, J., (ed) *Is Shakespeare Still Our Contemporary? Conference Discussions* (London: Routledge, 1990)

Engels, F., Marx, Karl *On Literature and Art* (Moscow: Progress Publishers, 1976)

Engels, F., *The Condition of the Working Class in England* (Harmondsworth: Penguin, 1987)

Erickson, P., *Rewriting Shakespeare, Rewriting Ourselves* (Berkeley Calif: University of California Press,1991)

Farrell, Brian A., *Philosophy and Psychoanalysis* (New York: Macmillan College Publishing Company, 1994)

Felman, S., and Laub, D., eds, *Testimony: Crises of Witnessing in Literature, Psychoanalysis and History* (New York: Routledge, 1992)

Felperin, Howard., *The Uses of the Canon: Elizabethan Literature and Contemporary Theory* (Oxford: Oxford University Press, 1992)

Ferguson, H., *The Lure of Dreams: Sigmund Freud and the Construction of Modernity* (London and New York: Routledge, 1996)

Ferguson, J., *A Companion to Greek Tragedy* (Austin, London: University of Texas Press, 1972)

Ferris, D. S., *Walter Benjamin: Theoretical Questions* (Stanford, California: Stanford University Press, 1996)

Fiedler, L., *The Stranger in Shakespeare* (London: Croom Helm, 1973)

Finkelstein, N., *The Ritual of New Creation: Jewish Tradition and Contemporary Literature* (Albany: State University of New York Press, 1992)

Fiorentino, *Il Pecorone* (1378) [one of the key sources for Shakespeare's *The Merchant of Venice*]

Fiorenza, E. S., and Tracy, D., eds, *The Holocaust as Interruption* (Edinburgh: T and T Clark, 1985)

Fisch, H., *The Dual Image: A Study of the Jew in English Literature* (London: World Jewish Congress, British Section, 1959)

Fish, Stanley, *Is there a text in this class? The Authority of the Interpretive Communities* (Cambridge, Mass: Harvard University Press, 1980)

Fokkema, D. W., *Literary History, Modernism and Postmodernism* (Amsterdam and Philadelphia: Utrecht Publications in General and Comparative Literature, 1986), XIX

Foster, Deborah, D., "The Blood Knot and the Island as Anti-Tragedy" *South African Literature* 1, ed., Stephan Gray (1982)

Foucault, M., *The Archaeology of Knowledge*, trans. by A. M. Sheridan Smith (London: Routledge, 1995)

Foucault, M., *The History of Sexuality: An Introduction*, trans. by Robert Hurley (London: Penguin), Vol I (1990)

Foucault, M., *The History of Sexuality: The Care of the Self*, trans. by Robert Hurley (London: Penguin), Vol III (1990)

Foucault, M., *The History of Sexuality: The Use of Pleasure*, trans. by Robert Hurley (London: Penguin),Vol II (1992)

Foulkes, A. P., *Literature and Propaganda*, (London: Methuen, 1983)

Fowler, A., *Kinds of Literature: An Introduction to the Theory of Genres and Modes*, (Oxford: Clarendon, 1982)

Freud, S., "Mourning and Melancholia" *Collected Papers*, Vol. 4. (London: Hogarth Press, 1947). Also see Penguin Volume, *On Metapsychology*

Freud, S., *Art and Literature,* trans. by James Strachey (London: Penguin), XIV (1990)

Freud, S., *On Metapsychology*, (London: Penguin), X (1991)

Freund, E., *The Return of the Reader: Reader-Response Criticism* (London: Methuen, 1987)

Friedlander, G., *Shakespeare and The Jews,* with preface by Maurice Muscovitch (London: Routledge and Sons, 1921)

Friedlander, S., ed., *Probing the Limits of Representation: Nazism and the 'Final Solution'* (Cambridge, Mass: Harvard University Press, 1992)

Fugard, A., *Statements: Two Workshop Productions Devised by Athol Fugard, John Kani and Winston Ntshona* (London, Cape Town: Oxford University Press, 1974)

Fugard, A., *Notebooks 1960–1977* ed., Mary Benson (London: Faber and Faber, 1983)

Furness, H. H., ed., *The Merchant of Venice: A New Variorum Edition* (Philadephia: J. P. Lippincott, 1888)

Fynsk, C., *Language and Relation . . . that there is language* (Stanford, California: Stanford University Press, 1996)

Gaggi, S., *Modernism/Postmodernism: A Study in Twentieth Century Arts and Ideas* (Philadelphia: University of Pennsylvania Press, 1989)

Gallop, David "Can Fiction be Stranger Than Truth?—An Aristotelian Answer" *Philosophy and Literature*, Vol. 15, No.1 (April 1991) 1–18

Gates, Jr., Henry Louis., *Loose Canons: Notes on the Culture Wars* (Oxford: Oxford University Press, 1992)

Gay, Peter, *Freud: A Life for Our Time* (London: Papermac, 1995)

Genette, Gerard., *Paratexts: Thresholds of Interpretation* trans. J. E. Lewin (Cambridge: Cambridge University Press, 1997)

Genette, Gerard, "Structuralism and Literary Criticism" in *Modern Criticism and Theory* (ed) David Lodge (London: Longman, 1993) 63–78

Geras, N., *Discourses of Extremity* (London: Verso, 1990)

Gill, C. B., ed., *Bataille: Writing the Sacred* (London: Routledge, 1995)

Gillespie, Stuart, *The Poets on the Classics: An Anthology of English Poets Writings on the Classical Poets and Dramatists from Chaucer to the Present* (London: Routledge, 1988)

Gilman, Sander L., *Jewish Self Hatred: Anti-Semitism and The Hidden Language of the Jews* (Baltimore and London: The Johns Hopkins University Press, 1986)

Goldberg, S., "Textual Properties" in *Shakespeare Quarterly* Vol. 37 (1986) 213–217

Goldberg, S., *James I and The Politics of Literature* (Baltimore: Johns Hopkins Press, 1986)

Gombrich, E. H., *Ideals and Idols: Essays on Values in History and in Art* (London: Phaidon Press, 1994)

Goodheart, E., *The Skeptic Disposition in Contemporary Criticism* (Princeton: Princeton University Press, 1984)

Goodman, R., ed., *Pragmatism: A Contemporary Reader* (New York and London: Routledge, 1995)

Goodwin, J., *Akira Kurosawa and Intertextual Cinema* (Baltimore and London: The Johns Hopkins Press, 1994)

Gorek, J., *The Making of the Modern Canon: Genesis and the Crisis of Literary Idea* (London: Athlone, 1990)

Gosse. Edmund, *Some Memoirs* ed., William Bellows (London: R. Cobden Sanderson, 1929)

Goux, J. J., *Oedipus, Philosopher*, trans by Catherine Porter (Stanford, California: Stanford University Press, 1993)

Gray, S., ed., *Theatre One: New South African Drama* (Johannesburg: Ad. Donker, 1978)

Greenblatt, Stephen Jay., *Renaissance Self-fashioning: From More to Shakespeare* (Chicago: University of Chicago, 1984)

Greenblatt, Stephen Jay., *Learning to Curse: Essays in Early Modern Culture* (New York, London: Routledge, 1990)

Greenblatt, Stephen Jay "Marlowe, Marx and Anti-semitism", *Critical Inquiry*, 5 (1978) 291–307

Grotowski, J., *Towards A Poor Theatre* (London: Methuen, 1981)

Guberman, Ross Mitchell, ed., *Julia Kristeva Interviews* (New York: Columbia University Press, 1996)

Guignon, C., ed., *The Cambridge Companion to Heidegger* (Cambridge: Cambridge University Press, 1995)

Guillory, John, *Cultural Capital: The Problem of Literary Canon Formation* (Chicago: University of Chicago Press, 1993)

Gumbrecht, Hans Ulrich, "Phoenix from the Ashes or: From Canon to Classic" *New Literary History* 20 (1988) 141–163

Gunner, L., ed., *Politics and Performance: Theatre, Poetry, Song in South Africa* (Johannesburg: Witwatersrand University Press, 1994)

Hall, S. Held, D. and McGrew,T., eds, *Modernity and its Futures* (Cambridge: The Open University Press, 1992)

Hall, S., ed., *Representation: Cultural Representations and Signifying Practices* (London: Sage Publications, 1997)

Hamilton, Donna, *Shakespeare and the Politics of Protestant England* (Lexington: University Press of Kentucky, 1992)

Hamilton, P., *Historicism*, (London and New York: Routledge, 1996)

Hanfling, O., *Philosophical Aesthetics, An Introduction* (Oxford: Blackwell and Open University, 1994)

Harrison, B., *Inconvenient Fictions* (New Haven: Yale University Press, 1991)

Harrison, C. and Wood, P., eds, *Art in Theory 1900–1990: An Anthology of Changing Ideas* (Oxford: Blackwell, 1993)

Harrison, J., ed., *Essays and Studies Presented to William Ridgeway* (Cambridge: Cambridge University Press, 1914)

Harrison, T., *The Common Chorus: A Version of Aristophanes' Lysistrata* (London and Boston: Faber and Faber, 1992)

Hassan, Ihab "Negative Capability Reclaimed: Literature and Philosophy *contra* Politics", *Philosophy and Literature*, Vol. 20, No. 2 (October, 1996) 305–324

Hawkes, T., *Meaning By Shakespeare*, (London and New York: Routledge, 1992)

Heath, M., *The Poetics of Greek Tragedy* (London: Duckworth, 1987)

Heidegger, M., *Being and Time* trans. by John Macquarrie and Edward Robinson, (Oxford: Blackwell, 1995)

Heidegger, M., *Basic Writings* ed., David Farrell Krell (London: Routledge, 1993)

Hernadi, Paul, ed., *What is Literature?* (Bloomington: Indiana University Press, 1978)

Hernadi, Paul, *Beyond Genre* (Bloomington: Indiana University Press, 1972)

Herrnstein Smith, B., *Contingencies of Value: Alternative Perspectives for Critical Theory* (Cambridge, Massachusetts: Harvard University Press, 1988)

Heywood, C., ed., *Aspects of South African Literature* (New York: Heinemann, 1976)

Highet, Gilbert, *The Classical Tradition: Greek and Roman Influences on Western Literature* (New York and London: Oxford University Press, 1959)

Himmelfarb, G., "Telling It As You Like It—Postmodernist History and The Flight from Fact" *The Times Literary Supplement* 16th October 1992, pp.12–15

Hirsch, E. D., *The Aims of Interpretation* (Chicago and London: University of Chicago Press, 1978)

Hirsch, E. D., "The Politics of Theories of Interpretation" *Critical Inquiry* 9 (1982) 235–247

Hoggart, R., *The Uses of Literacy* (London: Penguin, 1992)

Holderness, G., ed., *The Shakespeare Myth* (Manchester: Manchester University Press, 1988)

Hollingdale, R. J., ed., *A Nietzsche Reader* (London: Penguin, 1977)

Holub, M., *The Dimension of the Present Moment and Other Essays* (London: Faber and Faber, 1990)

Horkheimer, M., and Adorno, T. W., *The Dialectic of Enlightenment* (New York: Continuum, 1994)

How, Alan, *The Habermas-Gadamer Debate and the Nature of the Social* (Aldershot: Avebury Series in Philosophy, 1995)

Hoy, David, *The Critical Theory: Literature, History and Philosophical Hermeneutics* (Berkeley and Los Angeles: University of California, 1978)

Hulme, P. and Jordanova, L., *The Enlightenment and its Shadow* (London: Routledge, 1990)

Hutcheon, L., *A Theory of Parody: The Teaching of Twentieth Century Art Forms* (London: Routledge, 1991)

Hutcheon, L., *Irony's Edge: The Theory and Politics of Irony* (London: Routledge, 1994)

Hutcheon, L., *The Politics of Postmodernism* (London: Routledge, 1993)

Huyssen, Andreas, *After the Great Divide: Modernism, Mass Culture, Postmodernism* (Bloomington: Indiana University Press,1986)

Huyssen, Andreas., *Twilight Memories: Marking Time in a Culture of Amnesia* (New York and London: Routledge, 1995)

Innes, C., *Holy Theatre: Ritual and the Avant-Garde* (London: Routledge, 1994)

Iser, Wolfgang, *The Act of Reading: A Theory of Aesthetic Response* (London: Routledge and Kegan Paul, 1978)

Jameson, F., "The Deconstruction of Expression" (1984) in *Art in Theory, 1900–1990: An Anthology of Changing Ideas* (eds) Charles Harrison and Paul Wood (Oxford: Blackwells, 1992) 1074–1080

JanMohammed, A. R., Lloyd David, (eds) *The Nature and Context of Minority Discourse* (Oxford: Oxford University Press, 1990)

Jardine, Lisa., *Reading Shakespeare Historically* (London: Routledge, 1996)

Jauss, Hans R., *Toward An Aesthetic of Reception* (Minneapolis:University of Minnesota Press, 1982)

Jauss, Hans Robert, "Literary History as a Challenge to Literary Theory" in Walder, D. ed., *Literature in the Modern World* (Oxford: Oxford University Press, 1992) 67–75

Jay, Martin, "Experience Without a Subject: Walter Benjamin and the Novel" in *The Actuality of Walter Benjamin: New Formations* No. 20 (Summer 1993) 22–32

Johnson, G. "Hermeneutics: A Protreptic", *Critical Review*, Vol. 4, No. 1 and 2, (Winter-Spring 1990) 173–211

Kani, John, see Russell Vandenbroucke "Robert Zwelinzima is Alive" *Yale/Theater*, Vol. 7, No. 1 (1982)

Katz, J., *From Prejudice to Destruction: Anti-Semitism 1700–1933* (Oxford: Clarendon, 1980)

Kermode, Frank, *Selected Prose of T. S. Eliot* (London: Faber and Faber, 1975)

Kermode, Frank, *The Classic: Literary Images of Permanence and Change* (New York: Viking, 1975)

Kermode, Frank, "Forms of Attention" *The Wellek Library Lectures* (University of Chicago, 1985)

Kierkegaard, S., *Either/Or: A Fragment of Life* trans. by A. Hannay (London: Penguin, 1992)

Kierkegaard, S., *Fear and Trembling*, trans.by H. Hong (Princeton: Princeton University Press, 1983)

Kimmerle, H., ed., *F. D. E. Schleiermacher's Hermeneutics: The Hand-written Manuscripts*, trans. by J. Duke (1977)

King, Nicola "Autobiography as Cultural Memory: Three Case Studies" in *Cultural Memory: New Formations* No. 30 (Winter 1996–97) 50–63

Krieger, M., *Words About Words About Words: Theory, Criticism and the Literary Text* (Baltimore: Johns Hopkins Press, 1988)

Kristeva, J., *Powers of Horror: An Essay on Abjection* (New York: Columbia University Press, 1982)

Kristeva, J., *Strangers to Ourselves* trans. by L. S. Roudiez (New York: Harvester Wheatsheaf, 1991)

Kushner, T., *The Holocaust and the Liberal Imagination* (London: Blackwell, 1994)

Kushner, Tony, "The Memory of Belsen" in *Cultural Memory: New Formations* No. 30 (Winter 1996–97) 18–33

Kuspit, D., *The Cult of the Avant-Garde Artist* (Cambridge: Cambridge University Press, 1995)

Lacan, J., "The Mirror-Phase as Formative of the Function of the I" (1949) in *Art in Theory, 1900–1990: An Anthology of Changing Ideas* (eds) Charles Harrsion and Paul Wood (Oxford: Blackwells, 1992) 609–613

Lacan, Jacques, "The Essence of Tragedy: A Commentary on Sophocles' Antigone" in *The Ethics of Psychoanalysis: The Seminars of Jacques Lacan*, Book VII, trans. by Dennis Porter (London: Routledge, 1992)

Laclau, E., and Mouffe, C., *Hegemony and Socialist Strategy: Toward a Radical Democratic Politics* trans. by W. Moore and P. Cammack (London: Verso, 1985)

Lacoue-Labarthe, Philippe, "Neither an Accident Nor a Mistake" *Critical Inquiry* 15 (1989) 481–485

Lahr, John, *Light Fantastic: Adventures in the Theatre* (New York: Dial Press, 1996)

Landa, M. J., *The Jew in Drama* (London: P. S. King and Son, Orchard House, 1926)

Langer, L., *Holocaust Testimonies: The Ruins of Memory* (New Haven: Yale University Press, 1991)

Langer, Lawrence, *The Holocaust and the Literary Imagination* (New Haven: Yale University Press, 1975)

Larmore, C., *The Morals of Modernity*, (Cambridge: Cambridge University Press, 1996)

Leeming, G., *Wesker the Playwright* (London: Methuen, 1983)

Lefevevre, A., *Translation, Rewriting and the Manipulation of Literary Fame* (London: Routledge,1992)

Lefevevre, A., "Why Waste Our Time on Rewrites? The Trouble with Interpretation and the Role of Rewriting in an Alternative Paradigm" in *The Manipulation of Literature: Studies in Literary Translation* ed., Theo Hermans (New York: St. Martin's Press, 1985)

Levi, Neil, "The Subject of History: Gadamer, Lacoue-Labarthe, and Lyotard" in *Textual Practice* Vol. 5, No.1 (Spring 1991) 40–54

Levi, Primo., *The Drowned and The Saved*, trans. by Raymond Rosenthal (London: Abacus, 1993)

Levinas, E., "As If Consenting to the Horror" in *Critical Inquiry* 15 (1989) 485–488

Levinson, Jerrold "Art, Value and Philosophy" A Review of *Pictures, Poetry, Music* by Malcolm Budd (London: Allen Lane, Penguin, 1995) *Mind*, Vol. 105 (October 1996) 667–682

Lodge, David *Twentieth Century Literary Criticism: A Reader* (London: Longmans, 1985)

Loomba, A., *Gender, Race, Renaissance Drama* (Manchester: Manchester University Press, 1989)

Lovell, T., *Pictures of Reality: Aesthetics, Politics and Pleasure* (London: BFI Publishing, 1983)

Lovell, Terry, *Consuming Fiction* (New York: Verso, 1989)

Lunn, K., ed., *Traditons of Intolerance* (Manchester: Manchester University Press, 1989)

Lupton, J. R., and Reinhard, K., *After Oedipus: Shakespeare in Psychoanalysis* (Ithaca and London: Cornell University Press, 1993

Lyotard, J-F., *Heidegger and "the jews"*, trans. by Andreas Michel and Mark Roberts (Minneapolis: University of Minnesota, 1990)

Lyotard, J-F., *The Postmodern Condition: A Report on Knowledge* trans: by Geoffrey Bennington (1984)

Lyotard, J., *The Differend: Phrases in Dispute*, trans. by Van den Abbeele (Minneapolis: University of Minnesota Press,1983)

MacAloon, J. J., (ed.) *Rite, Drama, Festival, Spectacle: Rehearsals Toward a Theory of Cultural Performance* (Philadelphia: Institute for the Study of Human Issues, 1984)

Macann, C., ed., *Critical Heidegger* (London and New York: Routledge, 1996)

Macherey, Pierre, "The Text Says What It Does Not Say" in Walder, D. ed., *Literature in the Modern World* (Oxford: Oxford University Press, 1992) 215–222

Magnus, B., Stewart, S., and Mileur, J-P., *Nietzsche's Case: Philosophy as/and Literature* (New York and London: Routledge, 1993)

Mailloux, S., *Rhetorical Power* (Cornell University Press, 1989)

Mailloux, S., *Rhetoric, Sophistry and Pragmatism* (London: Cambridge University Press, 1995)

Mannheim, K., *Ideology and Utopia: An Introduction to the Sociology of Knowledge* (London: Routledge,1991)

Maranda, P., "The Dialectic of Metaphor: An Anthropological Essay on Hermeneutics" in *The Reader in the Text: Essays on Audience and Interpretation* eds., Susan R. Suleiman and Inge Crosman (Princeton: Princeton University Press, 1980) 183–204

Marcuse, H. "Art as Form of Reality" *New Left Review*, No. 74 (July-August 1972) 51–58

Marcuse, H., *Eros and Civilization: A Philosophical Inquiry into Freud* (London: Ark Paperbacks, 1987)

Marcuse, H., *One Dimensional Man* (London: Ark Edition, 1986)

Marcuse, H., *The Aesthetic Dimension: Toward a Critique of Marxist Aesthetics* trans. by H. Marcuse and Erica Sherover (London: Macmillan, 1979)

Marks, J., 'A New Image of Thought', New Formations: Michel Foucault: J'Accuse, 25, (1995), 66–76

Marowitz, C., The Dramatic Medium: Recycling Shakespeare (London: Macmillan, 1991)

Marsden, J. I., ed., The Appropriation of Shakespeare: Post Renaissance Reconstructions of the Works and Myth (Hertfordshire: Harvester Wheatsheaf, 1991)

Martin, J., Voice in The Modern Theatre (London: Routledge, 1991)

Marx, K., Early Writings (London: Penguin, 1975)

Matsuda, M. K., The Memory of the Modern (New York, Oxford: Oxford University Press, 1996)

McCole, J., Walter Benjamin and the Antimonies of Tradition (Ithaca and London: Cornell University Press, 1992)

McDonald, M., Ancient Sun, Modern Light (New York: Columbia University Press, 1992)

Melberg, A., Theories of Mimesis (Cambridge: Cambridge University Press, 1995)

Memmi, A., Dominated Man (Boston: Beacon Press, 1968)

Memmi, A., The Colonizer and Colonized introduced by Jean-Paul Sartre (Boston: Beacon Press,1965)

Merleau-Ponty, M., Phenomenology of Perception, trans. by Colin Smith (London and New York: Routledge, 1995)

Michelfelder, D. P., and Palmer, R. E., eds. Dialogue and Deconstruction: The Gadamer-Derrida Encounter (Albany: State University of New York Press, 1989)

Mill, J. S., On Liberty (London: Penguin, 1985)

Miller, Karl, Doubles: Studies in Literary History (Oxford: Oxford University Press, 1985)

Moi, Toril., Sexual/Textual Politics: Feminist Literary Theory (London: Routledge, 1985)

Morey, Adrian, The Catholic Subjects of Elizabeth I (London: Allen and Unwin, 1978)

Mphahlele, E., *The African Image* (London: Faber,1974)

Mphahlele, E., *Voices in the Whirlwind* (London: Macmillan, 1973)

Mueller-Vollmer, Kurt, ed., *The Hermeneutic Reader* (New York: Continuum, 1985)

Mukarovsky, J., "Aesthetic Function"(1934–6) in *Art in Theory, 1900–1990: An Anthology of Changing Ideas* (eds) Charles Harrison and Paul Wood (Oxford: Blackwells, 1992) 511–512

Mulvey, Laura, "Visual Pleasure and Narrative Cinema" (1973–5) in *Art in Theory, 1900–1990: An Anthology of Changing Ideas* (eds) Charles Harrison and Paul Wood (Oxford: Blackwells, 1992) 963–970

Murdoch, I., *Metaphysics as a Guide to Morals* (London: Penguin, 1993)

Ndebele, N. S., *South African Literature and Culture: Rediscovery of the Ordinary* (Manchester: Manchester University Press, 1994)

Nietzsche, F., *On the Genealogy of Morality* trans. by Carol Diethe (Cambridge: Cambridge University Press, 1995)

Nietzsche, F., *The Birth of Tragedy: Out of the Spirit of Music* trans. Shaun Whiteside (London: Penguin, 1993)

Nietzsche, F., *Thus Spoke Zarathustra*, trans. by R. J. Hollingdale (London: Penguin, 1969)

Nietzsche, F., *Untimely Meditations* trans. by R. J. Hollingdale (Cambridge: Cambridge University Press, 1994)

Niven, A., "Athol Fugard in Britain" *Commonwealth Newsletter* 7 (1975)

Nochlin, L., Garg, Tamar, eds., *The Jew in the Text: Modernity and the Construction of Identity* (London: Thames and Hudson, 1995)

Norris, Christopher, "Home Thoughts from Abroad: Derrida, Austin and the Oxford Connection" *Philosophy and Literature*, Vol. 10, No. 1 (April 1986) 1–25

Novitz, David, "Disputes About Art" in *The Journal of Aesthetics and Art Criticism* Vol. 54, No. 2 (Spring 1996) 153–163

Oliver, K., ed., *Ethics, Politics and Difference in Julia Kristeva's Writing* (New York and London: Routledge, 1993)

Orkin, M., *Drama and the South African State* (Manchester: Manchester University Press, 1991)

Osborne, P., *The Politics of Time: Modernity and Avant-Garde* (London: Verso, 1994)

Oudemans, C. W. *Tragic Ambiguity: Anthropology, Philosophy and Sophocles 'Antigone'* (Leiden, New York: E. J. Brill, 1987)

Palmer, Richard, *Hermeneutics: Interpretation Theory in Schleiermacher, Dilthey, Heidegger and Gadamer* (Evanston: Northwestern University Press, 1969)

Patterson, A., *Reading Between the Lines* (London: Routledge, 1993)

Patterson, A., *Shakespeare and The Popular Voice* (Cambridge: Blackwell, 1989)

Pavis, P., *Theatre at the Crossroads of Culture*, trans. by L. Kruger (London: Routledge, 1992)

Perret, Marion, *Shakespeare Studies: Research, Criticism and Reviews XX*, ed., J. l. Barroll (New York: Burt Frankling and Co, 1988)

Phelan, P., *Unmarked: The Politics of Performance* (London and New York: Routledge,1993)

Picard, M., *La Lecture comme jeu* (Paris: Editions de Minuit, 1986)

Pike, C., ed., *The Futurists, The Formalists and the Marxist Critique* (London: InkLinks, 1979)

Pippin, R., and others, *Marcuse: Critical Theory and The Promise of Utopia* (London: Macmillan, 1988)

Plato, *Early Socratic Dialogues*, trans. by Trevor J. Saunders and others (London: Penguin, 1987)

Plato, *Phaedrus and Letters VII and VIII*, trans. by Walter Hamilton (London: Penguin, 1973)

Plato, *The Last Days of Socrates,* trans. by Walter Hamilton (Middlesex: Penguin, 1978)

Plato, *The Republic*, trans. by Desmond Lee (London: Penguin, 1987)

Plato, *The Symposium*, trans. by Walter Hamilton (London: Penguin, 1951)

Plottel, J. P., and Charney, H., eds, *Intertextuality: New Perspectives in Criticism* (New York: New York Literary Forum), II (1978)

Rabinow, P., ed., *The Foucault Reader: An Introduction to Foucault's Thought* (London: Penguin, 1991)

Rabinowitz, N. S., and Richlin, A., eds, *Feminist Theory and the Classics* (New York and London: Routledge, 1993)

Reich, Wilhelm, *The Mass Psychology of Fascism* trans. by Vincent R. Carfagno (London: Souvenir Press, 1972)

Reinelt, J. G., and Roach, J. R., eds, *Critical Theory and Performance* (Ann Arbor: University of Michigan Press, 1992)

Rickman, H. P., ed., *Meaning in History: W. Dilthey's Thoughts on History and Society* (London: George Allen and Unwin, 1961)

Rickman, H. P., ed., *W. Dilthey: Selected Writings* (Cambridge: Cambridge University Press, 1976)

Ricoeur, P., *History and Truth*, trans. by Charles A. Kelbley (Evanston, Illinois: Northwestern University Press, 1992)

Ridley, A., "Desire and the Experience of Fiction", *Philosophy and Literature*, Vol. 16, No. 2 (1992) 279–291

Riffaterre, M., "Interpretation and Undecidability" in *New Literary History* Vol. 12, No. 2 (1981) 227–242

Riffaterre, M., "The Interpretant in Literary Semiotics" *American Journal of Semiotics* 3:4 (1985), 41–56

Riffaterre, M., *Fictional Truth* (Baltimore & London: The Johns Hopkins University Press, 1990)

Riffaterre, M., *Semiotics of Poetry* (Bloomington, Indiana University Press, 1978)

Roberts, J., ed., *Art Has No History: The Making and Unmaking of Modern Art*, (London: Verso, 1994)

Robinson G., and Rundell, J., eds, *Rethinking Imagination: Culture and Creativity* (London and New York: Routledge, 1994)

Rose, M., *Parody/Metafiction* (London: Croom Helm, 1979)

Rosenberg, Edgar, *The Jew in English Drama* (New York: New York Public Library, 1970)

Roskies, David, *Against the Apocalypse: Responses to Catastrophe in Modern Jewish Culture* (Cambridge, Mass: Harvard University Press, 1984)

Ruthrof, Horst, *The Reader's Construction of Narrative* (London: Routledge and Kegan Paul, 1981)

Said, E. W., *Culture and Imperialism* (London: Chatto & Windus, 1993)

Said, E. W., *The Politics of Dispossession: The Struggle for Palestinian Self Determination 1969–1994* (London: Chatto & Windus, 1994)

Said, E. W., *The World, the Text and the Critic* (London: Vintage, 1983)

Said, E. W., "Opponents, Audiences, Constituencies and Community" *Critical Inquiry*, 9 (1982) 1–26

Sallis, J., ed., *Reading Heidegger: Commemorations* (Bloomington and Indianapolis: Indiana University Press, 1993)

Salusinszky, Imre, *Criticism in Society: Interviews with Jacques Derrida, Northrop Frye, Harold Bloom, Barbara Johnson, Frank Lentricchia, J. Hillis Miller, Geoffrey Hartman, Frank Kermode, Edward Said* (London and New York: Methuen, 1987)

Santner, E. L., *Stranded Objects: Mourning, Memory and Film in Postwar Germany* (Ithaca and London: Cornell University Press, 1990)

Sapir, E., *Culture, Language and Personality: Selected Essays* (Berkeley: University of California Press, 1962)

Sartre, J. P., *What is Literature?*, trans. by B. Frechtman (Bristol: Methuen and Co, 1986)

Sartre, J. P., *Essays in Aesthetics*, trans. by W. Baskin (London: Peter Owen, 1964)

Sartre, Jean-Paul, "Why Write" in Lodge, D. ed., *Twentieth Century Literary Criticism: A Reader* (London: Longman, 1985) 371–385

Sass, L. A., *Madness and Modernism: Insanity in the Light of Modern Art, Literature and Thought* (Cambridge, Mass: Harvard University Press, 1994)

Scholes, Robert, *Textual Power: Literary Theory and the Teaching of English* (New Haven: Yale University Press, 1985)

Scott, M., *Shakespeare and the Modern Dramatist* (Wiltshire: Macmillan, 1993)

Seequeberhan, T., *The Hermeneutics of African Philosophy: Horizon and Discourse* (London, Routledge, 1994)

Shapiro, J., *Shakespeare and the Jews* (New York: Columbia University Press, 1996)

Shava, Piniel Viriri, *A People's Voice: Black South African Writing in the Twentieth Century* (London: Zed, 1989)

Sheppard, A., *Aesthetics: An Introduction to the Philosophy of Art* (Oxford: Oxford University Press, 1987)

Shils, E., *Tradition* (London: Faber & Faber, 1981)

Shklovsky, V., "Art as Technique" (1917) in *Art in Theory, 1900–1990: An Anthology of Changing Ideas* (eds) Charles Harrison and Paul Wood (Oxford: Blackwells, 1992) 274–278

Silverman, H. J., ed., *Gadamer and Hermeneutics: Science, Culture and Literature* (New York and London: Routledge, 1991)

Silverman, Hugh J., ed., *Derrida and Deconstruction: Contintental Philosophy II* (London: Routledge, 1989)

Simons, J., *Foucault and the Political* (London and New York: Routledge, 1995)

Sinfield, A., ed., *The Context of English Society and Literature 1945–1970* (New York: Holmes and Meier, 1983)

Sinfield, Alan, *Faultlines: Cultural Materialism and the Politics of Dissident Reading* (Oxford: Clarendon Press, 1992)

Sinsheimer, H., *Shylock, The History of a Character, or The Myth of the Jew* (London: Victor Gollancz, 1947)

Sisk, John P., "Bondage and Release in the Merchant of Venice" *Shakespeare Quarterly* 20 (1969) 217

Smith, P. J., *Social Shakespeare: Aspects of Renaissance Dramaturgy and Contemporary Society* (London and New York: Macmillan Press, 1995)

Smith, Robert, *Derrida and Autobiography* (Cambridge: Cambridge University Press, 1995)

Sontag, Susan., *Against Interpretation* (London: Vintage, 1994)

Soyinka, Wole., "This Past Must Address This Present" (Nobel Laureate Address: December 8, 1986)

Spivak, Gayatri. Chakravorty., "Who Claims Alterity?" (1989) in *Art in Theory, 1900–1990: An Anthology of Changing Ideas* (eds) Charles Harrison and Paul Wood (Oxford: Blackwells, 1992) 1119–1124

Spivak, Gayatri Chakravorty, *The Postcolonial Critic: Interviews, Strategies, Dialogues* (New York and London: Routledge, 1990)

Squires, J., ed., *Principled Positions: Postmodernism and the Rediscovery of Value* (London: Lawrence & Wishart, 1993)

Stallybrass, P., and White, Allon, *The Politics and Poetics of Transgression* (London: Methuen,1986)

Steiner, G., "The Long Life of Metaphor: An Approach to the *Shoah*" in *Encounter* Vol. 68, No. 2 (1987) 55–61

Steiner, G., *After Babel: Aspects of Language and Translation* (New York and London:Oxford University Press, 1975)

Steiner, G., *Antigones: The Antigone Myth in Western Literature, Art and Thought* (Oxford: Oxford University Press, 1989)

Steiner, G., *Heidegger* (London: Fontana Press, 1992)

Steiner, G., *Language and Silence: Essays 1958–1966* (London: Faber and Faber, 1990)

Steiner, G., *The Death of Tragedy* (London: Faber and Faber, 1961)

Stern, David, "Midrash and Indeterminacy" *Critical Inquiry* 15 (1989) 132–161

Sutrop, Margit, "The Death of the Literary Work", *Philosophy and Literature,* Vol. 18, No. 1 (April 1994) 38–49.

Szondi, P., *Introduction to Literary Hermeneutics*, trans. by M. Woodmansee (Cambridge: Cambridge University Press, 1995)

Szondi, P., *Theory of The Modern Drama* trans. by Michael Hays (Minneapolis: University of Minnesota Press, 1995)

Talfourd, F., *Shylock or the Merchant of Venice Preserved. An Entirely New Reading of Shakespeare* (London: Thomas Hailes Lacey, 1848) First Produced at the Royal Olympic Theatre, Monday July 4th 1853

Tambling, Jeremy, *Narrative and Ideology* (Milton Keynes: The Open University Press, 1991)

Tatham, Campbell, "Mythotherapy and Postmodern Fictions: Magic is Afoot" in Benamou, M., Carmello, C., eds., *Performance in Postmodern Culture* (Milwaukee, Wisconsin: Centre for Twentieth Century Studies, 1977)

Taylor, C., *Sources of the Self: The Making of the Modern Identity* (Cambridge: Cambridge University Press, 1996)

Thompson, E. P., *The Poverty of Theory and Other Essays* (London: Merlin Press, 1978)

Thompson, G., *Aeschylus and Athens* (London: Lawrence and Wishart, 1980)

Tillyard, E.M.W., *Shakespeare's Problem Plays: Hamlet, Troilus and Cressida, All's Well that Ends Well, Measure for Measure* (London: Penguin, 1993)

Todorov, T., *The Fantastic: A Structural Approach to a Literary Genre* (Ithaca, New York: Cornell University Press, 1975)

Todorov, T., *The Morals of History*, trans. by Alyson Waters (Minneapolis and London: University of Minnesota Press, 1995)

Todorov, Tzvetan, *Genres in Discourse* trans. by Catherine Porter (Cambridge: Cambridge University Press, 1991)

Trussler, S., "The State of the Nation's Theatre—Simon Trussler: An Editorial View—First Ask the Right Questions" *Theatre Quarterly* Vol. 3, No.11 (July-Sept 1973) 29–31

Veeser, H. A., ed., *The New Historicism* (New York: Routledge, 1989)

Verhoeven, W. M., ed., *Rewriting the Dream: Reflections on the Changing American Literary Canon* (Amsterdam: Rodopi, 1992)

Vernant, J. P., and Vidal-Naquet, P., *Myth and Tragedy in Ancient Greece*, trans. by Janet Lloyd (New York: Zone Books, 1988)

Vidal-Naquet, P., *The Jews: History, Memory and the Present* trans. and ed., David Ames Curtis (New York: Columbia University Press,1996)

Vidal-Naquet, P., *Assassins of Memory: Essays on The Denial of The Holocaust*, trans. by J. Mehlman (New York: Columbia University Press, 1992)

Von Hallberg, R., ed., *Canons* (Chicago: Chicago University Press, 1984)

Walder, D., ed., *Literature in the Modern World: Critical Essays and Documents* (Oxford: Open University Press in association with Oxford University Press, 1990)

Walder, D., *Athol Fugard* (London: Macmillan, 1984)

Walter, Simon, "Aesthetic", *A Journal of Modern Critical Theory*, Vol. 17, No. 3, November 1994 (Introduction)

Warnke, G., *Gadamer: Hermeneutics, Tradition and Reason* (Stanford: Stanford University Press, 1987)

Waugh, P., *Practising Postmodernism/Reading Modernism* (London: Edward Arnold, 1992)

Webster, Richard, *Why Freud Was Wrong: Sin, Science and Psychoanalysis* (London: Harper Collins, 1995)

Weigel, S., *Body and Image Space: Re-reading Walter Benjamin*, trans. by Georgina Paul (London and New York: Routledge, 1996)

Weil, Simone, *Intimations of Christianity among the Ancient Greeks*, trans. by E. C. Geissbuhler (New York: Beacon Press, 1958)

Weimann, R., *Shakespeare and the Popular Tradition in the Theatre: Studies in the Social Dimension of Dramatic Form and Function* (Baltimore, London: The Johns Hopkins Press, 1978)

Weinsheimer, J., *Gadamer's Hermeneutics: A Reading of Gadamer's Truth and Method* (New Haven and London: Yale University Press, 1985)

Weinsheimer, J., *Philosophical Hermeneutics and Literary Theory* (London: Yale University Press, 1991)

Weinsheimer, J., "Suppose Theory is Dead" *Philosophy and Literature*
    Vol. 16, No. 2, (1992) 251–265

Wertheim, Albert, "The Treatment of Shylock and Thematic Integrity in
    The Merchant of Venice" *Shakespeare Studies* 6 (1970) 75–87

Wheeler, W., 'After Grief? What Kind of Inhuman Selves?', New For-
    mations: Michel Foucault: J'Accuse, 25 (1995) 77–96

White, Hayden, *Metahistory: The Historical Imagination in Nineteenth
    Century Europe* (Baltimore & London: The Johns Hopkins Uni-
    versity Press, 1990)

White, Hayden, "The Politics of Historical Interpretation: Discipline and
    De-Sublimation" in *Critical Inquiry* 9, (September 1982) 113–137

Williams, R., "Dominant, Residual, Emergent" (1977) in *Art in Theory,
    1900–1990: An Anthology of Changing Ideas* (eds) Charles
    Harrison and Paul Wood (Oxford: Blackwells, 1992) 979–983

Williams, R., *Drama in Performance* (Milton Keynes: Open University
    Press, 1991)

Williams, Stanley Thomas, *Richard Cumberland: His Life and Dra-
    matic Works* (New Haven: Conn., 1917)

Wimsatt, W. K., and Brooks, Cleanth, *Literary Criticism: A Short His-
    tory* (London: Routledge and Kegan Paul, 1957)

Wistrich, Robert, *Anti-Semitism: The Longest Hatred* (London: Thames
    Methuen, 1991)

Wittkover, Rudolf, *Allegory and the Migration of Symbols* (London:
    Thames and Hudson, 1977)

Wohlfarth, Irving, "The Measure of the Possible, The Weight of the Real
    and The Heat of the Moment: Benjamin's Actuality Today" in *The
    Actuality of Walter Benjamin: New Formations* No. 20 (Summer
    1993) 1–21

Wolin, R., *Walter Benjamin: An Aesthetic of Redemption* (Berkeley,
    Los Angeles: University of California Press, 1994)

Wood, D., ed., *Christianity and Judaism: Studies in Church History*,
    29 (Oxford: Blackwell, 1992)

y Gasset, O., *The Dehumanisation of Art and Other Essays on Art,
    Culture and Literature* (Princeton: Princeton University Press, 1968)

Yates, F. A., *The Art of Memory* (London: Routledge and Kegan Paul, 1966)

Young, R., 'Foucault on Race and Colonialism' in *New Formations: Michel Foucault: J'Accuse*, 25 (1995) 57–65

Young, R., *White Mythologies: Writing, History and the West* (London: Routledge, 1990)

Zimmerman, M. E., *Heidegger's Confrontation with Modernity: Technology, Politics, Art* (Bloomington and Indiana: Indiana University Press, 1990)

Zizek, S., *Looking Awry: An Introduction to Jacques Lacan through Popular Culture* (Cambridge, Massachusetts: M I T Press, 1992)

Zizek, S., *The Sublime Object of Ideology* (London and New York: Verso, 1989)

Zuckert, C. H., *Postmodern Platos: Nietzsche, Heidegger, Gadamer, Strauss, Derrida* (Chicago and London: University of Chicago Press, 1996)

STUDIES IN
LITERARY
CRITICISM
& THEORY

Hans Rudnick, General Editor

The focus of this series is on studies of all literary genres that elucidate and interpret works of art in the context of criticism and theory. Theory and criticism are held to provide the hermeneutically most rewarding access to specific authors, works, and issues under consideration. Studies of a comparative nature with special reference to issues of literary history, criticism, and postmodern theory are the distinctive features of this monograph series. Emphasis is on subjects that may set trends, generate discussion, expand horizons beyond present perspectives, and/or redefine previously held notions about "major" and "minor" authors and their achievements within or outside the canon. Approaches may center on works, authors, or abstract notions of criticism and/or theory, including issues of a comparative nature concerning world literature.

For additional information about this series or for the submission of manuscripts, please contact:

Peter Lang Publishing
Acquisitions Department
P.O. Box 1246
Bel Air, Maryland 20104-1246

To order other books in this series, please contact our Customer Service Department:

800-770-LANG (within the U.S.)
(212) 647-7706 (outside the U.S.)
(212) 647-7707 FAX

or browse online by series at:

www.peterlangusa.com